Pragmatic Wisdom for the Sincere Student

The Complete Stoic Lessons Vols. 1-8

James Bellerjeau

A Fine Idea

Copyright © 2025 by James Bellerjeau

All rights reserved.

No portion of this book may be reproduced in any form without written permission from the publisher or author, except as permitted by U.S. copyright law.

Why Do Anything?

An Introduction to the Stoic Lessons

Dear friends. Join me on a journey to discover what it means to live a good life. Our inspiration in this quest is Seneca's Moral Letters to Lucilius, revisited and revised for our modern times. The search for what it means to live a good life was not new in Seneca's day, and it will not be old when we are all long gone.

Although these are not Seneca's letters, they honor both his wisdom and his instructions for new students. That is, we should grapple with deep thoughts and make our understanding of the truth personal.

Because no one has a monopoly on the truth, we can each contribute to the puzzle. **The reason to do anything is to answer a question that has not been answered, or at a minimum to answer it for yourself.**

In answering life's deepest questions, would it not be foolish for us to pass by the foundational stones laid by the great thinkers who labored before us? Seneca himself in search of inspiration says in his Letter 2:

> I am wont to cross over even into the enemy's camp, — not as a deserter, but as a scout.

Let us all be avid scouts of the great thinkers, seeking out their every camp with the mindset of anthropologists unearthing meaning from among the ruins. Although Seneca's words have been mined by many for centuries, each generation keeps turning up gemstones.

Thus, with this series of Pragmatic Wisdom for the Sincere Student, let us polish old stones to show them in a new light, and in washing off the mud and debris, reveal what fresh reflections may appear.

Be well.

Pragmatic Wisdom Vol. 1

Stoic Lessons on Work and Retirement

James Bellerjeau

A Fine Idea

Contents

1. On Being Busy — 5
2. On the Teacher's Duty — 7
3. On Retirement — 11
4. On Posterity — 15
5. On Sticking to Your Decisions — 19
6. On Instagram-Worthy Quotes — 23
7. On a Successor's Success — 25
8. On Defining Your Own Success — 27
9. On Bosses and Underlings — 29
10. On Dangerous Goals — 33
11. On Private and Public Service — 35
12. On Business as a Distraction — 39
13. On Losing One's Mind — 43

Chapter One

On Being Busy

Better an hour spent in quiet contemplation than a year mindlessly doing

G reetings dear reader!

Do not call yourself busy. Busyness is the fate of those who have relinquished control over their daily lives. They have ceded ground not honorably, like the battered general calling retreat to the troops after a hard-fought battle.

No, the busy today have put their fortune in the hands of strangers. They have done so without a fight and often without a thought. If you do not maintain the strictest control over your calendar, like a miser clutching his last coin, you will find your ledger soon overflowing, but with obligations, not credits.

Fear of missing out you say? Tell me, when did a mindless herd of cattle ever lead you to a destination you wanted to go to? You not only exhaust yourself trying to keep up with the herd, but you also end up bedraggled, dusty, and dung-riddled for your efforts. And no sooner has the lead cow paused than a random bull becomes the leader of the next charge.

Fear of becoming irrelevant you say? Show me a person who does not fear they are missing out, and I will show you a person who understands precisely the value of their time. I would rather hear a single person who says "No" calmly, than a hundred who vigorously cry out "Yes!"

Time that you do not waste is a deposit in the bank account of your life. The sheep stuff their day with the filling but ultimately empty blandishments of modern media. The more generously you cut out their bleating, the more you will clear your schedule, not to mention your head.

It's the busy person who occupies themselves with doing. But doing without thinking is the fate of beasts of burden, not you. With apologies to the Goddess of Victory, don't just do it!

Better an hour spent in quiet contemplation than a year mindlessly doing.

Be well.

Chapter Two

On the Teacher's Duty

Just because I am alone does not mean I am wasting my hours away

"Do you advise me," you ask, "to ghost the public sphere, and to be happy with my thoughts alone? How am I helping improve the world by withdrawing from society?"

This is not the contradiction that first appears. My aim in seeking seclusion is to create space for great work. Just because I am alone does not mean I am wasting my hours away. I hope that by taking time to think clearly, I can add to the storehouse of ideas as a service to all who come after me.

For all those who cannot see where they are walking because their faces are planted in their iPhones, it is my life's labor to remove stones from the path, so that we do not needlessly stumble.

Here is what I would tell them: Don't worry about what others think. Decide for yourself what success and happiness mean.

Rather than rejoicing in your latest raise, ask whether you are painting your silver handcuffs now with gold. Do you call your gilded shackles progress? If you wish to live happily, your every thought must be to disdain the normal trappings of success that hold so many in their spell.

We think possessions will satisfy us when all they really do is whet our appetites for more. The most unfulfilling meal is the lavish one you have given your very life to obtain. And worse, maintaining your standard of living at the highest-level chains you to a treadmill whose controls only ratchet upwards.

This shall be your rule of thumb — strive for functionality over form.

- Your feet and a bicycle will get you to most places as quickly or better than a Rolls Royce, and they're easier to park.

- A picnic lunch of a cheese sandwich by the lake will satisfy you as much or more than a feast of *foie gras* and lobster.

- Your Patek Philippe grand complication chronograph tells time not a whit better than a Timex automatic.

Adapt your circumstances to succeed with simple things, and you will train your mind in sufficiency.

I hear you asking "How do I reconcile a life of contemplation with the need to pay my bills?" Just as the opposite of busyness is not idleness, so too when you give up wants you do not become free of needs.

It is noble to work according to your nature and abilities to sustain yourself. The satisfaction of a job well done is its own reward, besides keeping your ledger in the black, and is also one of the paths to finding meaning.

When I tease out such lessons for myself and future generations, am I not providing a greater service than when I review the hundredth sales contract, draft the latest annual report, or rage on in Twitter wars?

Rather trust that at least some who are seen least in the public eye are engaged in higher pursuits.

But now I stop and balance the scales with a contribution in kind. I pay not with my own currency, but with that of the Chinese philosopher Confucius:

> The more man meditates upon good thoughts, the better will be his world and the world at large.

I expect you are wondering why I am quoting other philosophers to such an extent, rather than relying on the established Stoic canon. Can the Stoics lay claim to being the only ones to have laid bare and mined a rich vein of wisdom?

If the Greeks and Romans themselves never pretended to have had every worthy thought, then why should we?

Nothing brings me greater joy than to know that great thoughts have emerged and re-emerged from every corner of the globe, across time and distance. I trawl willingly the waters of Asia, Europe, and the Americas, and my travels have not gone unrewarded.

You, my sincere student, may take this as a free gift, for it is not mine to hoard but the world's to share.

From the Japanese Zen, my nets have hauled up this treasure, reminding us that it is not only the teacher who has a duty:

> To a sincere student, every day is a fortunate day. Time passes but he never lags behind. Neither glory nor shame can move him.

Be well.

Chapter Three

On Retirement

How much better to choose the time of your leaving yourself?

I am never so happy as when my mailbox yields an e-mail from you. They contain confirmation of your progress, and this is no small thing. I urge you to continue on in this way, and this urging is for your benefit more than any other.

You are now at the point where you must decide the next stage of your life: Will you stay on the raging white waters, bending your oar to keep the ship straight, or will you turn off onto a quieter tributary, where eventually all the waters will end up?

You face the deliberate choice of whether to slow your pace, ease your burden, and let someone else serve as captain.

Though some swear they will die tethered to the helm, and will even go down with the ship, it is only natural to pack it all in when the load that once seemed light starts to weigh you down.

How much better to choose the time of your leaving yourself? You otherwise risk others choosing it for you in circumstances that are unlikely to be to your liking.

"I am still at the peak of my powers," you say. "What if I am leaving too early?" So, no one is yet pushing you out the door. What is it exactly that has you clinging to your desk?

Ambition is what got you to your current position. Will you let ambition goad you on for the sake of accomplishment alone?

You need no further accolades to know you have achieved more than most. Your competitive nature is what gave you the drive to succeed, but will you let it drive you into an early grave?

Even the fastest racehorse will lose the race of time, and in the waning years will lose to many lesser horses she could have bested in her prime. Why stay on the field when the odds are inevitably stacked against you?

There is a certain pride some people take in knowing they have accumulated more wealth and possessions than their peers. I have warned you many times about the dangers of measuring your worth by your holdings.

If you need reinforcement beyond my own words, I can give it to you from an authoritative voice in the form of Seneca himself:

> No one is compelled to pursue prosperity at top speed; it means something to call a halt ... instead of pressing eagerly after favoring fortune.

Seneca understood that the choices we make voluntarily are the most meaningful compared to the ones that are forced upon us.

A well-ordered mind can find peace with either, but the choices you make when no one is making you are the ones that make you who you are.

Any voluntary choice carries risks, but what of it? Firstly, nothing of value is gained without effort and risk. Did you gain your current position without taking any chances? Looking back over your life so far, were there not many skirmishes where you emerged the victor but could have been vanquished?

And secondly, remember that you are always choosing, whether you do it by design or by default: if you choose not to decide, you still have made a choice. (Lest you think I borrow too freely without settling my accounts, I give thanks for this formulation of wisdom to the Canadian band Rush in their song Freewill.)

So age and decrepitude will have their way with you, whether you prepare for their workings or hold your breath and hope to wish them away. And that's if you are lucky, for a long life is not guaranteed to any of us.

You have long since passed the point of having what you need. Have you reached the point of having enough?

Every luxury you learn to live without is a payment on the insurance policy for a happy life. Fine food, expensive wine, sports cars, vacation homes; you can have them all and enjoy them all, but they will all be taken from you, one by one, as surely as the grains of sand drop from the top of the hourglass to the bottom. He that fortifies himself by relinquishing such pleasures voluntarily will suffer no loss from their absence.

My sayings above may have settled our accounts to today, but I wish to be sure I am not leaving you expecting more. I thus draw once more from the reserves of Seneca, who says:

> If you keep turning round and looking about, in order to see how much you may carry away with you, and how much money you may keep to equip yourself for the life of leisure, you will never find a way out. No man can swim ashore and take his baggage with him.

It is in anticipation of luxury and the accumulation of things that we forget the best things cannot be acquired with money. The best-rewarded effort is the work we put into ourselves.

Be well.

Chapter Four

On Posterity

We want some part of us to continue, to survive the ages

"How will I be remembered?" Is this what is keeping you from letting go of your position, dear reader?

I ask you, are you making a mark only insofar and for so long as you are holding the reins of power? There is no end to powerful people who are forgotten the moment they step foot out their office doors.

But you would be mistaken in thinking that it is your office that makes you memorable.

Let's consider what makes someone noteworthy not just in the moment, but for posterity.

- We can all bring to mind great literature and art, and often, though not always, this is intimately tied to the name of its creator.
- Renown declines rapidly when we consider music, where there is but a handful of composers from just the last few centuries whose work remains.
- And what shall we say of movies, television, and speechmaking? Even though only a few will make their names here, still these entertainments are fleeting and ephemeral, holding influence for a generation or two before fading.

Things that people find enduringly valuable are valuable because they speak across time.

- Paintings of the hunt drawn on a cave wall 25,000 years ago call to us today because they contain a fundamental truth: we are part of nature, and we must fight for our position in the world.

- The Venus of Willendorf fertility statute of a similar age carries a similar message: we want some part of us to continue, to survive the ages.

- What better way than passing our genes through our children and their children? Every person alive today can trace their ancestry back to a common parent if we unravel the tapestry of genealogy sufficiently far back.

Fiction in the form of plays and theater amuse us for an evening. Those that endure are the ones that elaborate on fundamental aspects of human nature.

- Tragedy, comedy, pride, these we can recognize immediately, though they are acted out on a stage thousands of years old.

- Shakespeare's renown is unmatched, not only or even chiefly because he wrote so well, but because he wrote with insight about our true passions and desires, of the human condition in all its folly, foibles, and majesty.

Philosophy is aimed at uncovering enduring truths. The human condition has changed little since the first civilizations emerged.

People were worried about living a good life thousands of years ago, and chances are good that they will be interested in this question a few thousand years from now.

What is human thought, what drives human motivation, and what guides human interaction? Address these questions, dear reader, and you will never lack an attentive audience.

History will enshroud almost all of us in murkiness as surely as death shrouds our worn-out bodies. Most or all of what we do will be lost. Make your efforts meaningful to the human condition and you may extend your renown beyond your lifetime if that is what you want.

Of the billions who have gone before us, precious few have made a lasting mark, and even fewer because of the office they briefly held. If you wish to represent more than a ripple from a pebble tossed in a pond, bend your efforts toward answering questions of basic human motivation.

And to do this, you need *less* of the company of your fellow man, not *more* of it. To think deeply and correctly, you need solitude. You need to make space for your thoughts to ramble, you need stillness for your voice to be heard.

We all know that one cannot serve two masters well. When you are about the affairs of the state, you cannot state the true nature of affairs to yourself, let alone others.

Rather than watching your pebbles vanish into the depths, carefully place your foundation on solid ground. Lay your stones one atop another, until the tower you have erected can be seen from the horizon and stand for the ages. This is surely difficult for all of us, and it is the reason that so few manage to make a lasting impression.

I will pay you today with a cornerstone, on which you may continue to build. For this stone may be used over and over, by builders of every kind. It comes from the workshop of Epictetus, whose chisels rang out with this truth:

> Wealth consists not in having great possessions, but in having few wants.

I have drilled this lesson into you to such an extent that I need not elaborate. Today I urge you to note that you may apply the principle of this proverb to many areas of human endeavor.

- Do you wish to accomplish great things? Do not attempt to do more but focus on less. Better pick a single priority and focus on it until you have found success than to spray your efforts like mist in a hurricane.

- Do you yearn for better relationships? Rather than numbering your Facebook friends in the hundreds, lavish your time and attention on your family.

- Are you looking for the perfect vacation or trip or experience? It is folly to cast your nets wildly in every direction in the hopes of catching a prize. Bait a single hook and sit quietly in one place until you have calmed your mind. You will realize that satisfaction cannot be fished up by dredging anywhere other than within you.

TLDR (too long; didn't read)? I leave you with a gift from the Greek tragedian Euripides, which encapsulates the lessons of this letter:

> Our lives ... are but a little while, so let them run as sweetly as you can, and give no thought to grief from day to day. For time is not concerned to keep our hopes, but hurries on its business, and is gone.

Euripides advises us to pay no heed to what bothers us daily, for fear the daily troubles become thieves of our happiness. His words survived for centuries because he spoke of human values, not because he was aiming for fame.

Be well.

Chapter Five

On Sticking to Your Decisions

Whether you are advancing or retreating, be fully committed to what you are doing

Each person has to take their own stock of when is the proper time to step away from their working life. It will be different for different people, with different safety nets deemed necessary, and no one else can determine this for you.

I caution you though, dear reader, don't make yourself unhappy while you are pondering your future. Whether you are advancing or retreating, be fully committed to what you are doing.

Make it your business to do a good job with what is before you, and the next step comes more easily and naturally for you and all around you. If, rather, you make yourself miserable by musing on what you have not yet achieved, you are sabotaging your chances of success.

Accepting your tasks and doing your very best at what is before you also means embracing the consequences of your decisions.

Who cares what other people think about success, accomplishment, and living a good life? Others do not live with the consequences of your decisions, you do. If you are properly guided by your own thoughts, and achieve the outcomes you intended, what of it that another has set their sights differently?

I wrote to you about standing out among the many who will be forgotten. An iconoclast will stand out by challenging conventional wisdom. Do not challenge the status quo for the sake of being contrarian, but simply to ensure you come to your own conclusions, and that you think for yourself.

I consider Steve Jobs a modern-day skeptic; he put it this way:

> Your time is limited, don't waste it living someone else's life. Don't be trapped by dogma, which is living the result of other people's thinking. Don't let the noise of others' opinions drown out your own inner voice.

What would I tell those just embarking on their careers?

- I would tell them not to fear failure, but rather to make sure they learn from every experience. It is more harmful to your prospects not to try than it is to mess up every now and then.

- Next, consider that those who have gone before you thought just like you did. As a result, try to imagine *why* they did what they did before you try to tear it down.

- Finally, chase growth, not money, at least as soon as you have enough money to pay for your basic needs, and use development as your metric to decide when to make a change.

Once you have made up your mind to change your job or give it up altogether, the decision on how to proceed is entirely up to you. To successfully execute, you must reconcile yourself to a change in circumstance, that is all.

If you seek retirement, yes, you will relinquish the office, the company car, the perks, and some status. Decide what you love more: The trappings or your freedom.

And remember this, my dear reader, many complain without end about the burdens associated with their position. But if it is your position that affords you advantages you can't afford to live without, what sense is there in complaining? You are held captive by your desires, and so you desire your captivity.

There must be an end to desires. You can never earn enough if you measure your worth by your earnings.

But you can take none of your wealth or the possessions they enable you to buy with you into death. And many more do not survive their wealth, in the sense that the pursuit of wealth drives them to an early grave.

You can take nothing of your belongings with you. Consider the Pharaohs' elaborate tombs and burial chambers, filled to overflowing with material goods. Though their spirits passed away, their possessions stayed resolutely behind.

My finger hovered once more over the send button until I realized you are missing your customary words of wisdom.

To show you that lessons may be drawn from any source and that it is the content that counts and not the wrapper it comes in, I offer you inspiration from the American televangelist Robert Schuller:

> I'd rather attempt to do something great and fail than to attempt to do nothing and succeed.

View your decisions over the course of your career as a grand adventure. They deserve your best effort and undivided attention, and you shall be as dedicated as any general is to their campaign. Once you have made a decision, commit to it with the fervor of Cortés in his colonization of the Americas.

Though you do not burn your bridges, for you can always use connections to those who have journeyed with you and helped you along the way, by all means, burn your ship so that there may be no retreat from your chosen path.

Be well.

Chapter Six

On Instagram-Worthy Quotes

You mustn't take the headline for the whole of the message but rather read on

What has become of my closing quotes, you wonder, where I shared wisdom collected from sages across the ages. Am I no longer able to reinforce each letter with the lessons duly noted from earlier masters?

Fear not, my store of pithy sayings has not been depleted.

The Stoics alone numbered many who became adept at condensing their knowledge into rich kernels, making them easy to pass on and share. One sees their influence across the intervening centuries, in students as diverse as Shakespeare, C.S. Lewis, and Steve Jobs.

The Stoics, in turn, represent but a fraction of notable thinkers who have grappled with great truths. Thus, from sources without end, we have a rich menu of maxims to choose from.

Moreover, for any single idea, you can call upon ten or twenty formulations, each of which either reiterates or reformulates a central theme.

The sayings we collect and repeat do serve laudable purposes: They whet our appetites to know more, they refresh our memory of what we have already studied, and they provide a glimpse through an opened window of what truths lie beyond.

But just as the container is not the content, the maxim is not the full message, only a key for interpreting the map. Though one may memorize a thousand sayings, and repeat them back in any setting, are they any better than a trained parrot?

A chatbot may respond to any of a hundred programmed questions, but are you having a meaningful interaction? Alexa on your countertop has become your daily conversationalist, but if you probe beneath the surface will you find anything of substance?

Thus I caution you, my dear reader, that to know why an idea is worthy of study at all, you need to digest more than Instagram-worthy morsels. Such light fare may be eagerly sought by the masses, but not the sincere student.

You mustn't take the headline for the whole of the message but rather read on. Read widely and deeply.

I want you to walk the grounds that gave root to an idea, wallow in the soil that nourished it, and be drenched by the summer storms that gave it strength. If you tend to the garden of ideas in this way, you will know not only how the fruits there came to ripen, but you will enjoy an abundant harvest.

Now consider this: No matter how strong the seed stock you start with, would you be a mere tender of another's crop, or will you add something new to the storehouse of humankind's bounty?

When you are the master of your garden, you can cross-pollinate ideas and bring whole new lineages of thought into being.

I think that although you may start out with what others thought, you need to end up with what you think.

Be well.

Chapter Seven

On a Successor's Success

If the sincere student is not ready, the teacher is not done

I cannot tell you what joy it brings me to be well replaced! To know that what you have built will be maintained and expanded is to know that you have not toiled in vain.

The master carpenter lays down tools all the more willingly when the apprentice is waiting and eager to take them up.

How to explain, then, the many who clutch jealously to the reins and refuse to relinquish them?

We talked elsewhere about the dangers of mistaking one's work for one's meaning. Besides those who have not found their purpose outside their labor, I suspect what keeps many in the saddle well beyond their comfort is fear.

This fear comes in two forms: First, that their successor will outshine them, and second, that they will not.

"What can this mean?" you ask. "How can both the one and its opposite be the culprit?"

They are alike, my dear reader, in that they both arise from flawed thinking about the relationship between teacher and student.

- The one who is afraid of being outdone does not understand that the renown of the student reflects favorably on their teacher.

- And while the other avoids this particular trap, they have fallen prey to another: Namely, lacking confidence that they have done enough to prepare their pupil.

- Just as renown redounds to the teacher, so too does failure lie properly at their feet. For if the master fears the student is not ready, does the apt pupil not also know it?

It is folly to hand over the keys while sweating and flinching at the thought of what the new driver will do on their first solo trip.

If the sincere student does not understand, the teacher has not been clear. If the sincere student is not ready, the teacher is not done.

Humankind progresses when we do our utmost to ensure that the steps we've taken do not need to be retraced and that the lessons we've learned are not lost.

Consider how much farther the next runner in the relay race can advance if we take care that they do not start behind us, but rather from the very tip of the baton in our outstretched hand.

Just as you are a sincere student, I aim to be no false teacher. I rejoice in seeing you progress, as much for my own sake as your own, because it means I am fulfilling my duty as you fulfill your promise.

Be well.

Chapter Eight

On Defining Your Own Success

To follow your own mind, especially when it directs a course that goes against all others, is the greatest achievement

If you would be a true friend to your friend, then advise him to stand firm on his decision to stand down from his position. The title, the prestige, the pay, these are but little compared to his peace of mind.

The many who challenge him and call him crazy for quitting in his prime do not know him. If you consider how hard we must work to know ourselves, what chance is there that another knows us better?

No, the critics flail about not because they know his heart, but for another reason: To go along with the crowd is comforting because it requires no thought.

When one pushes off confidently in another direction, they must be crazy, for otherwise what does it say about the crowd? People will happily convict a person who challenges their unspoken convictions so as to avoid challenging themselves to think.

"He is lazy," claims this one. "He is afraid of failure," says the next.

When people accuse others, they often are giving you a window into themselves. Because our imagination is weak, we see in others the things we feel in ourselves.

And I do not need to tell you that there is another kind of friend, the one who wishes secretly to see you fail. Your value to such a friend is that they feel superior to you.

This one does not rejoice in your joy but feels only envy when seeing your success.

Upon seeing one who, knowing his own mind and dealing honestly with the results of his thoughts, makes a hard decision, do we give courage or cast doubt?

You are no false friend. As such, congratulate your friend that he has finally come to know himself.

To do what everyone does requires no thought and little effort. To follow your own mind, especially when it directs a course that goes against all others, is the greatest achievement.

Compared to this, no amount of riches or power amounts to anything. And without self-possession, no amount of possessions will satisfy.

If you wish to capture success, the greatest weapon you can arm yourself with is not a physical thing.

- It is not bargained for with money, or even bought with bonds of loyalty.
- Though you surround yourself with things to serve as legions of defenders on every front, still the enemy slinks undetected into your tent and into your thoughts.

To protect yourself from harm, you do not need to add to your army but rather subtract from it: lose the fear of loss and give up wants.

If you yourself can take these things away, no one can take anything from you. Then you will have cleared the field and made the way for satisfaction and joy to win the day.

Be well.

Chapter Nine

On Bosses and Underlings

It betrays real cruelty to knowingly treat another as beneath you simply because they serve you

I am pleased to observe that you behave the same no matter the company you are with. You can tell much about a person by how they treat those around them.

"That's just an employee," your colleagues will say. Are we not all employed in one pursuit or another?

"Servant!" Yes, and do you not also serve many masters?

"Stranger!" No, they are but one we haven't met yet.

Reflect how often we would treat worse those whom we know nothing about, who have done us no harm, over those we know best and who have surely given us cause for complaint.

I wrote you that your social class is no bar to becoming a philosopher. Why then does achieving an elevated status serve for so many as a barrier to treating people well?

We all know the executive who scurries from the door of their chauffeured limousine to the express elevator waiting to whisk them to the top floor of their building.

- A selection of powerful seconds-in-command is on hand to fill their ears with affirmations before they adjourn to the executive dining room to fill their bellies with delicacies.

- And should they need relief after their indulgence, they retire to their private bathrooms where they discreetly conduct another sort of business.

They imagine their power makes them lonely because no one can understand the burdens they bear. Undisturbed in their isolation, they think they are unobserved.

Better see them for what they are, which is unobservant, for a horde of underlings circles around them always:

- Who chauffeured them from their manor to the office, or kept the lobby clear of obstacles and the elevator doors open and waiting?

- Who keeps the printer toned and full of paper, the trashcans emptied, and gilded faucets gleaming?

- Does the food so tastefully described in the menu of the day materialize unaided by human hands, like the miracle of the loaves and fishes?

I suspect the boss who fears having too frequent interaction with the common employee knows the encounter risks reminding both that their differences are slight.

Better that they surround themselves with the trappings of power, reinforcing a distinction in appearance if not in substance. Though if they only paused to consider what sort of difference they were drawing with this thinking, they might think twice.

Give one person a low position and raise another up high. Have you done anything to either's sharp hearing, far-seeing, or clear thinking?

The lowly perceive in an instant every false note from their bosses, just as those seniors are shutting their senses to all beneath them.

Worse than the boss who blinds themselves to what is going on around them is the boss who convinces themselves that they have become better by virtue of their elevation.

They may have failed basic math and be hopeless at adding single-digit sums without a calculator, but they become geniuses at calculating their respective status on the social ladder.

ON BOSSES AND UNDERLINGS

There is no sadder spectacle than a boss who berates their secretary while toadying up to the board committee members overseeing compensation.

It betrays real cruelty to knowingly treat another as beneath you simply because they serve you. But to do so out of ignorance of their inherent worth is an even worse offense to your own worth.

For what kind of person says a colleague is to be prized because of their tailored suit and Rolex watch, while another is base because they lack them?

I will tell you what kind of person, dear reader, and pray you do not find yourself among their number.

You have seen this person out of their business setting but still in their element: they stroll without a blush to the front of the security line because they are in a hurry and have a plane to catch.

It effortlessly escapes their attention that every person they've walked past has an identical objective, and some will be on the same plane, and it is as well they have averted their gaze for they would otherwise see murder in a thousand eyes.

Well before you arrive at the restaurant door, you hear this person enunciate the words that serve as their passport to prominence, "Don't you know who I am!"

It is a declarative statement, not a question, for no answer other than an abject apology for the delay is acceptable. What goes unsaid by the maître' d' and all others in earshot is this: "I know exactly who you are, and you are a fool."

But this person is a fool who will be gladly suffered for the sake of parting them with their folding cash.

When you are welcomed with air kisses and open arms into the boutique or gallery that would turn away all but the most well-heeled, consider whether it is your person or your wallet that is being courted.

Things that have true value are not counted in money. People are not properly measured by their outward appearance.

A boss that places their faith in money and appearances may gain both in the short term, but it is their fate to be forgotten.

They retire to their golf courses on the East Coast barrier islands, and no one marks their passing as a loss. Though their gated communities are virtual barriers to the poor, they are nonetheless filled with the unworthy.

Be well.

Chapter Ten

On Dangerous Goals

How many unhappy professionals do we know who, upon reaching the pinnacle of supposed success, are plagued by doubts about whether the sacrifices were worth the prize?

You thought your parents, teachers, and friends wanted what's best for you.

From your earliest days, they told you "You can do anything you want. You can be anyone you want!" Though our cheerleaders may wish us well, in practice their statements have the worst of effects on us.

Even when every hand would lift us up, still we are weighed down by others' expectations when we make them our own. Better that we were nurtured by wolves than have our expectations raised to such heights.

The YouTuber who becomes a millionaire in their teens. The rapper who becomes a star in their twenties, flashing brilliance along with their golden chains and diamond watches.

For every astronaut, celebrity baker, senator, or hedge fund billionaire, there are countless watchers who set their goals accordingly: I will be rich, I will be powerful, I will be famous.

When you set any of these as your goal, you set yourself on a path of guaranteed hardship and likely disappointment.

It is a lucky few who learn at the end what they should have asked themselves at the beginning: How can I be happy?

There are two problems with goals, dear reader: The first is that in themselves goals do not contain the blueprint for success only the seeds of suffering.

They are a marker for what you say you want, but they give no clue as to the roads you must choose and how steep will be the tolls you pay to travel towards your destination.

The second problem is that goals guarantee dissatisfaction unless and until they have been reached, by which time the damage wrought in their seeking often outweighs the benefit you hoped for.

How many unhappy professionals do we know who, upon reaching the pinnacle of supposed success, are plagued by doubts about whether the sacrifices were worth the prize?

How many celebrities who decry the relentless intrusion of the very attention they so desperately sought to attract?

Conspicuous consumption is noticeably absent from the habits of the wise person with a well-ordered mind.

If by wanting things you find yourself wanting for peace and satisfaction, leave off the setting of such goals and set yourself to understanding the value of things.

You can never achieve that which you do not understand, even though the ingredients for your success may be stored away in your pantry to pick up at will.

You cannot satisfy your hunger until you understand it is a sickness of the mind that ails you and not a lack of nourishment.

Cure your illness by cutting off the source of the pathogen that infects you: the expectations of others, and your own ill-considered goals.

Be well.

Chapter Eleven

On Private and Public Service

The true meaning of public service is not those offices that are most visible, but those deeds that have the greatest impact

We do things in the reverse order: We encourage young people into public service and positions of power before they have learned wisdom, and we urge our elders to withdraw from public view when they are most likely to be of service to humankind.

At different stages of their lives, each person should consider how they can make a contribution to the world, and this starts with learning how to better themselves.

A broken ruler will never yield a straight line, no matter how many times you put it to service, so your first task is to learn what is true.

Rarely does an education in life come for free, though you may not pay the tuition in money. Experience is a hard teacher, dear reader. I would have said unforgiving, but that's not true. For though we cannot control everything that comes our way, the consequences are applied evenly for all.

The teacher of life is strict but consequent, and a lesson learned need not be repeated. The fact that some of our companions may need multiple sessions is not the fault of the professor but of the inattentive student.

A sincere student is watchful, attentive, and above all humble. To know when you do not know is to gain the key that will open the door to wisdom.

Certainty is a key that will turn many locks but open no doors.

Think of your life as a series of stages. In your youth and early adult years, you should be best friends with curiosity. Be a sleuth, observe much, say little. Inquisitiveness is your watchword.

Strive to make every sentence begin with "Why ...?" Most of what you hear in response will be wrong, misguided, or irrelevant. Scattered among the inaccuracies will be grains of truth, but how to tell which is which?

You will note that what people say and what they do are rarely in harmony. Listen to their words and watch carefully their deeds. Gaining an insight into the human motivations behind both talking and doing gives you X-ray-like perception, allowing you to see beneath the surface of things.

In time, you will develop rough models for not just how the world works, but also why. Incentives are everything and I will come back to this another time.

In the second stage, let's call it middle age though it may come at any age, you will have working hypotheses. You will be able to say the words, "In my experience ..." and it will not be the start of an empty sentence.

You will still watch more than you talk, because you are conducting experiments to test your hypotheses, not yet publishing the conclusions of your studies.

Besides checking whether your predictions regarding people and events are accurate, you may begin to wonder how best to direct the course of events.

If what people say is an unfaithful guide to their actions, and they can be influenced without even realizing their minds are not their own, may you not put human motivation to use for your own purposes?

By this time in your life, most of your peers will have given up on trying to see behind the complexity of affairs and will accept the surface appearance of things. They will not think explicitly this is so, but their convictions about how the world works will steadily calcify, reinforced by the fact that everyone else believes the same as they do.

When all around you say, "More money is good, more responsibility is best, more possessions are pleasurable," who are they to disagree?

This is when you are at your most dangerous and when you must watch yourself with the vigilance of a prison guard whose every inmate has escaped multiple times before. For you are like a child grasping a sharp knife. You know that it cuts deeply, and which end is pointed, but you do not wield it confidently or accurately.

At the next stage, your values become paramount because they are put to the test. For the first time, you have the power to direct the course of events in a material way. The young student may not know much, but they also cannot influence much.

You have learned much, including not only how and why things work, but also how to make them go in the direction of your choosing. Will you be wise in your choices?

For with your greater insight, you are now in a position to make choices on behalf of others, not just yourself. Though the sheep believe they are making their own choices within the comfort of the herd, the shepherd knows they are controlling the flock's direction, guiding and steering with a tap here, a word there, a sharp whistle from time to time.

In this third stage of your life, you are ready to make the move away from the private service of bettering yourself towards the public service of bettering humankind.

This does not mean you must take up public office. That is but one possible avenue of service, fraught with many pitfalls and as much likelihood of doing harm as doing good.

For most, I say you are better served by serving in obscurity. Best that none know your name or position, though your influence may be widely felt.

"Why is this?" you ask, "What is the harm in being transparent and gaining recognition for your works?"

The risk in prominence is two-fold, dear reader. The first comes from yourself, and the second comes from others. To the first risk, when you act for the benefit of others, fame and recognition are false currency, feeding your pride more than they do your reason.

The reward for being altruistic cannot be to burnish your vanity. Otherwise, your own motivations will be corrupted to gain acclaim rather than to do good. Only infrequently will you find these two in harmonious company. You must maintain a watchful guard over your mind to stay alert, for your wisdom has not permanently vanquished your ego, only temporarily subdued it.

The egos of the masses present then your second risk. Do you think any will be happy to learn of your manipulations? That you have had not only the idea but also practice trying to influence their actions?

That you say it is for their own good will not dim their outrage. Do you think they will delight in hearing that everything they value, all they have placed stock in, has been misguided?

We would rather be told sweet lies, blindfolded and only steps away from the guillotine, than be told that we are naked and exposed with a long way to go till paradise.

Tell the truth at your peril, for the ignorant will not understand, the wicked will not care, and the great many will hate you for making them doubt their own beliefs.

Thus, you must serve in silence if you wish to preserve your ability to maneuver. The greatest good is done by those with the least need to talk about it. The true meaning of public service is not those offices that are most visible, but those deeds that have the greatest impact.

And remember this: You may change the world more with a single honest idea than you do by leading the mightiest army.

Be well.

Chapter Twelve

On Business as a Distraction

It is impatience in business affairs, as much as in life, that leads us to be distracted from potentially more valuable pursuits

There is a feeling I've had more than once lately, dear reader, and it is an unwelcome one even though I know I bring it fully upon myself.

You ask me a question and I recognize the topic. I am familiar with the issue, and I know I have worked on it at length before. But I do not recall enough of the answer to feel confident that I should speak without refreshing my memory.

Once not long past I had all my thoughts firmly about my person, available for ready use at a moment's notice, "without a thought," so to speak. Now I fear that I am shedding recollections like cats and dogs shed their hair: Carelessly, profligately.

I have scattered behind me a steady trail of thoughts in WIKI entries, chats, emails, memos, and one-pagers. Like Hansel and Gretel thinking their breadcrumbs would remain untouched such that they could retrace their steps, I am probably wrong to assume I will be able to call indefinitely upon my own markers to recall my state of mind when I created them.

Thus, I will not answer your latest question off the top of my head. I need consultation with my crumbs before I can reply to you, my dear reader. I trust you are not so impatient as to require an immediate response, in which case I would have to rely on my gut rather than my head.

It is impatience in business affairs, as much as in life, that leads us to be distracted from potentially more valuable pursuits. There is always something urgent clamoring for our attention and often enough we are confronted with a perceived or actual crisis that crowds out everything else.

When our hair is on fire, it seems only natural to postpone all that is not urgent and tend to the flames, but this runs the risk of forever keeping us from attending to that which is important.

To be the director of your own play, to stage your own actions rather than being danced about like a marionette on invisible strings, this seems like the greatest luxury to the busy worker. It is a kind of torture to feel pulled by events toward actions you would otherwise not have chosen to pursue.

All the more so when you are aware of the time lost from your studies in pursuit of a well-ordered mind. I think this is why so many give up trying to control the turbulent flow of work that streams into their office. To fight against the current is a herculean task, and not one that many can maintain for long.

"I already know what you're going to say," I can hear you sigh. But do not despair, dear reader, for my message today is not one of hardship and sacrifice, or at least not toil without end.

Yes, it is true I do not counsel you to "go with the flow," because this carries you only to places you do not wish to go. But nor will I urge you to swim upstream. Rather, turn your gaze to either shore of the river, and start to make your way to dry ground.

Though you are still being carried along by the raging waters, you can swim the short distance to the shore. What awaits you on the banks? Nothing more than the realization that though you do not recall diving or being pushed into the water, no one and nothing forces you to stay in and drown.

You can be content by not competing for the same carnival prizes that all your companions scramble after. Your happiness need not be related to your busyness, or your success in business. Your possessions need number little more than your self-possession.

If your mind is the motor that propels you along in life, your reason is the rudder that helps you steer around obstacles and put safely into port. Would you scrape off barnacles, scrub the decks spotless, and maintain everything on your boat except the motor? Would you be eager to board a charter when you observed no one's hand was on the rudder?

Why then do you think you'll be well served in responding to every urgency of business when this prevents you from the all-important business of maintaining your mind?

Rather than praying for a drought to dry up the stream of your desires, take seriously the duties of captain and carefully steer your ship away from useless wants and groundless fears. The Coast Guard is not coming to save you, you must save yourself by setting yourself free.

If you will allow me to stretch the analogy a bit more: You save yourself by donning the life vest of philosophy, grasping tight to the lessons we have been discussing lest you lose the progress you have made.

If you feel at this moment like you would rather slip under the waters if only it meant you would not need to hear me urging you on, then use the words of Naval Ravikant instead of my own as the lighthouse to guide your way:

> I value freedom above everything else. All kinds of freedom: freedom to do what I want, freedom from things I don't want to do, freedom from my own emotions or things that may disturb my peace.

I value you too much, dear reader, to let you go unaided. I will continue to offer my assistance for so long as I am able.

Be well.

Chapter Thirteen

On Losing One's Mind

Am I of sound mind when I tell you I believe I can control the elements? You need but lace up your shoes and join me to experience the phenomenon yourself

You asked me to relay the details of my day and to omit nothing. This must mean you have developed a tolerance for my overly wrought descriptions.

Perhaps you feel my actions will serve as an example of how to behave yourself, in which case you are placing great faith in me as your teacher. Or could it be that you have digested well the lesson of mine that a person serves as an example regardless of the merit of their behavior: If they behave wisely you may emulate them, but if they are foolish tell yourself to avoid their mistakes.

Either way, let my day be your object lesson today!

The course of my days has changed in recent times as I have moved from being master over others to focusing more on being master over myself.

For years I woke to the blare of an alarm clock, pulled usually from some fitful dream brought on by obsessive attention to a topic. A difficult employee situation, a contract dispute, an intense strategy session.

Other times it was a recurring travel nightmare my alarm freed me from. No matter how many times I travel, and I once traveled every week in four crisscrossing the globe, I dream I will be late — to wake, to catch the train, to check-in, to board the plane, to make the connection, and so on in a series of endless ways to lose out by losing time.

However drawn from slumber, my routine was to dress and have a quick bowl of cereal while catching up on emails before getting in my car and driving the half hour to the office.

This commute was the quietest time of my day and I used it to change my mental state: On the way to work to get in the necessary hardened mindset and on the way home to leave that hardness behind and become fit for family interaction.

At work, twelve hours would pass, and I will spare you a recitation of those details so as not to unnecessarily strain your politeness. Suffice it to say that I learned to tell myself regularly that upholding the rule of law is so vital to a healthy society that it must justify even the most mundane lawyerly tasks.

And though I needed to thus fortify my tasks in my head to consider them vital, still the days would often pass without my noticing the time. It was only upon looking up and seeing the sun was long gone that I realized my kids would already be asleep in their beds and my dinner tucked away under plastic wrap, and take once more to the now empty roads on my solitary commute home.

But you were not asking what I *used* to do, patient reader, but what I *do now*. I ask you to indulge this reminiscence if only to draw a contrast to a typical day today.

You know I have reduced my work pensum to 50%, though compared to the hours I formerly toiled, in actuality I have gained back far more than half my day. I have largely laid claim for myself the first half of each day and have been experimenting with different pursuits in this newly found freedom.

I wake now to the rhythm of nature and my body. I have let the battery in my alarm clock dim and die as I often wished it would when I was working. If I need time to sleep and to dream, I take it.

When I awaken, I indulge in a cup of coffee before I leave the snug ensconce of my bed. This simple pleasure brings me such satisfaction. Aaahhh. Caffeine is a vice I will gladly continue to suffer if such benefits can be had at such a small price.

I first started by reading the newspaper in bed, cover to cover while still safely under my covers. This too was an indulgence, for I never had time to linger on any story before. No more would I skim the headlines for anything relevant to our business, perhaps some regulatory development or an enforcement action we should be concerned about.

Though it seemed a small luxury to read at my leisure, I began to feel this came at the much greater cost of my peace of mind. This is a threat to my reason that I cannot afford to let linger.

I don't know when it happened exactly, dear reader, but the news has turned from the business of informing minds to the business of inflaming passions. When profits are driven by clicks, and outrage keeps readers engaged, should we be surprised when our reporters turn to fiction? What they do not invent, they cherry-pick to present the most extreme side of every story.

Habits are truly our friend, though, in helping to both cultivate the good and excise the bad. By simply not picking up my iPad, I soon did not miss reading the paper in the morning or indeed at all. The few times I was drawn in again come evening, I was amazed at how irrelevant the day's news felt as the day drew to a close.

I do of course eventually arise from my bed, lest you think I spend not just the night on my back but also the day. Now up, my self-directed pursuits are found in reading, writing, and running, often in that order.

Instead of descending into shameful reporting that leaves me feeling tainted for having read it, I may pick up a letter from Seneca to Lucilius to see what these old friends were discussing and to what end. This usually inspires me to write to you and see if I can wrestle some thoughts from my head onto the page.

And when I feel the need for a break from mental gymnastics, I switch from exercising my mind to exercising my legs.

Though I run alone most days, I feel like I have a multitude with me. There are first the voices of the scholars I have been reading and communing with. I hear them as if they were talking aloud. I argue with them, imagining they are running beside me to hear my words.

I try to have five or six companions such as this at any given time. Right now they include Seneca, Epictetus, Confucius, Richard Feynman, and Jordan Peterson.

Later in the summer as the days lengthen and warm, I plan to have Cicero, Marcus Aurelius, and Charlie Munger joining me. I also want to visit once more with my former running partners, Jean Jacques Rousseau, John Stuart Mill, John Rawls, and the Federalist Papers.

In fact, I feel the Olympic stadium is filled with onlookers who at a moment's notice can be beckoned down from the stands to rejoin the race. We are blessed to have so many companions to choose from.

I cherish these voices, as much as I do yours, my dear reader, because they help drown out my own insistent thoughts. This is the one voice I can never outrun.

You would think after more than 20 years of running I would have learned to accept my limits, to know what I can safely do, and what I should leave to younger, fitter men.

But how easily I can bring to mind my old running coach, Martin. He is the kindest of persons though he has a mad glint peeking out behind his easy smile. That glint says "Go ahead, I dare you! Let's see how much you can do. Run as fast as you like, I'll never be further than one step behind you."

Truly we ran in fear of his imagined pitchfork at our backs as much as we did for the joy of it. I now carry with me in my brain my own mad Martin, urging me on and saying crazy things. It is best to pay that voice little heed, except perhaps when I need him to finish a race.

So, I find solace in these other companions, though I do all the work of carrying them with me on my rounds.

My madness does not stop with these thoughts about running. I would go so far as to tell you that I am reliably insane in several other areas.

For one, I am as gullible as Charlie Brown when Lucy invites him yet again to kick the football from her treacherous hands. My downfall is the weather app on my phone. How many times have I been fooled by a forecast only to find myself cursing the weather gods in the middle of a downpour?

Refusing to learn at least this lesson is apparently also habit-forming, for no matter how many times I find myself flung into a momentary rage upon needing to wring myself dry, still I check the forecast every single time before I set foot outside the door.

I would do better consulting the Farmer's Almanack from last century for tomorrow's weather. At least then I would have no illusions about what to expect.

Am I of sound mind when I tell you I believe I can control the elements, dear reader? You need but lace up your shoes and join me to experience the phenomenon yourself.

- When we start out on the path together you will marvel at the bracing headwind that whisks away our sweat.

- Though we run an out-and-back course, or even run in circles, you will marvel even more to note that the headwind prevails no matter our direction.

- Or consider the course that you would swear was flat when we ran it one way, but which turns into a hill upon our return.

- Just today I experienced a horizontal wall of rain (unforecasted of course) driven by a wind so strong that sailors' spouses would quail in fear that their loved ones would safely come home.

As god of the elements, I just hold onto my hat and keep putting one foot in front of the other.

My insanity is at least temporary, for I do not give it a long leash outside the arena of running. Pity those who lose control of their minds on a more permanent basis.

I am talking about the afflictions of envy, anger, and greed. Many give themselves over fully to these passions, though it deprives them of their right reason and well-ordered mind.

I condemn too lust, if not love. We say a person is "head over heels" in love. If we consider what state of mind and what activities give rise to this condition, shouldn't we rather say the person is "heels over head" in lust?

Take care that you limit your own insanities to times and places where you can be sure of quickly regaining your mind. I do not ask you to be perfect at all times, but to be perfectly aware when you are not.

Be well.

Pragmatic Wisdom Vol. 2

Stoic Lessons on Avoiding the Public Eye

James Bellerjeau

A Fine Idea

Contents

1. On Consuming Social Media — 51
2. On Friends, Not Followers — 53
3. On Public Opinion — 55
4. On Attending to Yourself — 59
5. On Introverts — 61
6. On Keeping a Low Profile — 65
7. On Looking Within — 69
8. On Word Games and Worthy Matters — 73
9. On Those Who Will Not See — 77
10. On Seven Popular Places — 81
11. On Philosophers, New and Old — 85
12. On Abiding in One Place — 89
13. On Mind Viruses — 93
14. On Popular Authors — 97
15. On the Greatest Threat — 101
16. On Treading Safely — 103
17. On Slogans — 107
18. On Being a Nonconformist — 113

Chapter One

On Consuming Social Media

A steady diet of social media will leave you bloated but undernourished

Greetings dear reader!

Judging by your latest message to me, I am positively inclined about your prospects. You do not flit from topic to topic or overly engage yourself with the latest story to trend.

The frantic hunt for likes and retweets is a sign of a distracted mind. The truest measure of a well-focused person is the extent to which they can leave aside the passions of the day in favor of the priorities they previously set.

A steady diet of social media will leave you bloated but undernourished. You will grow fat with trivialities as quickly as you grow unhealthy in your thinking.

In contrast, the proudest result of deep thought is a truth that you can express in a few words. Even though it may be devoured in a single bite, the healthy nugget of truth will nourish the wise. It is possible, but unlikely, to find deep truth in social media; remember most miners will go bankrupt.

Your challenge in separating the wheat from the chaff grows daily. The sheer volume of voices crying out to be heard threatens to deafen even the most astute listener.

Your chances of finding useful content today are like plucking up a handful of sand and expecting to sift out a diamond ring. You might bulldoze the entire beach and end up with nothing but silica for your efforts, not to mention a large bill for diesel.

What is a hungry consumer of a sensitive disposition to do? Rather than sample a thousand dishes in the hope of finding one that is not poisoned, better engage the services of a seasoned taster.

Find a Sherpa to lead you up the mountain, and to shoulder the bigger part of the load while they're at it. Unlike the mission facing the crew of the Starship Enterprise, this territory has been explored and mapped and its secrets laid bare.

Your challenge then is not to walk every inch of the land yourself, but to leverage the mapmakers' toil. Concretely, I tell you this: Select no more than five trackers whose navigation skills you trust. What lights guide their sojourns in the wilderness of the web? The best of them will give up their secrets willingly, for they want other pilgrims to join them on the path.

What compass guides my step, you ask? Honestly, ask first if you should step out your door at all. Consider whether you need to depart your oasis, for the desert is deep and wide and unforgiving.

The greater portion of what mankind has learned was uncovered long ago, and the sands of time have not buried it yet. Seneca, Marcus Aurelius, and Epictetus are some of the best guides you will find in any age.

But if you are compelled to seek out fresher fare, try the Farnam Street blog, and the Almanack of Naval Rivikant. These alone are deep enough wells from which to drink richly whenever thirst comes upon you.

Enduring truths are available freely to all. I would anyway urge caution when dealing with truthtellers who seek compensation for their wisdom. By selling their wares, they must give thought to their attractive presentation.

A lasting truth cannot be possessed, only uncovered, and once uncovered is made greater by sharing.

The wise profit from sharing their thoughts, not from selling them.

Be well.

Chapter Two

On Friends, Not Followers

A true friend will tell you when you are being a fool

Greetings dear reader!

You ask whether to congratulate the latest pop star to attract one hundred million followers on social media. Rather offer your condolences to Justin Bieber than your praise.

Followers want nothing more than to consume you, while a friend wants to see you nourished. Do not celebrate another cannibal joining the banquet when you are the main dish.

"But," you say, "am I not made greater by the acclamation of the masses?" If wisdom is rare in individuals, even fainter is your chance of finding it among the multitude.

This is because the masses are but one step removed from the mob, and the mob knows no morals. The mob knows only that it must do more of whatever it is doing at that moment.

Better a single voice speaking reason, thereby calming the passions of the throng, than a stadium of spectators cheering the games along.

"But my post was upvoted a hundred times and shared by two hundred more!" I hear you already. "Surely that demonstrates the truth of what I say."

I tell you, look at our politicians raining cash down upon a welcoming public. Should Congress take comfort in the wisdom of its course because polls show a majority approve?

Say you offer guests at your next dinner party the boon of carrying away the silver plates. Surely a supermajority of them will upvote your largesse. Now just imagine schoolchildren's universal chorus of likes when you declare candy for lunch and homework is forbidden.

The only thing such numbers tell us is that a great number of people can be greatly wrong about a great many things.

A true friend will tell you when you are being a fool. A true friend will risk your ire by not praising that, which is not praiseworthy.

You do not need a thousand to point out your flaws. A single friend will do, if they truly know you and if you listen truly.

And better the heartfelt praise of a single one who knows you, than the thunderous applause of thousands who are blind.

Be well.

Chapter Three

On Public Opinion

Nothing is more dangerous to your reputation than exposure to public view in the circus of social media

Greetings dear reader!

Do you ask me what you should avoid above all else? Public opinion, I say; for as yet none have managed to navigate it without peril. And no one ever ventured forth into the public arena without being tainted by what they encountered there.

When you swim in sewage you can't help but come away smelling sour. To court public attention is to court disaster because there is no chance that you will not be confronted with the basest and vilest among us. The more you seek to spread your reach, the greater your risk of getting your fingers smacked.

Nothing is more dangerous to your reputation than exposure to public view in the circus of social media. By crying out in this arena, you draw the attention of the mob that has no interest in building you up, but only in tearing you down.

It matters not what you say or mean; it only matters how what you say can be misunderstood. We are challenged enough to make our point clear in a debate with equally armed combatants, where there are no limits on our time to speak, and our opponent is primed to listen. Even here, a meeting of the minds is the rare outcome of hard-fought sparring.

What chance, then, can you hope to have in the social media sphere, where every tongue is sharpened, and your words are deliberately twisted in knots to tie you to positions you do not hold?

- "Can you believe how bigoted he is," the crowd bays.
- "He offended me," wails another.
- "I am offended on behalf of another!"

That you have committed no actual harm is irrelevant, and there need be no sin. When the crowd's bloodlust is aroused and the tweets are flying, the question is never whether there will be a cancellation, only whose turn it is in the dock today.

And don't think you can throw yourself upon the mercy of this court. Mercy only grows in soil watered by compassion and understanding, of which this mob has neither in abundance. The only water flowing on these grounds is the raging flood that etches first channels and then ravines into even the firmest bedrock.

Nay, no matter how abject your apology, absolution will not be forthcoming. Rather, we observe the opposite: the stronger your apology, the graver must have been your offense!

But the greatest harm is to your own soul. By offering an apology where none is due, you give credence to the false claims against you. Do not weaken your conviction by submitting to unjust jabs. Just as the valid argument does not become so by virtue of the multitude's praise, nor does the jabbering of a lunatic horde render your point defective.

"But surely it is worthwhile to put down enduring truths. For even though many will misunderstand, and even more will not hear, still the benefit will be real to some." True enough, dear reader.

If you do expose your thoughts to public opinion for this noble purpose, make sure that you have first built up your defenses as carefully as you have built your arguments.

Until you are ready, it is safest to withdraw into solitude and contemplation. In the quiet, your mind can expand and roam. Spend your time with a small group of friends, who are equally committed to self-improvement.

These friends will identify the flaws in your ill-considered arguments, but will not declare *you* flawed as a result. Your own thoughts are improved by refining away these flaws, and thus the battle leaves you strengthened rather than worn.

Lest you think that I write for my own sake alone, I shall share with you three excellent sayings along the same lines. Consider the first in payment of my debt to you and the others as advance deposits.

Epictetus serves up this reminder that the persons we surround ourselves with are vital to our progress:

> The key is to keep company only with people who uplift you, whose presence calls forth your best.

You might think it was his great wealth and power that led Bernard Baruch to this next thought, but the wisdom in it is equally available to the pauper:

> Be who you are and say what you feel, because those who mind don't matter, and those who matter don't mind.

And the third saying, from modern-day philosopher Henry David Thoreau, reminds us that we need nothing so much as our own well-ordered mind:

> I never found the companion that was so companionable as solitude. We are for the most part more lonely when we go abroad among men than when we stay in our chambers.

Take these words to heart, dear reader, to fortify your resolve neither to be shaken by praise nor blame.

True goodness comes from within, and thus your focus lies there.

Be well.

Chapter Four

On Attending to Yourself

There is no one with whom you more profitably spend time than yourself

I mean what I say: You should scorn public opinion, shun social media, and be shaken neither by praise nor blame.

Do not trust a thoughtless person. Leave them all if you can but trust yourself.

Build a foundation within yourself and it cannot be eroded by what others say or do. If you rely for your strength on others, it may be taken away at any time.

As the Buddhist scriptures enshrined in the Dhammapada urge us:

> Better than a hundred years not considering how all things arise and pass away is one single day of life if one considers how all things arise and pass away.

When you are true to yourself, you need not fear the judgment of time. Though your fellow man may judge you, aroused by anonymity, anger, and spite, you can rest assured that you are true to a higher purpose. Better solitary confinement to preserve your peace of mind!

Here is how I wish to see you. No, rather what I already see, for a wish is an empty thought: there is no one with whom you more profitably spend time than yourself.

You are already showing your understanding and strength of character by confidently putting our lessons into practice. Many hear, but few listen. I rejoice that your ears are open, and wise words are falling on the fertile ground of your mind.

A sound mind is a foundation that can support the grandest structures. Continue on in this way, and nothing will slow your progress.

As is now my habit, I send you along your way with a token. It is another true wisdom from the mind of Henry David Thoreau:

> What you get by achieving your goals is not as important as what you become by achieving your goals.

The masses foolishly mistake the goalpost for the goal. They spend their mortal lives on the idea that accomplishment is measured in things.

You, however, will appreciate that real wisdom comes in understanding that it is the daily shaping, turning, and grinding of the stone on the wheel that makes the gem, and not the shiny bauble that any fool can simply buy.

Be well.

Chapter Five

On Introverts

Introversion is not something that is remedied by exposure. If anything, repeated forays out of comfortable seclusion only strengthen the desire to return to safety

I talked recently with your friend D. after a lecture. He is capable and gives the impression immediately that he is a sincere student.

When I challenged him, he was at first hesitant to respond. I could see him drawing away before he pulled himself back, and I fault him not. It is a natural instinct, particularly among the inexperienced, to avoid a confrontation and retreat to safety.

An introvert is never so safe as inside their own head.

And I do not doubt that though he will be cured of the affliction of youth, he will continue to shy away even as his experience grows.

Introversion is not something that is remedied by exposure. If anything, repeated forays out of comfortable seclusion only strengthen the desire to return to safety.

Examples of accomplished recluses come easily to mind: Howard Hughes was fantastically wealthy and freakishly eccentric, all but guaranteeing he would be of constant interest.

He could so little bear interaction with others that he would shut himself away; he spent four months in a studio screening room without once leaving. Upon checking in to the Desert Inn in Las Vegas, he refused to leave, eventually buying the hotel to avoid confronting the owners.

Or consider Harper Lee, who blazed into the public eye after publishing *To Kill a Mockingbird*. We could not get enough of her, but she had her fill of us and so retreated into isolation and published nothing more for over half a century.

Some types of people thrive on exposure, while others wilt and withdraw.

As I noted, practice alone cannot undo the introvert element of human nature. If we could simply wish to change our nature and make it so, wishes would rule the world.

An introvert by birth will be an introvert at death, no matter how often they force themselves into public interactions to lessen the power of their feelings.

But you need not worry if you yourself or another you encounter has introvert tendencies because all that your progress requires is within you.

It is time now for my parting remark. Listen and learn from this lovely lesson:

> When witnessing the good action of another, encourage yourself to follow his example. Hearing of the mistaken action of another, advise yourself not to emulate it. Censure yourself, never another.

This dear reader is the wisdom of the Zen practitioners, who remind us we can behave correctly when there is no one about to correct us.

The introvert need never be separated from both good and bad examples, and from both, they may take their lessons though they stay secluded.

When we bring to mind a virtuous act, it serves as an example for us to emulate. And observing the foolish in their cavorting, we see clearly the line we know not to cross.

Blessed are they who, by keeping both the worst and best in their thoughts, know which paths to avoid and which to favor.

Though we may shun all others as a measure of our self-sufficiency, we can still measure ourselves against the standards of humankind.

Be well.

Chapter Six

On Keeping a Low Profile

I say this: The mob will hate you if you are wrong, and they will hate you even more if you are right

It is worthy to cultivate a sound mind in a sound body.

Our peace of mind is threatened most by three types of worry:

- of the many failures that can afflict our bodies,
- that we will lack the things we think we need, and
- what other people think of us.

Of these, the interaction with your fellow man creates the greatest potential for trouble.

All that the hermit lacks in possessions, comfort, and interactions, he gains in being free of the affliction that is neighbors.

In solitude, you can focus on your own thoughts. In a neighborhood you can scarcely be heard among the din of silently competing boasts: The Pelosis installed a $20,000 refrigerator, the Bidens bought a second home, and the Trumps have gilded their very bathrooms.

You are making do with a three-year-old BMW, and your last vacation was to Boston, not the Bahamas. Oh! for the days when you only had to keep up with the Jones.

Just as you cannot help but notice the crazed consumption of your neighbors, never be lulled into thinking your actions are beneath their regard.

And though you feel you must wither under your neighbors' condescension when you are outdone, that is a faint breeze compared to the furies you will unleash if you temporarily pull ahead on the hedonistic treadmill.

Our fellow man hates us least when we know our station, and that is always comfortably below our fellow, wherever the level may be. We can suffer grievous physical injuries and carry on, but an injured pride is fatal to many a friendship.

You cannot hide from prying eyes, short of taking up your own hermit's cave, but you can try not to draw attention, either positive or negative.

Remember, you can be hurt by the one, by the few, or by the many. If you wish not to be mauled, don't stroll through the zoo wafting meat perfume.

Putting a sign on your lawn bearing a political message will draw the ire of different-thinking neighbors like ants to crumbs at a picnic.

If you hold opinions that may inflame passions among arsonists, do not blow on them in the hopes of making them grow, because it is you who stands directly in front of the fire. Rather whisper such seditious thoughts to yourself.

"But," you say "do you really counsel letting the ignorant masses stifle free speech and clear thinking? It is the mob who are mistaken, and by remaining silent, do I not enable mindless tyranny?"

I say this: The mob will hate you if you are wrong, and they will hate you even more if you are right.

By speaking out as an individual, you threaten the consensus. Nothing is more harmful to the shallow-minded, because they instinctively grasp that their fragile foundations are built on sand. Thus, they cannot permit a wise voice to even puff in their direction.

By withdrawing from the public eye, you must take care not to present yourself as an easy target. A drop of blood in the water attracts sharks from fathoms away.

So too is a need for affirmation fatal to your safe passage. You withdraw not because you fear the public's opinion, whether good or bad, but because it does not concern you.

What concerns you is your well-ordered mind and your self-possession, and this no mob can plunder. In needing only basics and eschewing luxury, you find sanctuary within your own four walls. You then can busy yourself with the job of clear thinking.

Much like a road needs to be cleared of all obstacles before you can safely navigate it, your mind speeds along that much more expeditiously when cleared of extraneous fears, worries, and wants.

There is one exception to the basic rule of keeping a low profile: When passions are inflamed to such an extent that you may not be silent, lest a negative inference be drawn.

When silence is not an option, neither is meekly submitting to the mob.

Though they would tear you limb from limb, you must not say things you do not believe are true. This will erode your soul, and in short order your body as well, as surely as the mob's pitchforks and torches, but with the difference that you inflict the wound on yourself.

You may know a great truth and keep it to yourself because the mob's ears are shut. Fair enough. But you cannot lend your voice to a mob committing wrong, for this is both to perpetuate the wrong and give the mob power over the one possession that is truly yours, your self-possession.

You eagerly await a final truth that I should now share with you. Such is the quality of this addition to our store of wisdom that we may shout it from the rooftops, hear all who may.

> It is not the man who has too little, but the man who craves more, who is poor.

Here I return to our most trusted of guides, the Stoics, and that towering figure among them, Seneca. It was his particular gift to collect, curate, and sift the wisdom of the ages, and his courage to make it available for all with the desire to know it.

Man is the only animal that can instantly create both scarcity and abundance with the exact same quantity of material.

You are poor when you think you lack something, and you are as rich as your appreciation for what you have.

Be well.

Chapter Seven

On Looking Within

For us to know the true worth of something, we must look beyond the packaging. And this takes time

You are making a sound investment, one which will pay dividends, if you do as you describe in your letters, in regularly training your mind.

There are many before you who will stand as gatekeepers, and not all of them are benevolent:

- from the university administrators who say you cannot be educated without their degree,
- to the licensing bodies who claim you cannot run your business without their certification,
- to the self-help authors who say you cannot be happy without buying their book.

When it comes to achieving a well-ordered mind, none of these are required. They are in fact obstacles to progress, but only for those who listen to them. All you need to advance is within.

Think of the gardener quietly tilling the soil, patiently weeding, and enjoying the feel of the sun on her face as she watches her seedlings sprout and grow. It was no diploma or license that enabled this wholesome and satisfying work.

The poet putting pen to paper is tapping into a spring that flows purest when it is free of external pollution. The self-help book might as well be called the self-doubt book for all the good it will do someone who is trying to master their thoughts and emotions.

We are easily fooled by outward appearances because we are encouraged to be productive.

"What do you mean?" you say, "Is it not correct to be about our business in an efficient way? What harm is there in productivity?"

I will tell you, dear reader, where the harm lies. When you have set your goals around productivity, you are enabling yourself to do more. The more you can do, the more you agree to do, and the more productive you become. Except in your headlong rush, you have learned that you must make quick decisions, and hence you look no further than the surface of things.

- "This one has many followers and is popular on the talk shows. I will listen to him because he must have something important to say."

- "That one has accumulated great wealth and has three companies. I will work with her because she must be a brilliant businessperson."

- "This book is a New York Times bestseller. I will read it because it must contain important truths."

Can you ever be wrong in following the masses? Going along with the crowd brings you certainty, yes, but it is comfort only that you will not be alone in your beliefs, not that they are necessarily true.

For does not the crowd celebrate a person for their designer clothes, their sports car, and their expensive watch? When this tells you almost nothing about the person inside those clothes and that car, except that they have put faith in flashy displays.

A full head of elegantly coiffed hair is no guarantee of intelligence within. A sharply dressed man may be dull as a rock when it comes to what they understand of the world.

For us to know the true worth of something, we must look beyond the packaging. And this takes time.

Better that you sit with a single book and work your way through its pages, than to skim a hundred dust jackets and think you have gained wisdom from primary colors and blurbs.

Better that you engage in deep conversation, where you actively listen to your companion before you decide whether there is substance to their words.

And when you are building your own substance, do not look to the surface but look within. You are most productive when you attempt the least but do so thoroughly and completely.

Those who would judge you by your appearance are blind to your true value. The thing we should prize above all is invisible to a superficial inspection.

What is that, you ask? It is a well-ordered mind, working in harmony with circumstances and nature to bring about reason.

A person who can bring reason to bear in every situation is not led astray by emotions or bribery or threat of harm. They live content, untroubled by everything that plagues their fellow man.

Be well.

Chapter Eight

On Word Games and Worthy Matters

People spend their time in want and worry, and their earnest efforts are destined for futility because they are working towards ends that can never make them happy

You ask me to study your lengthy query, and I worry that your hand grew as weary as my eyes as you piled up the pages.

I shall be at leisure in my review, to give you a reply worthy of your own effort. Though I will not reply in kind, at least when counted in words. Rather, I will deliberate with care so that I may respond decisively.

In this I seek to be the good man that Confucius meant when he said:

> Does not the difficulty of deciding what is right to do necessarily imply slowness to speak?

And when it comes to what is right, let us remain a moment with Confucius to distinguish further:

> Better than one who knows what is right is one who is fond of what is right; and better than one who is fond of what is right is one who delights in what is right.

There are many who delight in wordplay, and they mistake their cleverness for wisdom. I am not overly fond of these, my dear reader, and neither should you be so easily amused.

When used to gain an unfair advantage over the unwary, words of influence are a stealthy tool in the hands of the adept.

But an audience brought to your side by trickery is like a nest built high in a swaying tree: It rests on an unstable platform and can be swayed again when the winds blow from another direction.

When your fragile point tumbles to earth, not only do you lose the high ground, but you have also given the crowd reason to question your own reason. Fool me once, shame on you. Fool me twice, shame on me.

"But," you say, "I am not talking about words used to convince, but rather to entertain."

If you spend any time with words, you will surely appreciate being brought to a smile by virtue of words being brought together. I think of the words from the Irish band U2 in their song *Running to Stand Still*:

> You've got to cry without weeping, talk without speaking, scream without raising your voice.

Although entertainment can be serious business, such word games are rarely the mark of a serious student. What they offer is but a distraction, and it is not harmless to distract yourself, let alone others.

The business of philosophy is to help man master reason, not to lose it.

People spend their time in want and worry, and their earnest efforts are destined for futility because they are working towards ends that can never make them happy.

- They want possessions, promotions, and power, and worry that what they have obtained will be taken from them.

- They are bothered by what others think, say, and do.

- They have time and waste it, good friends they take for granted, and have let luxuries deprive them of the enjoyment of simple pleasures.

- They turn a cold shoulder to the guests in their living room as they twitch the curtain aside in search of the ones they invited who do not arrive.

- Both responsibility and its absence torment them, and illness and death await, unbidden but unavoidable.

For all of these challenges, philosophy holds an answer. Shall we not dispense with play and get to the business of discerning what is right reason?

Knowing what is right, shall we not make sure that we climb down the ladder of our own desires to not only fondly consider the right path but to delight in leading the way?

You undermine both your case and yourself when you spend too much time in the company of word games.

It is not hurtful to tell the truth to those seeking wisdom; the real cruelty is keeping the truth to yourself for fear it will go unheeded.

And even though none hear your words, let your life serve as an example for any who are watching, now or later.

If you could wear a billboard about your person and stand in front of the doors of the bank, the car dealer, and the shopping mall, what words would you put upon it?

"It won't make you happy ..." deserves to be writ large on your front, and "The end is nigh!" upon your back.

Knowing that all things end, end your attachment to things, and you will find yourself on the path to happiness and nothing external can dislodge you.

Be well.

Chapter Nine

On Those Who Will Not See

Many people are the architects of their own misery, never realizing that with similar effort and much less worry, they could just as easily be about the building of a personal paradise

As if I needed yet another reminder that time is not one of the things given to humankind to control, I received your letter only today, though you mailed it many weeks ago.

- Was it COVID lockdowns that kept your missive locked in a dormant mailroom?

- Was it a canceled flight that kept your letter grounded and prevented it from flying to me with its usual dispatch?

- Or perhaps it was an overfull shipping container plugging the Suez Canal that kept your words from me, just as they kept shopfuls of sneakers and cheap cotton t-shirts from the shelves.

Although your words were missing in action for months, I trust that you have not been idle yourself but have been about the business of bettering yourself.

And what better way to do this than by remembering that the business of others troubling you is really just you causing trouble for yourself.

"What can you mean?" you say, "I am not causing others to behave the way they do. Should I now take credit for the sun setting and the moon rising?"

I would grant few people agency over their own actions, dear reader, let alone the actions of others.

No, what I refer to is how you respond to what happens, for this is the one thing that is always within your control.

Many people are the architects of their own misery, never realizing that with similar effort and much less worry, they could just as easily be about the building of a personal paradise.

What Plutarch wrote of Cicero in "The Parallel Lives" applies equally to many people today:

> He was prevented by many public affairs which were contrary to his wishes, and by many private troubles, most of which seem to have been of his own choosing.

We can wish for what we have not and so make ourselves unhappy and choose to consume our particular poison and so make ourselves unwell.

But who says we can only wish for and choose that which makes us miserable and sick? I grant you full agency over your thoughts, my dear reader, and I urge you to see clearly and use your power wisely.

Seeing clearly is something that the ancient philosophers did surprisingly well when one considers that they had no benefit of corrective lenses, not to mention the corrective surgery, that we take for granted today.

Perfect eyesight is available to us today in the form of laser eye surgery, seamless bifocals, and daily disposable contact lenses. We are not to be without our prescription, be it in our sunglasses or in our specially formulated blue-phase shifting glasses designed for viewing computer screens.

If only our vision could be as clear as our eyesight.

For all of our 20–20 eyesight, I would say that we are more blind than ever to what is truly important.

- We run after riches, and we tell ourselves that we cannot get by on anything less. Then there are the pursuits we busy ourselves in.

- The farther you travel from the countryside, the less likely you are to find people who work with their hands.

- You may create virtual worlds in your coding and be transported to new heights on the backs of unicorns. But if you have lost thereby the simple pleasure of digging a furrow in the dirt, planting a seed, and nurturing it to flower and eventually fruit, you are less attached to the ways of the real world in a materially important way.

"Must I grow my own crops to be well fed," I hear you ask, "and travel about on horses shod by my own blackened hands to travel well?"

This is not my message.

If you would be satisfied with a day's labor, ask first if you have satisfied anyone's needs beyond your own, and then what harm you have wrought in bringing about your ends.

- Have you made people see and appreciate their lives more clearly by devising new methods to keep their faces planted to their screens?

- Have you made people see and understand their civic duties with more fidelity by rewriting history to suit a new narrative of systemic oppression?

- Does manipulating people to part with their money with the twaddle you call marketing bring into sharp relief that their happiness lies not in things, or are you throwing sand in their eyes?

"We are just giving people what they want," the professional classes cry. "And if we were not selling things of value, why are we being showered with money for our efforts?"

If there was ever a false indicator, it would be to follow the flow of money.

When you spend your day snuffing out one after another each of the faint lights that line the path to reason, do not then express wonder that all now wander aimlessly in the dark.

When with your distractions you poke a stick in the eye of mankind's ability to sit quietly in contemplation, I say you are no blindfolded judge of people's natural desire to see.

But though all voices are clamoring for our attention, and all hands are pushing us steadily away from our desired course, still we have it within our powers to see clearly.

Pull away the blinders from your eyes, for no one holds them to your head but yourself.

Free yourself of the burden of doing what others do just because they do it, and you become free to see the way back to the path of reason.

Be well.

Chapter Ten

On Seven Popular Places

If you do not wish to be tempted, do not wander blithely through the bazaar of modern desires

Every place is the same as every other, dear reader, in the sense that we are all planted on the same earth, and the sun rises and sets equally on us all.

Why is it that some places seem destined to become places of wonder, whereas others bring out only the excesses in us?

I would have you avoid popular places altogether, at least until you have learned to tame your passions, for fear that in chasing what others call desirable you lose sight of what you should find valuable.

There are three types of modern-day meccas calling out the secular masses on their pilgrimages of tourism, adventurism, or debauchery.

For the tourist, consider the modern-day list of the seven wonders of the world:

- there is the Great Wall of China;
- the statue of Christ the Redeemer looking down from Corcovado mountain in Brazil;
- the Incan citadel of Machu Picchu in Peru;
- the Mayan ruins at Chichen Itza in Mexico;
- the Colosseum in Rome, Italy;

- the Taj Mahal in Agra, India; and
- the former capital of the Nabataean empire in Petra, Jordan.

Note that all but two of these are ruins, mute testament to great civilizations gone under. Most visit them to marvel at their accomplishments, though what we should be pondering are the reasons for their decline.

The grand adventurer is called to the great heights of the Seven Summits tour. To climb the tallest peak on each continent is to reach the penultimate height. Everest, Aconcagua, Denali, Kilimanjaro, Vinson, Elbrus.

"Penultimate height," you ask, "why what could be greater than this feat?" Remember that when it comes to one-upping our fellow man, humans display creativity unmatched by any less selfish pursuit.

The seventh peak varies, you see, according to the explorer who lays claim to a new route to fame: Puncak Jaya, Kosciusko, Mont Blanc, Mauna Kea, Mount Wilhelm.

I do not doubt that some molehill is even now having its stature reconsidered if it will yield an alternative route to the Guinness Book of Records.

All these intrepid climbers are deemed mere amateurs, however, upon the addition of the North and South poles to the Explorer's Grand Slam.

I do not need to slam the lesson home for you, dear reader, to eschew the routes of both the "grand tour" tourist and the "grand slam" explorer.

You have a greater sense than that. But I sense you are showing a weakness for the third type of popular destination, and that is the party spot, one of the places people go to blow off steam and where we let human emotions run free.

These riotous pools of excess humanity are exemplified in the following seven ways:

- on Spring Break in Fort Lauderdale and South Beach in Florida;
- in the bars and beaches of Cancun, Mexico;
- among the beads tossed from balconies during Mardi Gras in New Orleans;

- anywhere in the clubs of Benidorm, Spain, or dotting the Levante and Poniente beaches;

- amidst the sweaty dancers of Carnival in Rio de Janeiro, Brazil;

- behind the painted masks of the 72 hours of madness that is Dame Fasnacht in Basel; and

- ahead of the thundering hooves of the running of the bulls during the nine-day festival of Sanfermines in Pamplona, Spain.

What these all have in common is reckless abandon. The revelers give up their reason to bathe in emotion.

"For all the rest of the year that we are dutiful citizens, give me these few days to run free!"

If I wish to see people acting crazily, I do not need to see them drunken and heading for a night of unprotected sex. I do not need to hear them shouting and singing on their way to being hunched over a gutter spilling their guts in other noisy ways.

I can tell you without looking that their faces will be lined with dark circles and regret as they line up to board the charter flight back home to their "normal" life.

No, if I want to discern true madness, I will observe the office worker in their tower, the suburban parent about their errands, and the mall walker making their rounds.

Their "normal" lives are just as insane as when they are on holiday taking a "break" from their senses. Why is this?

Because they have set their whole lives in pursuit of things they know do not satisfy them or make them happy, and then they do it again and again expecting a different result.

For those who are training their minds, solitude may be the best way to avoid early unwelcome tests.

If you do not wish to be tempted, do not wander blithely through the bazaar of modern desires. If you struggle to tell what looks good from what will feel right, do not surrender your emotions to the passions of the ungoverned mob.

Better a single hour spent sitting in contemplation, cultivating your well-ordered mind, than a hundred hours lost to mindless revelry. How many hours do we spend in scrolling through TikTok videos or in never-ending games of Candy Crush?

We are so much more easily led astray than we are led forward, and once having left the path we find our way back only with difficulty.

It is not the places that lead us astray, dear reader, but our minds.

I would have you remember, though, that the places you are of a mind to go will shape your thinking, and may keep you from moving from the place you are in.

So heed my advice to avoid all places that allow you to avoid thinking, and you will think better of yourself for it.

Be well.

Chapter Eleven

On Philosophers, New and Old

Such is the bounty of philosophy: Though all are capable of being fed with what is already on offer, still we are ever creating new dishes to suit the palette of modern tastes

I am never so engaged with companions as when I am sitting by myself in my study.

When I am with friends, we converse about the topics of the day. These are the things that excite us and are designed to outrage us.

For the news is entertainment first and foremost, and information is secondary at best. Indeed, relevant information presented in context has the tendency to calm passions, not inflame them, so you will not find it often in today's media.

We talk of friends, absent and present. Your name came up, and talking of you gives me joy second only to being with you.

Much of the talk of friends is mundane. A promotion, an acquisition, a setback, a fall; parents moving from frailty to illness to death's door; children and their youthful mistakes.

Knowing what pitfalls lie ahead on the path is no safeguard against stumbling. It does not help a parent to tell their child such things, for some mistakes must be lived to be learned.

And, amidst the necessary lubrication that smooths all conversations, there is periodically a topic of worth and weight. But how few are the moments when such topics are safely raised.

If any are feeling stressed or unprepared, or if another has some news they wish to share, or if someone is distracted by a ping from their phone, the moment is gone, extinguished before it had a chance to flame into a meaningful exchange.

In my office, I have a most attentive audience.

They eagerly await my return, and I can almost hear them saying, "Finally! Someone has come to treat with our ideas."

Here there are no distractions I do not create myself, no interruptions I do not myself introduce, no superficialities to keep me from delving beneath the surface of things.

All the examples I need are on display before me:

- the good deeds I can revisit, and ponder the reasons why;

- the failures, faults, and blows of fortune I observe from a safe distance, and I need not offer condolences for these deeds are also done and gone.

- I have nothing less than the condensed wisdom of the ages, the best from thousands of years and millions of people.

What kind of person would I be if I were unmoved in the presence of this multitude?

- Confucius and the Buddha, half a world apart, yet closer in spirit than many who live on neighboring streets.

- The Bible and the Quran, seemingly leading down opposite paths, yet treading the same ground more often than not.

- Plato and Aristotle, Seneca and Marcus Aurelius, each building on the solid foundations of the last.

- And I haven't even gotten to the contributions of the last two millennia, dear reader!

We each have the materials at hand to keep building the palace of human knowledge and wisdom.

Whether we are merely dusting off cobwebs in an existing great hall, rekindling light to shine again out freshly washed windows, or renovating a room that has fallen into disrepair from lack of use.

Some of us will go so far as to commence construction of an entirely new wing, for humanity is growing, and the many mouths need shelter and nourishment.

Such is the bounty of philosophy: Though all are capable of being fed with what is already on offer, still we are ever creating new dishes to suit the palette of modern tastes.

The goal of the meal is the same — to bring succor and feed life — but each generation is given the instructions to the printing press and encouraged to add to the book of recipes.

Though I may never leave the four corners of my study, I roam the halls of our human palace of wisdom freely and widely.

And where I find a window shuttered or a door blocked, and sometimes even a brick wall in my way, I am resolved to break through, pick up the rubble lying about, and keep on building.

Be well.

Chapter Twelve

On Abiding in One Place

Progress is inversely proportional to the breadth of your focus. Include in your scope many things, and you will make little progress. Focus on one thing, and you will advance it the most

When I advise you to be steadfast in your thinking and your decisions, I urge you to abide in one place both physically and mentally. This does not mean that you make no progress.

"What can you mean?" you ask, "If I am bound to one spot, in my thinking, my abode, my actions, how am I making any progress? Life requires action, motion. I do not want to sit around doing nothing."

The answer is simple, dear reader, but also profound. I will give you several ways of looking at the solution, and you may choose the angle that suits you best. To start, let me ask you a few questions in turn.

- Do you think someone who drives their air-conditioned car 100 miles a day has learned more of the landscape than the person who walks daily the same quiet streets of their neighborhood?

- Does the politician who changes their mind hourly upon checking the prevailing wind of opinion have more profound thoughts by virtue of having had many conflicting thoughts?

- Is the person who purchases their weekly lottery tickets before returning home to their day trading more of an investor than the person who automatically directs a percentage of their income to an index fund and never thinks of it?

Just as the opposite of busyness is not idleness, busyness is no guarantee of productivity. How many busy people do we know who prodigiously waste their time?

When I say abide in one place, I mean three things: That you focus your efforts on one thing at a time, that you avoid distractions and temptations, and that you bend your will to making steady progress in a consistent direction.

In this way, you will move mountains. Continuous improvement is disarmingly powerful because it does not matter how slight the incremental steps are, just that you keep moving.

Progress is inversely proportional to the breadth of your focus. Include in your scope many things, and you will make little progress. Focus on one thing, and you will advance it the most.

The reason we do not prioritize is because we fear the consequences of prioritization. To say "This is the most important thing I should be working on right now," is to say implicitly, "And everything else is less important."

Most people would rather drown themselves in work than admit that some things are more valuable than others. And though we know this is true, but do not act accordingly, what does this say about us?

Do not let yourself off the hook. Do the hard work of thinking about what is most important before you undertake any tasks, and you will have set yourself up for success.

Having set yourself up for success, shut the door to the many sneak thieves who would rob you of your progress. Distractions and temptations take many forms:

- Friends, gossip, the news, social media, TV and movies.

- Changing jobs, changing cities, vacations, travel.

- New information, more information, a better way.

- An urgent task, an emergency, a new priority.

I say barricade yourself in a fortress against the army fighting for your attention.

"You have gone mad," you say, "if you think the best course is for me to shut myself in a monk's cell and cut off all contact with friends, with information, with the real world."

If I am crazy, dear reader, it is for thinking that saying the truth will make people believe the truth. For I am telling you nothing but the truth here, though, of course, I exaggerate to make my point.

Yes, you need interaction with others, you need to pay attention to making your way in the material world, and you cannot stop time by putting your watch in a drawer.

But I urge you to consider that every moment you spend on something other than what you have decided is your most valuable pursuit is a theft you commit on yourself.

By no means do I expect you to work every hour of the day. No one is so disciplined, nor need be, although we can train ourselves to be more focused than we might at first believe.

The way to handle your rest, relaxation, and recovery is to make it something you actively plan and direct, rather than something that slips unbidden upon your consciousness and spirits it away.

When you take a break for exercise, when you meet up with friends for dinner, or when you leave your studies for a vacation, it will be because you decided it was the most important thing to be doing at that moment.

Give your rest and recovery the same priority that you would your work, and you will get the most benefit from it. Let yourself be pulled away from either your rest or work by giving in to distraction, and you are wasting your time in both cases.

The last component, steady progress in a consistent direction, is easier to believe in after you have seen its effects for yourself. For now, trust me when I tell you that taking but a single step each day will bring you further along than all those whose efforts are heroic but sporadic.

You may still have days of mighty progress, and they will be welcome. But you should be just as happy to accomplish a tiny, incremental step, so long as it is self-directed and in the direction of your choosing. Because this means you are staying true to yourself, working on what you have decided is most important, and making progress.

I call upon American President Thomas Jefferson to reinforce today's lesson. His own actions were the proof of the truth of his words, judge for yourself:

> Determine never to be idle. No person will have occasion to complain of the want of time who never loses any. It is wonderful how much may be done if we are always doing.

Be well.

Chapter Thirteen

On Mind Viruses

The mind viruses are vices such as jealousy, greed, ambition, spite, and fear

So, I gather you think I have been rather informal in my emails of late, addressing weighty topics more like a casual encounter than a formal lecture with proper respect given to the subject at hand.

It is true that when I put my hands on the keyboard I imagine you are before me and we are simply talking. But do not mistake a comfortable conversation for one that lacks seriousness, dear reader. We are discussing important matters and their significance is not lessened though we try to keep our spirits light.

I do grant you that cleverness is no guarantee of correctness. In fact, the glib speaker who uses every oratorial trick is one whom you must attend to even more carefully. We are easily fooled by the surface of things, especially if they are pleasing to the eye, or in this case the ear.

Be especially wary of the hypocrite, the one whose actions in private do not match their flowery words in public. I work to achieve consistency of thoughts and deeds, and when I stray my wife is there to remind me.

I follow the dictates of my own thinking, and I am striving always to tell you what I think. If I also strive to string together my words in a pleasing fashion, let me do so in ways that shed light rather than merely dazzle.

We are always at risk of being dazzled because there are many things to distract us. A shiny new car, a sleek phone, and brightly-colored displays: These are specifically designed to entice us, and a great deal of thought and effort goes into making them appealing.

What then are we to think of the handsome and well-coiffed politician, promising to solve all our problems with other people's money and assuring us that nothing that happens to us is our fault?

- Is the politician also not an item on display, offered for sale to the buying public?

- And just how has he or she been designed to appeal to us? Is it to our better virtues or is the appeal to our fears and prejudices?

We are in a never-ending battle for our well-ordered minds, dear reader. For every hard-won step of progress we make in seeing through the surface of things to the substance beneath, a hundred new temptations and distractions are paraded before us.

It may help to think of your mind like a powerful computer, capable of performing the most amazing feats, but with this flaw: the input/output channels are hardwired to be completely unprotected against viruses.

Do you think you are safe because you have avoided being infected by such obvious conspiracies as QAnon, Bill Gates' plan to inject us all with microchips in vaccines, or the idea that the World Economic Forum is really a cover for the Illuminati seeking our subjugation via the so-called "global reset?"

I say take no comfort from the follies you have spotted. Say you have taken fifty steps safely in a minefield. Does that mean you should kick up your heels and run freely? If a sniper has fallen silent for a while, will you be the first to poke your head above the parapet?

And coming back to our computer, what would you think of the person who says "Oh, don't worry, I ran the anti-virus program two years ago when I set up my desktop?" You would back away from them slowly, just as you would an unexploded land mine because this person is a danger to themselves and others. That they are oblivious to their condition is sad, but no less dangerous.

This is your choice, dear reader: Either take regular steps to be on your constant guard or risk becoming a ticking time bomb of discontent, ready to explode at the slightest provocation of Fate not going your way. Once you realize that the mind is not immune from viruses that come in many forms, you will see the necessity and wisdom of running your personal anti-virus program daily.

"Tell me more about these viruses," you say, "and what is the protection program you speak of?"

The mind viruses are vices such as jealousy, greed, ambition, spite, and fear — all things that we know of and have been trying to put in their proper place. Just like a computer virus compels the CPU to perform destructive actions against its programming, so do mind viruses compel you to actions that erode your contentment and happiness.

Being infected with vices blinds us to the true value of things and causes us to pursue things of little or no value at the cost of our peace of mind.

Your protection is reason applied by the well-ordered mind. By checking every input and every stimulus against your pre-programmed list of personal values, you can identify when you are being offered a false good or false emotion.

Remember this: There are very few "trusted sources" in the world. Virtually all minds have been infected by bad ideas and sloppy thinking and thus their course of thought has been corrupted.

Though they may have the power of life and death over your person, do not give them unfettered access to your mind! It is the one place you can be secure in your self-possession, but only if you do not throw open the gates to any vandals who seek entry.

I do not mean to tell you to cut all connections to the world, tempting though that seems at times. We are social creatures, with moral responsibilities not just to ourselves, but to those close to us as well as to broader society.

Open the connection to let the world into your mind but filter it as carefully as you would drinking water from a muddy stream. Your connections to others bring you life's essence, but only so long as you do not poison yourself by consuming everything offered.

Be well.

Chapter Fourteen

On Popular Authors

By using your reading as a mirror into your own thoughts, you train yourself to pay attention to your mind

I have told you to spend your spare time in reading to train your mind. That you should read widely and well, sampling many authors across time.

That when you read, you should seek to make the lessons more than fleeting by taking them to yourself, for example by summarizing them in your own words. In time, you will be able to build your own new structures using the materials you have stored in your warehouse.

I may have left you with the impression that your leisure reading must be on weighty subjects by serious authors if you are to add value to your stores.

No doubt you gain from studying the greats, because these will give you strong foundations to build upon, steel girders that can hold the weight of the tallest towers. But remember that the materials abundant in most buildings are more common stuff: Walls and ceilings made of drywall, concrete blocks, and bricks and mortar.

No matter whether you expect to learn the most from the masters, it is worth considering why the less serious topics and more popular authors have such reach.

Why do they sell books in such abundance, and how do they keep their readers eagerly clamoring for more? The academic dismisses these questions easily because they know that critical acclaim is no indication of correctness.

Indeed, the worst insult a certain type of scientist can levy on a colleague is that they are a mere popularizer of science, and not substantive in themselves.

But I ask you, what is wrong with making something understandable to many? Writing on complex topics in a manner that only a few can decipher is no great feat and not uncommon. It is a far greater task and eventual accomplishment to take a complex topic and make it understandable to all.

For the moment, let us ensure we are not ourselves snobs, but ready to take wisdom wherever we find it. Is there wisdom to be found in the best-seller list, and if so, why?

At this moment I expect you are calling to mind all the times I told you to avoid the self-help aisle like an active minefield. Though I gave you permission to sneak one or the other volume from these explosively dangerous shelves, am I now giving up my caution by opening the shopping cart to this year's summer read?

I think it is a mistake to dismiss Stephen King as no more than "America's schlockmeister," even though he himself says he is resigned to this fate, or to say that J.K. Rowling is not serious because she writes of wizards and magic.

Do we value less Elmore Leonard's gift just because he wrote crime fiction? Michael Lewis writes no fiction at all, but do we relegate him to the top of the display of "popular titles" because he writes individual vignettes tied loosely together rather than weaving tightly wound grand theories?

What do all these authors have in common?

- Stephen King delves into our deepest fears. What he finds there is not pleasant, but can anyone deny that it is a true reflection of what lies hidden within humankind?

- J.K. Rowling spins daydreams, fantasy, and wish fulfillment into epic tales shot through with darkness, suffering, and pain. This combination of the delightful with the spoiled, the pure with the soiled, is no less true than Stephen King's visions.

- Elmore Leonard had a gift for writing dialogue so true to life that you felt yourself a bystander in every scene. You feel less like you are reading an Elmore Leonard novel than living it alongside the characters.

- Michael Lewis's gift is to see the uniqueness in each individual and to let them speak in their own voice. By shining a spotlight on so many individual foibles and peccadillos, we have a chance to recognize ourselves in others.

The thread tying them all together is that they speak honestly and truly about the human condition and about our emotions: What we long for, what we fear, and what makes us angry, sad, and happy.

You would think that because we all feel these emotions, it would be a trivial matter for an author to describe them honestly without omission or exaggeration. And yet it is rare.

Do I take away some of your enjoyment when I tell you to take a lesson from your reading?

I would say do not let me detract from such pleasant times, read and enjoy what you are reading. But if you would be a sincere student and not just idle away your hours without profit, then periodically stop and ask yourself why.

Why did you enjoy that last chapter so much, and why did that other disturb you? What was it exactly that transported you effortlessly from your couch to another world?

The answers to these questions will give you insights into the human condition, but even more so into your own condition.

Your own condition varies from day to day, though you may feel always like the same person. Has it ever happened that a book you loved suddenly turns odious and you find yourself loathe to pick it up, let alone finish it? Has the author turned treacherous, or is it you who has come into a different state of mind?

Both are possible, and you will know the truth if you are mindful in your reading.

By using your reading as a mirror into your own thoughts, you train yourself to pay attention to your mind. This helps form the conditions for following the reason of your well-ordered mind in other things.

In this way, your reading for pleasure will be no less useful to you than your most dutiful studies. If the latter teaches us what we should do, the former can help guide us in how to do it.

Be well.

Chapter Fifteen

On the Greatest Threat

You are never closer to danger than in the presence of your fellow humans. You are safer tucked away in contemplation of ancient wisdom

If you pay too much attention to the news, you will come away worried about all the wrong things.

- Will you be caught up in a twister, carried away by a flash flood, or struck by an errant bolt of lightning? And that's just from watching the weather channel.
- Other channels of doom will tell you to live in fear of dying from lead-poisoned water, radon-suffused earth, and second-hand smoke-filled air.
- Then there are the industrial accidents, derailed freight trains, and collapsing bridges you must assiduously avoid.

That such things happen is undeniable, dear reader. That they are rare indeed is never mentioned, and you could be forgiven for placing wrong odds on your chances of encountering misfortune in such a newsworthy manner.

We do not talk of the greatest danger to people, which is immeasurably more likely to rain down upon us than a piece of space debris falling from the sky.

"What is this great danger," you ask?

It is our fellow people.

You are never closer to danger than in the presence of your fellow humans. When provoked by the tiniest of slights we are something to behold.

And we do not need to be angry to be destructive. Our capacity to do capricious harm also knows no bounds.

- Did early settlers not shoot tens of millions of buffaloes to death out of nothing more than boredom, leaving carcasses to rot across the western plains?
- Carrier pigeons once flew in the billions across the summer sky, hurried now to their graves by the wanton destructiveness of humankind.

If we were better judges of the truly dangerous, we would free all the animals in the zoo and relegate the human visitors to locked cages for the safety of all.

You cannot eliminate your danger from this source, only reduce it.

Be aware that *any* provocation risks being too much, because it is viewed through the eyes of the recipient. You may think you are being amusing or that your insult was but a little thing. Murderous rage has sprung from a wayward glance, the corners of the mouth turning down at the wrong time, to say nothing of an actual encounter with someone prone to violence.

You are safer in the company of the dead, which is one reason I tell you to have your philosophy books about you in great numbers. When safely tucked away in contemplation of ancient wisdom you are less likely to give offense to the living.

However, you give offense even by your absence because we are annoyed by everyone who stands out.

"What, the world is not good enough for you that you feel it necessary to withdraw into seclusion?"

You will be misunderstood in the presence of your fellow person, and you will be misunderstood alone. But at least you make yourself less of a target when you quietly study, and that is something.

Be well.

Chapter Sixteen

On Treading Safely

Remember that being polite costs you nothing while being indifferent may cost you everything

I take it from your response that you think I was too pessimistic in my recent assessment of our fellow person.

"You have exaggerated once again the situation," you say. "Surely it is not so dangerous to be out among humankind."

I say that I have not been dire enough in my warning if you still doubt the point. I am deadly serious, dear reader, but my point was not to have you live in fear or live in seclusion.

Let me thus tell you how you can more safely co-exist in the world.

I told you that people are dangerous and now let's consider specifically what makes them dangerous. No doubt you will readily agree that much harm springs from the passionate emotions of others like envy, hatred, and fear.

Let me consider them in turn and arm you with your defensive weapons against them.

You do not need much for people to envy you. In fact, when you probe your own feelings, you will be forced to concede that the condition of envy is not brought about by abundance but merely by difference.

No matter how little a person has, you will be tempted by envy if they have more than you. No matter how much you have, if another has a penny more you will not rest easily.

The only way to avoid envy is to avoid scrutiny. If you flaunt your possessions do not expect adoring acclaim, only envy.

I do not ask you to become a hermit but give thought to your public displays. The less you show publicly and the more you can content yourself with private displays, the safer you will be among your fellows.

Hatred arises so much more easily than we think. It does not take a great provocation to create passionate hatred.

Why this should be so I do not know, but we can observe it readily enough.

- A driver cuts you off on the way to work, and in that moment, you are ready to abandon your commute, your respectable profession, and everything else.

- For a moment a grim fantasy plays through your head of following that driver to the ends of the earth so you can grind them to dust under your unforgiving boot.

- And then they raise a hand in acknowledgment that they momentarily inconvenienced you, and all is forgotten.

If a murderous fantasy can be called to life by something as trivial as a few seconds' delay in traffic, believe me when I tell you that to interact with people is to engender hatred.

At a minimum, do not deliberately provoke people. I say go a step further and be alert to potential inadvertent slights. Be quick to apologize for all things.

Remember that being polite costs you nothing while being indifferent may cost you everything.

You can use the words of that great counselor Seneca to guide you. The wise man

> will not misinterpret a word or a look; he makes light of all mishaps by interpreting them in a generous way. He does not remember an injury rather than a service.

Now comes fear. There is nothing we will pursue more avidly than attempting to crush out that which strikes fear in us.

Observe how one who fears spiders will crush their lives out and spray poison in copious quantities. The response is out of proportion to the threat, but it is the injury to our peace of mind that drives the overkill.

When you make someone afraid of you, they may appear subdued. But in their minds, you are a threat to their peaceful existence, and they cannot rest while you are a threat.

How do you avoid being feared? Do not avenge slights. Make light of them. Remember the Buddha's words:

> You throw thorns. Falling in my silence they become flowers.

Call to mind the sound advice of Epictetus:

> You will meekly bear a person who reviles you, for you will say upon every occasion, 'It seemed so to him.'

So far, I have been talking about the harm others can do to you, and how to arm yourself against these dangers. There is one danger greater than all this that I would have you avoid, and that is the danger you do to yourself.

I refer now to the failure to behave honestly and honorably in your actions. Bring to mind the Buddha's words here as well when he says:

> So long as an evil deed has not ripened, the fool thinks it is as sweet as honey. But when the evil deed ripens, the fool comes to grief.

Your misbehavior will arouse in others the emotions we have been discussing. But it will also give rise to painful emotions of your own. Doubt, shame, fear of exposure. All these are a steep price to pay for the temporary satisfaction of giving in to your base desires.

When you behave wrongly, the punishment of the state is but confirmation of the sentence you have already laid upon yourself.

So these are your instructions for how to make your way more safely in this world, dear reader. I sleep more easily knowing that you are well-armed for modern life.

Be well.

Chapter Seventeen

On Slogans

It is precisely when you find your emotions aroused by a small handful of words that you must force yourself to pause. Someone is almost certainly trying to manipulate your thinking for their own ends

You know I am no fan of sayings in philosophy. I object to them when they serve as a substitute for the hard work of thinking about and understanding underlying principles.

They have their place as reminders for the scholar and reinforcement for the student. But too often they take the place of thinking and are taken for the substance of an argument rather than merely the headline of an article.

Recently I was reminded of my distaste for superficialities in another context, politics. I sometimes reminisce on the happy hours I once spent reading a favorite newspaper. I am probably misremembering because really the media has done me a favor by becoming so blatantly partisan.

I now no longer have the slightest expectation of being objectively informed when I read a "news" story. I consider each article to be pure propaganda and the only question is whether the author made any attempt to hide their agenda.

I feel like the unsophisticated investor talking to the Wall Street banker: It is not a question of *whether* they are trying to screw me over, just a matter of *how* they are trying to do it this time.

I do not see any distinction in attempted persuasion between the opinion pages and the news section. In fact, I consider opinion writers to be the more intellectually honest. At least they openly purvey their views under an accurate banner.

The whole industry is moving to the realm of subjective opinion, though. Newspaper employees and pundits have largely dropped the pretense of objectivity altogether, whatever the header says above their byline.

There are some journalists who it appears have refused to pervert their writing to partisan ends or sell out their integrity for clicks. You will not find many working for major publications or on television. They have gone underground because the mob has declared open season on honest views, honestly stated.

Books are pulled from store shelves; electronic copies disappear not only from the online store but from your downloads as well. If there was ever an argument for paper copies of important books, it is that small-minded totalitarians have a harder time eliminating them from the world.

Book burnings serve to illuminate only the hatred on the faces of the zealots throwing volumes on the fire.

Where have these honest journalists found their havens? Where will you find them today, speaking out bravely against the unthinking erosion of all the progress humankind has achieved? On private servers and members-only sites that place barriers to public view. How ironic that the spread of free ideas today takes place in secret behind locked doors.

If you want to see examples of our much-diminished breed of free-thinkers, dear reader, here is where you can still find them: Look to Substack and Medium to find independent authors, Locals for communities of content from creators of all types, Rumble for videos that are not censored for political correctness, and X for unfiltered speech.

"I see the same developments as you do," you say "and I agree that it is tragic. But what does all this have to do with slogans, or have you forgotten the point?"

I have not forgotten the point, dear reader, although I thank you for keeping me from straying further. The reason philosophy fails to find more adherents in any age is that thinking is hard.

For the same reason that we ourselves find it tempting to give in to our vices, to let go of our discipline, to tell ourselves sweet lies: It is easier than accepting the hard truth that real progress requires hard work, in all arenas of life.

- If I want to be physically fit, I have to put in effort and make sacrifices. I need to pay attention to what I eat and plan tactically to expend my energy. I need to work on my fitness.

- If I want to advance in my career, I need to first let go of the daydreams of shortcuts and the resentment at unfair treatment I see all around me. I need to work at my job.

- If I want to be happy, I have to gain the upper hand on my otherwise untamed mind and bring its wild excesses within the control of reason. I have to work on maintaining reason.

All this is hard work, and there are limits to how much effort any person is willing or able to sustain. So we find ourselves relaxing, first in little things, and in just a few areas.

But see how our indulgences grow with the least of efforts! I had salad for lunch, so I could have a Big Mac for dinner. I parked a little farther out on the parking lot today, so I will take the elevator and avoid the unforgiving flights of stairs. I was at the office late last night, so I am playing a round of Angry Birds now.

These transgressions you can at least easily observe, for you see them with your own eyes. The indulgences we grant in our thinking are invisible but just as insidious. Because thinking is hard, and the conclusions can be painful, we devolve to slogans.

"At last," you say, "he is coming to the point!"

Be patient, dear reader, for I am trying to teach you a lesson as well in *how* I teach my lesson. I could have given you the point in a single paragraph, but would you have understood it as well without knowing the reasons why? Would it stick in your mind beyond the minute it took you to read it?

I would have you avoid the same trap of shallow thinking that is the result of consuming only sayings or slogans because they are an easy substitute for thinking. So, though it seems like I wear out your patience with my plodding, at least remember there is a method to my meandering.

The examples in politics that brought me to this way of thinking come from all sides:

- Make America Great Again and America First *versus* Black Lives Matter and Antifa

- Defund the Police *versus* Law and Order

- Follow the Science *versus* Science Denier

Listening to what passes for public debate today, you could be forgiven for concluding that our attention span has diminished to encompass no more than three or four words.

And yet, could anything be clearer than the fact that a few words can move mountains? That passions can be inflamed by nothing more than fifteen or so letters, strung in a particular order?

Philosophers know better than most that ideas are powerful and can have an impact on the mind far out of proportion to the size of a sentence. Propagandists have learned this lesson all too well.

Moreover, propagandists are much cleverer than philosophers in expending their efforts. While we spend hours debating the substance behind our ideas, they content themselves with the catchy slogan.

They know the inherent laziness of people means they will be satisfied with the surface appearance. A few words impel the masses to action. The fact that there is but little substance beneath the surface is irrelevant because the crowd is already on the march!

I am not suggesting there is no substance behind the slogans I listed above. The reason the words are powerful is precisely because they touch on matters of great importance.

My complaint is that they are doing just that — touching the surface and relying on human laziness in thinking to do the rest.

Two people hearing the word "Antifa" will imagine very different things. The one will say, "I am against fascism, and Antifa means 'anti-fascism' so I must be in favor of Antifa."

The other will say, "Antifa members are behaving like anarchists. They protest violently, destroy property, and advocate the overthrow of government. I am against all those things, so I cannot be in favor of Antifa."

One person reading about a study that makes a conclusion that is to their liking (say drinking red wine and eating chocolate lowers the risk of heart attack), feels justified in their behavior and virtuous for "Following the Science." That the study was funded by the Alcohol and Cocoa Foundation, its results were taken out of context, and then misleadingly reported by a journalist who didn't bother to read the study is not important.

The nutritionist who tries to provide a broader perspective is labeled a "Science-Denier" because this is much easier than trying to nurture a nuanced understanding of an issue. (If you think I am being too trivial with my example, see what happens to your brain if you substitute the words "climate change and global warming" for "red wine and chocolate," and you will understand my approach.)

I would go so far as to say this: You cannot achieve a deep understanding of a substantive topic if you limit yourself to slogans.

It is precisely when you find your emotions aroused by a small handful of words that you must force yourself to pause. Consider first that someone is almost certainly trying to manipulate your thinking for their own ends.

Will you be such an easy mark, a willing dupe? Not you. Force yourself away from following your gut response. Rather put in the effort to apply your reason. This will help inoculate you from the mind virus that is spreading via slogans.

One final word of caution, dear reader. Just because you may have vaccinated yourself against a particular virus in the form of a slogan, remember that the virus is still spreading wildly among the unprotected public. This is why you see competing slogans so often.

Propagandists on all sides are trying to infect the public first, not with the kind intention that we reach any kind of herd immunity, but to ensure that their ideas are the ones that take root in unsuspecting minds.

If you needed another reason to avoid social media and what passes for public discourse, this would be it.

Be well.

Chapter Eighteen

On Being a Nonconformist

The anarchist beats in all our chests, and it is only through the collective surrender of certain freedoms that we retain any freedom to pursue meaningful lives

Nonconformism is a phenomenon primarily of youth.

If it is a badge of honor to rail against the system in passionate youth, we call the person who carries it on into middle age a dropout, never-do-well, or malcontent. It is somehow embarrassing to be a forty-year-old hippie, never having seriously joined the fray but residing always on the frayed edges of society.

A small glimmer of hope remains. If the nonconformist maintains their attitude into old age, they can regain a certain respectability if for nothing more than their dogged consistency. But at best this person is regarded as an eccentric or a curmudgeon.

Why do youth find nonconformism so attractive? For some, it is a reaction to the early adulthood realization that society is attempting to mold them. What they previously never questioned or unthinkingly took for benevolence they now see as little distinguished from brainwashing.

"You want me to do *what* for the rest of my life? And you want me to do it so I can go into debt to buy a house and a car, and continue building debt to raise children of my own and then send them into the maw of the same educational machine that molded you and me?

"That's what you have on offer? No thanks! Screw your hard work and sacrifice, and loyalty to a greedy corporation that has no loyalty to me. I think I'll travel the world instead."

There is a reason the Peter Pan story holds allure, dear reader. How lovely to think that we can stay children forever, never having to take up the world's cares.

Others go a bit deeper in their thinking, realizing that their childhood must one day end.

These individuals understand that they will assume burdens as adults and that societies perform useful functions in curbing humankind's worst excesses. They grasp that if we left everyone to their own unstructured devices, the result would be far from paradise.

But they do not accept the system at face value, first because they were given no choice in the matter (the brainwashing almost worked!) and second because the system has such obvious flaws.

They will ask, "How can any system so riddled with problems, injustice, and unfairness be the best way to proceed?"

This latter group has come further in their thinking, but they are still reacting to the surface of things and that is a dangerous place to stay.

It is a trivial thing to point out problems.

We must say to this group, "Sorry, my young friends, you will get no reward for finding the flaws abundantly distributed throughout life. In landing on the gaping cracks in the system, you have jumped over the much more important question: Why was the system established the way it was? What other systems were tried, and what was the outcome of those systems?"

I understand why youth lack humility because they also lack experience, which is a most able teacher. It takes multiple examples of the world not behaving as you confidently predict for you to begin to accept that you may not be perfect after all.

While I can forgive the confidence of youth, I do not forgive their ignorance. After all, the reason your ire is aroused is because you've realized you are in a system that is trying to shape you. In saying you will not be so easily duped, you have traded one set of blinders for another.

You say democracy is bad because it creates income inequality, and the rich appear to be getting richer. You say, because it seems a wonderous thought to you, that everyone would be better off if no one had more than anyone else, or at least if some wise person took wealth from those who have it and distributed it more fairly to those who lack it.

All fine. Here is what we say in return: "Before you step further in seeking to implement this change, do your homework. If you don't want society to think for you, think for yourself. How has this forced redistribution worked out in the societies that have tried it? Did you think you were the first one to have this idea?"

This line of thinking is most helpful to a large number of people and brings them back onto productive tracks in their lives.

- They realize that the collective efforts of millions of people over thousands of years have not just been random bumbling.

- They understand that despite obvious flaws in what we see around us, *if there were obvious fixes* we would have implemented them.

- They accept that sometimes a cure is worse than the disease and it is also possible to kill the patient.

A small number of nonconformists remain who are strong in their convictions. They know what they know — not only is the system corrupt but the people running it are corrupt. The system is not just flawed but broken.

And in what I find to be the most breathtaking leap, they believe they know how to fix it. With this group before me, I could forgive not just confidence but even ignorance if only they were not consumed with arrogance.

Especially when we consider that their "fix" requires first destroying our system so they can replace it with their new idea. And, finally, that they are the first humans in history to be without flaws, and hence they will not be corrupted by their new system.

Many calling for equality of outcomes are not looking for equality at all, but to upset the existing hierarchy.

- If others have power according to the current hierarchy, then let us tear this hierarchy down to the ground.

- We will reframe it in a picture more to our liking, in which the advantages you currently enjoy are taken away and given to us.

I suppose we are still talking of nonconformism, dear reader, but it seems the more descriptive word is anarchism.

With this last group, you can have no reasoned discussion or debate. Their purpose is not to learn, and certainly not to work within the established system. Their purpose is to uncreate, to destroy.

But nor can we simply wish them away.

No, the existence of this group of anarchists is the very reason societies came into being. We need civilization to tame our wild and destructive natures because they are dangerous if left unchecked.

The anarchist beats in all our chests, and it is only through the collective surrender of certain freedoms that we retain any freedom to pursue meaningful lives.

Let us not spend time wondering "Why are humans made so? What is it that makes us so dangerous to ourselves?"

We can more profitably answer the question "Discontent is a fundamental aspect of the human condition. What can we do to help avoid discontent becoming malcontent that leads to mass suicide?"

This is where philosophy's lessons hold their greatest promise. By teaching us humility and patience and instilling a desire to look beyond the surface of things.

And ultimately, teaching that conforming to our nature is not giving in to the bonds of servitude but opening the door to the happiness of a life well-lived.

Be well.

Pragmatic Wisdom Vol. 3

Stoic Lessons on Living and Dying

James Bellerjeau

A Fine Idea

Contents

1. On the Quest for Immortality — 119
2. On Aging — 123
3. On Exercise Routines — 127
4. On Senior Citizens — 131
5. On Reaping What Has Been Sown — 135
6. On How All Things End — 139
7. On Knowing Your Limits — 143
8. On Existence and Its Opposite — 147
9. On Living a Full Life — 151
10. On the Proper Measure of Grief — 153
11. On the Will To Live — 157
12. On Our Duty To Live — 163
13. On Training To Improve — 167
14. On the Utility in Catastrophe — 171
15. On the Length of Life — 175
16. On Mourning the Dead — 179

Chapter One

On the Quest for Immortality

What drives the quest for immortality? At its root, it is an excess of greed and fear

Greetings dear reader!

Your studies do you credit, and your progress will pay you dividends. For the sooner you find answers to the questions that vex you, the longer you will live in an enlightened state.

An hour spent in quiet contemplation is better than a hundred spent in confusion and so imagine the rewards for ordering your mind.

You should desire an ordered mind because you have an excellent chance at a long life. Ponder for a moment the amazing increase in life expectancy in just the last century and a half.

- In 1870, global life expectancy was a mere 29 years.
- By 2019, it had leaped to 73 years.

You would think humankind would cry out with joy at this almost tripling in our lifespan. We hear not cries of joy but lamentation.

We lament that if some have already lived to 120, why can't we all? If we can eradicate disease, if we can manipulate the very DNA that makes us what we are, can we not eliminate aging itself?

And perhaps boldest of all, if we can digitize every moment of every day, can we not simulate in our computers worlds indistinguishable from reality, and so achieve immortality, at least in code?

What drives the quest for immortality? At its root, it is an excess of greed and fear. Greed for more of what tastes sweet, for unending pleasure and consumption.

Can anything be more ill-considered? You may eat delicacy upon delicacy until your stomach groans, true. Even children soon learn gluttony comes with a price.

Radical life extensionist Ray Kurzweil himself concedes that a corporeal immortal would suffer existential ennui, running out of not only things to do but ultimately even new ideas.

Not least, achieving immortality would mean the end of humankind. If none die, none may be born. For even though we add just one per century, in an eternity an infinity would come to be. Thus, to allow eternal life means to end new life. What could be more arrogant and selfish?

All that have come before you have yielded their spot on the stage. What possible claim could we have to deny a place to all who would come after us?

"Not at all," the critics claim. "We will create all worlds digitally, all that ever were, and all that will ever be. There is space for everyone and everything." In ones and zeros, they aim to "live" forever, never growing bored or running out of new things to consume.

But nothing gains in value by being added up infinitely. As the last King of Lydia, and after conquering the Greeks, King Croesus's gold hoard was the greatest in the world, but even this was insignificant compared to what the mythical King Midas could create with a touch. Who came more to regret his lust for gold?

The value of luxury lies in scarcity; what all can possess infinitely, none will value highly in possessing.

Does the solution lie in finding some limit? Not infinity, say, but a thousand years? This would never satisfy those who fear death. Because what they fear is fear of missing out. But can anything be more foolish?

Whether your life is fifty years, one hundred, or a thousand, it shrinks in insignificance on the scale of the universe. What is a million years compared to the billions our cosmos has spun without us, and will spin on to come?

To truly avoid missing out, you would have to master not only immortality for all time yet to come but travel backward in history to sample the eternity already swallowed by time.

So, no limit can satisfy, and without limits, we destroy the value of life. The inevitable conclusion is to give up the fantasy of immortality.

By striving for what you cannot have, and would not want if you could have it, you destroy your peace of mind today.

An ordered mind knows the value of life is precisely that it is limited.

Be well.

Chapter Two

On Aging

There is no greater pleasure than being able to look back on a life of proper thoughts and actions

Everywhere I look I see signs of my own obsolescence. I cleaned out my office this week and was struck dumb by the extent to which tools I once cherished have been left to gather dust.

My HP LaserJet printer that faithfully produced thousands of pages lies beached in a corner, its power cord and printer cable laying akimbo to snare the unwary. Now my pages pass through the air wirelessly to a monster shared printer of such complexity that the architects of the moon launch must look on in wonder.

I have uncovered not less than three once miraculous devices for storing and playing my music, each compacter than the last, and concentrating more goodness into more tininess: From my first pink iPod mini to an iPod shuffle, to the iPod Nano.

Am I surprised that the next stage in development has been to shrink the iPod into invisibility, which is to say it too has become obsolete? The airwaves now carry what needed a battery, a white wire, and two earbuds to convey.

And I fairly weep to consider the fate of my most cherished guides to wisdom and universal truths: Books and printed matter.

Where once I was surrounded by reassuringly weighty volumes and binders of yellowing paper, I now see a welter of cables powering a veritable graveyard of successive e-readers.

I can mark their progress by a similar shrinking in size, though I stopped counting the generations at ten. At this rate, the population explosion we need to fear is not humankind's, but that of chips and lithium-ion batteries.

Kindle is a word that all fellow seekers of knowledge should cherish, but I admit it arouses in me now only a sense of loss. For what we have surely gained in convenience and access we have traded for competence.

The dog-eared volume, cracked spine, and underlined passages that were once the mark of the serious scholar have all given way to impermanent effervescence.

What good does it do to dip into all the libraries of the world if we do no more than browse idly for minutes before crashing on to the next electronic distraction?

I could go on chronicling the electronic wreckage, from laptops and mobile phones to rows of castaway monitors staring back at me with blank screens, but it is enough to say I am reminded that each day I am one day closer to death.

In my own case, I am not melancholy, for a purposeful life is not wasted, no matter how brief it may be.

There is no greater pleasure than being able to look back on a life of proper thoughts and actions. When you are young, everything lies before you, and you are overwhelmed by potential. What great things you are capable of, there are no limits to what you can do!

How comforting to be at the pinnacle looking back on what you have accomplished, though your journey is soon done, than to have the climb ahead of you.

And how wonderful it is to finally put an end to appetite and ambition. No more will you be goaded onwards and upwards, a donkey laboring under the stick; you now enjoy the well-deserved rest of the already done.

"Wait," you cry, "doesn't this mean you are starting to hear the stealthy footsteps that harbinger your own death?" Death does not take us in order of our age but plucks from across our ranks.

We are each of us replaced by the next generation and not only should we not resist but rejoice. I am as happy for another day as any, but I do not need it to feel fulfilled.

I bring this letter to a close.

"You do not mean," you say "to leave me hanging without a nugget of wisdom?"

Have no fear, dear reader, I bring a small offering, which packs a punch above its weight. For what is more weighty than the following words that this letter conveys:

> The man who does something under orders is not unhappy; he is unhappy who does something against his will. Let us therefore set our minds in order that we may desire whatever is demanded of us by circumstances.

Indeed. There is no binding that can hold a person who is free in his mind.

"These are Seneca's words," you note, "and how is it that you put them to use for your own purposes here?"

I will quote Seneca and any other without end to remind us the truth belongs to us all, and not to the one who utters it.

The best ideas cannot be owned by one, only discovered and rediscovered by us all.

Be well.

Chapter Three

On Exercise Routines

Your body is a machine that deserves tending to be sure, but are you the engineer or merely a mechanic?

It is normal to want to be fit. A sound body is a worthy goal, but your aim must be to master the body and not to become its servant.

Your fitness tracker faithfully counts your steps for you, but do you not feel its electronic whip if you falter? Many are consumed by consuming daily their avocado toast, fruit smoothie, and lean protein.

Your body is a machine that deserves tending to be sure, but are you the engineer or merely a mechanic? Do not lean too far into the role of perfect tender, lest you neglect the values that are truly dear: The vessel is not the content, no matter how fine.

When people think of fitness, it is usually only physical fitness that springs to mind.

We all know people who have entered into a holy pact with themselves to maintain the temples of their bodies. From their Spandex shorts and functional outerwear to their latest sports watch and space-age shoes, their commitment is apparent to all.

And though it is appropriate to preserve the body, we should reserve our worship for another less visible kind of fitness: That of the mind. Mental fitness is the proper goal for the philosopher.

Lacking a solid mental foundation, the hyper-athlete is no more than fast-twitch muscles under hormonal orders. What use is it to run a marathon a month if your direction is aimless?

I will tell you, dear reader, how to keep your body in shape, without encroaching on the time and space necessary for your mental athletics.

You will recognize the truth in what I say because you have heard me say it before: Follow systems rather than goals and leverage continuous improvement principles.

Your systems are simple daily habits that you inculcate and then let run routinely, without any exercise of willpower. Feel free to walk the length of the great wall but do it a few kilometers each day as part of your normal routine.

Stock your household with nourishing food and drink, not indulgences. What comfort can you take from "comfort" food, if it leaves you steadily less fit each time you pamper yourself? You should eat to live, not live to eat.

The dedicated athlete will need all manner of supplements to maintain performance: Protein shakes to build muscle torn down by stress, electrolytes to replace salts lost to sweat, and magnesium for cramps brought on by overuse.

In both exercise and eating, you gain the most by reducing. Short, focused sessions of intense activity (high-intensity interval training), together with eating less frequently (intermittent fasting).

Your body is a most wonderful machine, capable of self-repair the best auto mechanic could only dream of. But to do its work, the body needs stillness and rest.

"Am I to lounge about," you ask, "doing nothing all day before heading to an early rest?"

Not at all, for strenuous effort is still required of the sincere student. Expend your effort, however, in being mentally strong and thinking deep thoughts.

Just as habits and routines are the keys to unlocking physical fitness, so too are they the tools for building mental strength. Establish and follow rituals in which you think, read, and write.

The more you bend your mind to following these habits, the more eagerly will your mind take to the tasks you put before it.

And because mindfulness does not require idleness, you can attend to your mental training while also going about the business of maintaining the physical machine. A meditative walk is good medicine for both the body and the soul.

I grant you now another boon, which is an insight from that most dedicated athlete of the mind and fellow Stoic, Marcus Aurelius. Let it serve as a reminder to us that all we need to successfully exercise the mind and body is within our grasp at all times:

> If you work at what is before you, following right reason seriously, vigorously, calmly, without allowing anything else to distract you, expecting nothing, fearing nothing, but satisfied with your present activity according to nature, you will live happy.

I wish for you to live happily, so I will extend this thought a bit further. When you expect nothing and fear nothing, it means you already have all that you need.

There is nothing that you need to attain to be successful. You may give yourself no small comfort by remembering how much you have already attained, and how this puts you ahead of the vast multitude of people on the earth.

Be grateful for what you have but be more grateful for who you are.

Be well.

Chapter Four

On Senior Citizens

If we want a true test of our training, we must check our thoughts against the one fate we can be sure is destined to come our way

I was writing not long ago about coming to terms with my ongoing obsolescence.

I fear I have left obsolescence behind and entered the realm of the antique. One still expects some functionality from the out-of-date, but the ancient is beyond function.

I have not fallen so far, so you can place me somewhere between the going and the gone.

But I am not going to complain, my dear reader, for I am still here, and you are still here. Or as the modern-day musician and author Chad Sugg put it so memorably:

> If you're reading this ... Congratulations, you're alive. If that's not something to smile about, then I don't know what is.

In my case, my essence remains, while most of my rough edges have been worn away.

With the clamoring of youth behind me, the cares of middle age put to rest, I am left with the companionship of an aged but well-ordered mind. It tells me that I have earned hard-won peace, and who am I to contradict myself?

Though I am careful not to take full credit for arranging my thoughts in this way, because the mere passage of time does a measure of the work for us all.

If I am perfectly happy to no longer reach for the same heights, is it because I no longer feel the need? Or because they are beyond my grasp?

"But," you ask, "is it not a loss to see the steadily encroaching decline of your capabilities? To know that you will never again do more than before, but only less?"

It is the nature of all living things to decay and die, dear reader. I would rage as successfully against the wind as against the inevitable decline all people face.

Let me make a claim against Lucian, whose accounts I have not yet plundered, but whose satiric riches are available to all:

> The world is fleeting; all things pass away; or is it we that pass and they that stay?

That which is inevitable I am wise not only to not fear but to actively embrace.

Things that are uncertain preoccupy our minds and occupy our time. Not so the things that are certain.

If we want a true test of our training, we must check our thoughts against the one fate we can be sure is destined to come our way.

It is our habit to prepare for many things that may not come to pass, for in this way we ready ourselves not to be bothered if they do. How much more valuable the preparation for our own deaths, which should come as a surprise to no one, though we may be taken off at short or no notice.

I take comfort that my lessons have taken root. I hear them in my thoughts when no one is listening, and I feel them in my soul, which no one can touch.

Here to help pay my debts I call upon the 16th President of the United States, Abraham Lincoln who reminded us:

> It's not the years in your life that count. It's the life in your years.

I have lived, and I have no issue with either the number of my years or their nature.

And even if I was so unwise as to be ungrateful with my lot, I know that we need no more than a single day to put things right.

I am thinking of what English novelist Mary Ann Evans said, better known in her day under the name George Eliot:

> It is never too late to be what you might have been.

Be well.

Chapter Five

On Reaping What Has Been Sown

For all the time that we spend worrying about things that may never happen, how much do we contemplate the one thing we can be sure of?

We pack our elderly relatives off to old folks' homes and we tell ourselves we do it so that they may be well taken care of in their dotage. Or that the burden is beyond our capabilities.

Or often, with no sense of irony, that we have no time. I suppose this last is at least true, in the sense that not one of us possesses the ability to dole out extra time to ourselves let alone another.

Our end is sealed from the beginning, dear reader, for it is the fate of all humans to perish. Rather than face this fact head-on, some hide from all hints of aging as if turning a blind eye to age can prevent it from creeping up on us unbidden.

But death is stealthy and unstoppable, part sneak thief and part mighty army, carrying away both the careless and the well-protected with equal ease. Whether you cower down in terror or stand tall in defiance, the reaper's scythe cuts as cleanly.

The question is, then, not what future awaits us, but how we await it. For all the time that we spend worrying about things that may never happen, how much do we contemplate the one thing we can be sure of?

It is one thing to dream about winning a lottery, and quite another to know with certainty that your number will be called.

Some of us fill our days with as many activities as possible as if there was a prize for getting the most things done. The more we do, though, the more we feel like we are missing out on other things we could be doing.

The American poet Stephen Dobyns put it hauntingly so:

> Each thing I do, I rush through so I can do something else. In such a way do the days pass — a blend of stock car racing and the never ending building of a gothic cathedral. Through the windows of my speeding car I see all that I love falling away: books unread, jokes untold, landscapes unvisited...

But if simply doing is not the path to joy, what is?

To contemplate an unavoidable outcome and order your mind accordingly, you must not only not look away but purposefully direct your gaze to the end.

Rather than sending off your aged parents to lonely exile, you are better served by inviting them into your life and spending your best hours with them. The benefit this will bring to them is great, but it is secondary to the benefit that accrues to your account.

Their wrinkled faces and spotted skin serve as a daily reminder of what fate holds in store for you, and that's if you are lucky. And because no outside diversion can long distract you, you are regularly encouraged to prepare yourself for the fate that awaits you.

I give you this advice freely, dear reader, and you need not subtract from my balance. Let me add to it with this contribution from Steve Jobs, whose words show he was a sincere student for the ultimate test:

> No one wants to die. Even people who want to go to heaven don't want to die to get there. And yet, death is the destination we all share. No one has ever escaped it, and that is how it should be,

because death is very likely the single best invention of life. It's life's change agent. It clears out the old to make way for the new.

Now pay heed to me a little further. Preparing for the inevitable does not mean that you seek to hasten its arrival.

Though your reward is lasting peace, and freedom from all that pains you here on mortal earth, still you should not be overly hasty in concluding your journey. The point of the practice is not to desire your end, but to end your desire for life without end.

By rambling on so, I fear you will desire this letter to end before your life force is fully drained from you.

Time is allotted to us in unequal measures, and we are unevenly prepared when our measure of time is up. Think about this so that you are ready for what comes whenever it comes.

Be well.

Chapter Six

On How All Things End

I woke up one day to see some potion had taken its effect and wizened my face before I managed to bring wisdom to my eyes

I had thought myself by now master of my senses, but I had yet another reminder today that they are still my master. For my self-possession was torn from me by something as simple as the smell of thyme in a market.

I was instantly transported to the hills of southern Spain, where herbs grow freely in the brush of the foothills cascading down from the reddish peaks to the Mediterranean.

And your face, my dear reader, was just as quickly before me recalling to mind the hikes we took with the family up and down those rocky ravines among those hardy herbs.

It seems we were just there together, basking in the buildup of afternoon heat and languishing through days where the sunlight never seemed to fade.

In my memories, time becomes a disordered jumble. I can pluck a scene from my pre-teens that feels as near in time to me as other dramas that played out when my own children were that age.

My parents never seemed to age, frozen in one unchanging state, but time's invisible passage has left its visible marks upon them.

Now I have aged myself, though I similarly did not note time's magic as it worked upon me. I woke up one day to see some potion had taken its effect and wizened my face before I managed to bring wisdom to my eyes.

Though these memories in my mind tell me that everything is yet as it was, I need but look around me to see that my internal map has not kept up with the landscape:

- Shall I count the number of gravestones bearing silent witness to the fact that the ranks of our comrades have been thinned by death's scythe?

- Not many of these were taken in their prime, and what does that say about how stealthily time lulls us into submission?

I look up and see buildings gone, entire blocks upheaved and remade, cities that bear the same name but whose streets I do not know by heart, like the goat paths we used to tread as children.

At this rate, can we doubt that the very mountains we once clambered up will be gradually worn down and themselves swept into the sea?

Some get so swept up in the course of their campaigns that they consider only current affairs and give no thought to what brought them to that pass, or in which direction they are heading.

In my case, I cannot say that I was unaware while events unfolded, for mindfulness has been my practice for many a year.

- I recall my decision to study law after abandoning the pursuit of the study of the mind (how light a decision for something that would prove so weighty over my life!),

- meeting the love of my life in law school (though the vision of her distracted me mightily from my lessons!),

- the rites of passage accompanying my passing the bar (what a low bar it now seems for such a high pursuit, and would that we set it much higher to maintain the rule of law!), and

- the joy at turning my love of words into the otherwise laborious practice of law (how something so pure can be turned into something so base when every principle comes with a price tag attached!).

No, dear reader, in my head I am still in all of these states simultaneously: Chomping at the bit to start the race, undisciplined and prodigious in my expenditure and waste of energy, finding my easy rhythm and stride, one day rearing up accomplished and experienced, then at one moment first noticing the load I was pulling, and now feeling the full weight of that load inexorably slowing me to a halt.

The more I have accomplished, the more I find myself looking backward rather than looking forward.

I tell myself this is only natural, and moreover, it is the correct course because no lesson is as well learned as the one you have taught yourself. But this introspection also gives me pause, because I realize time never pauses for us.

We are but poor judges of time, for we never once correctly estimate that time's passage is the same for us all and is the same at all times.

- In our childhood we are heedless, and this makes time seem endless.

- In our youth we are reckless, and this makes us wasteful of time.

- In our middle age, we take note and start to enjoy the finer notes of life and time.

- And as we approach the finish line, we are alarmed, for we realize the race we've been rushing through awards a prize that none would jump the line to receive early.

Knowing finally that every hour contains but sixty minutes, and every minute but sixty seconds, each moment seems infinitely more precious to us precisely because we know they are slipping through our fingers, never to return.

What irony that it takes a lifetime to learn that we should take none of our lives for granted!

If it was in my power to change just one part of the human condition, I would make memory work in both directions. That is, let us remember our futures as clearly as we do our pasts.

If as youths we could call to mind not just the small number of things already done, but the vast number yet to come, we would realize the fullness of life as it is happening, rather than after it has passed.

Be well.

Chapter Seven

On Knowing Your Limits

Awkwardness, thy name is Smalltalk!

If you are looking to convince me of your latest pet theory, dear reader, you should make the attempt now, for I was recently convinced to once again attend a social dinner.

It was an honor to be invited; the attendees counted select law school faculty and local legal luminaries. The occasion was a lecture arranged by the Europa Institut, and if I should manage to stick to the public portion of these events I would be a happy man.

I was drawn from my solitude, lured once again by the outstanding quality of the speaker, though I knew well what giving in to this temptation would entail:

- the pre-talk private meet and greet, presenting a chance to shake hands and perhaps get a favorite volume signed; and even more enticingly,
- the post-talk dinner for invited guests, and the forced intimacy that comes from assigned seating.

No, I will not say which event it was, because that would not be fair to any of the participants. Suffice it to say there are few opportunities indeed for one such as me to be put face to face with Ambassadors, Federal judges, and even Justices of the United States Supreme Court.

Perhaps to the layperson, the names Alito, Ginsberg, and Scalia call to mind only thoughts of vague European heritage, but to the constitutional lawyer, they are blazing stars in the night sky.

"Sounds delightful," you say, "and yet I detect a hint of complaint. What am I missing?"

Truly I am an ungrateful wretch, but I will tell you that these events make me wretched, for all that I cannot stay away.

Imagine how you would feel meeting a genuine inspiration, a hero whose works you have studied and admired from afar. My stomach flutters and my intestines are tied in knots. Prone to sweating from the lightest of exertions, I become a sticky mess affixed to my place by the buffet table.

To avoid acting a fool and not just looking like one, I raise my glass and join the toast. The last thing my gut needs is food and drink, which just roils my belly much as my thoughts and emotions are already roiled.

Social trivialities in the presence of such weighty people and ideas seem the greatest waste to me, but I never seem to navigate safely the path between banalities or a boring inquisition on something significant but out of place in this setting.

Awkwardness, thy name is Smalltalk!

And to know that I will inflict myself on an unwitting dinner table with my unwitty remarks makes me wish most fervently to return to my hermit's cave.

I venture forth each time for the same reason, dear reader: Nowhere else are the chances better of hearing unvarnished truth and wisdom.

These speakers and judges are at the peak of their careers, brimming with knowledge, experience, and insight. They are also typically near the *end* of their careers, and because Federal judges are appointed for life, this means they are near the end of their lives.

I've often thought the invitation to speak at these series is like an advance copy of one's obituary. Considering how many have passed away not long after speaking, I'd be superstitious about not passing up an invitation to speak.

They have gained confidence because of their age and experience. More importantly, they've typically gained wisdom, not least in having learned not to care what other people think.

ON KNOWING YOUR LIMITS

Consider what happens if you are presented daily for decades with opposite sides of every issue and forced to decide which is correct, or whether neither is correct and a third way is appropriate.

This will make you very good at deciding, and to stay sane you must also believe you are making good decisions. Remember, at the level of the Supreme Court there is no further appeal, so yours is the last voice.

For us to hear such learned people speak their minds without regard to what others think, and with neither the intent to flatter nor offend, is a rare blessing.

Philosophy holds out this blessing to each of us, without the agony of gilded invitations to pre-talk toasts or post-talk parties: The chance to hear and understand the unvarnished truth, for any whose eyes and ears are open to the message.

Yes, it is uncomfortable to be confronted with one's failings and frailties. To not look away because there is no hiding from oneself, no higher court to take up the appeal.

But to admit a weakness is to put a name and a face to that weakness, which is the first critical step to overcoming it and becoming stronger.

Philosophy helps us not because it tells us that we are perfect, but in holding up a mirror to our faults. By helping us recognize our limitations we can most profitably direct our efforts to where we need them most.

Are you warned to be wary of wants? Then pay attention to the signs indicating you are wanting more than you need.

Are you plagued by worry over what other people think? By ordering your mind to understand the true nature of things you learn that ignorant opinions carry no weight and so should not burden you.

Philosophy ultimately arms us against all that ails us, but we must first let her indicate that we are ill.

Be well.

Chapter Eight

On Existence and Its Opposite

What does it say if you cannot say you are living today, but only preparing for a tomorrow that may never come?

Are you happier knowing the instrument of your end, or remaining ignorant of it?

Though we are at the peak of health and can complain of no ailment, still we carry the seeds of our end with us at all times.

- Accidents carry some away in their prime, and the one consolation is that the end comes quickly.

- Cancer can strike at any age, and its cruelty is a lingering finish.

Imagine the feeling that not just a general end at a future time but a specific doom hangs over you.

For some, getting notice of a terminal illness is a death sentence to their happiness. "All that I could have done, would have done, want to do!"

What a pity that they ruin the remaining life they have because they do not have longer to live. For consider, there is not one of us who could not be carried off today.

What does it say if you cannot say you are living today, but only preparing for a tomorrow that may never come? What does it say if you cannot be happy today unless you think you will be around to be happy tomorrow?

I say it is a blessing to be confronted with our mortality, dear reader, and that it should not only not make us morbid, but rather joyful for what we have.

Knowing that your time is limited, do you not value it more highly than if your days were to run into each other to eternity?

If you find your perspective still lacking, consider the relative flicker that is human existence compared to the broad sweep of time.

- Whether you live a year, a decade, or a century, you are but a pinprick on the long ribbon of unfurling time.

- You missed all that came before you came into existence, but did you suffer any pangs or pains for your loss? You did not, because you were not.

- Will you suffer after you are gone? I believe not, because you will not be.

You will recognize me as carving onto the page here the Epicurean epitaph:

Non fui, fui, non-sum, non-curo (I was not, I was, I am not, I do not care).

Our existence is but the briefest moment, dear reader. See to it that you do not merely exist.

Order your mind so that it neither dwells too long in the past nor resides chiefly in the future. Stretch too far in either direction, and you will anyway be among the non-existent.

The ordered mind comes about from choosing your state of mind. You cannot be compelled to do anything that you do willingly.

So whatever your circumstance is at the moment, make a game of turning an unexpected turn to your favor.

What seems to be your worst luck can also be your best luck, if you simply turn the frame of reference in the right direction.

- Your train is late? You have more time to listen to the birds and feel the sunshine on your face.

- Oh no, it's started raining! You now have an unscheduled demonstration of your hardiness to inconveniences.

- Your flight is cancelled? You have just won an unplanned holiday and a chance to experience a new city first-hand.

"These are but trivialities," you say. "Do you really expect me to be happy in the face of serious misfortune?"

I do expect it, for your own sake I do, and I urge you to think about it now.

- Your job is eliminated? This gives you the opportunity to get away from annoying colleagues and start that side business you've been dreaming of.

- Your doctor returns holding your x-rays and says "We have to talk" in a grim intonation? You will soon have the uncertainty of your end cleared up, and all the burdens and struggles and pains and worries will be eased from your shoulders. Others will carry on and carry the load for you.

There is a distinction I would have you learn. To accept your end cheerfully does not mean you seek to hasten its arrival.

Would you consider a man wise who, upon spying a $100 bill at his feet, walks on by, saying "I do not need it." Only the foolish spurn what is on offer, just as the wise eagerly receive that which others would push away.

The distinction is that you learn not to want what you cannot have, and to appreciate and value what you *do* have.

Just because you do not need good health, wealth, and long life to be happy, you do not give them up to demonstrate your independence from them.

I must end now, and take my leave. Before I go, I leave you with this summary: to know your specific end is to know that we all must end, but no one said we need to end in tears.

Be well.

Chapter Nine

On Living a Full Life

We tell ourselves we'll be happy if only we can achieve something else. But this treadmill only speeds up the faster we run

Let us stop behaving as if we are living a dress rehearsal and can fix our lines and redo our actions tomorrow.

This has been my singular aim for some time now, dear reader. I do not assume I will have more time, that I will be able to complete later all that I have left unfinished today.

- I tell myself this may be the last breakfast I will enjoy.
- I am writing as if this was my last letter.
- My son is off to work, my daughter about her studies, and my spouse on the way to the grocery store, and do I tell myself we may never see each other again?

You may think such thoughts would train one to be melancholy, but in my experience, they foster tranquility and joy.

Reflecting on the scarcity of the present makes it seem infinitely precious to me.

The past is gone, and may it stretch out emptily for eons behind us for all the good that it will do us today. To live in the past is not to live at all.

Look to the future then! But the future may never arrive, and by casting my thoughts ahead I rob the present of my watchful presence.

We put things off for two reasons: we don't want to do them at all, or we *do* want to do them but we assume we'll get to them later.

In putting off that which we dread, do we assume we'll be more successful than the ostrich in avoiding troubles? When we raise our heads from the sand, will we find our unpleasant tasks have gone away, or have only multiplied in our self-imposed blindness?

Learn this lesson dear reader, and you will live a happy life: Tell yourself that you do nothing against your will; that though the task may be strenuous or unpleasant it is done by your own choosing.

You do not dread that which you do willingly. So no matter the chore, put yourself fully behind it and you will be successful regardless of the outcome.

The temptation to put off supposed burdens is at least understandable. But why do so many put off living joyfully in fulfillment? Isn't that the goal we're striving towards?

We tell ourselves we'll be happy if only we can achieve something else. But this treadmill only speeds up the faster we run.

The only sensible course is to step off the treadmill, to step off and take stock of all you have at this immediate moment.

It sounds trite, but you can be satisfied today if you only set aside disappointment — just as you choose your actions, choose your attitude and you will be similarly successful.

If you assume your time is limited to today, you will waste less of it and enjoy more of it.

Be about the business of living, then, and live each day fully, and you will not be troubled by either the past or the future.

Be well.

Chapter Ten

On the Proper Measure of Grief

If you would treasure your times with true friends, you will every now and then permit yourself to imagine life without them

Your friend J. has succumbed in his battle with cancer, and we mourn. You are right to be sad, but I would have you avoid turning a pure thing into a selfish thing by mourning to excess.

If I were to tell you that you should not mourn at all, you would think me to be asking too much, although in truth you'd be better for it.

But it takes a person of rare self-possession to be above all bother about what occurs on the mortal plane. Even such an elevated person would note the passing of a dear friend, but their noting would not turn into a drawn out dirge.

In our case we may let our sorrow show, so long as we can then show that we have let it go.

You do not need to harden your heart to feeling strong emotions. That is not what I am advising.

You need merely observe the cries and carrying on that accompany the bereaved, though, to be warned of over-acting.

"Acting," you say, "are my feelings for my friend not genuine?"

I do not doubt your feelings are real, dear reader, but consider whether they are well-placed, and, equally, well-timed.

Some people seek to demonstrate the depth of their feeling by the depth of the tears they shed upon a loved one's passing. Too often this is a display for the benefit of the living, to prove as it were, that their feelings were real.

Were their feelings as intense when their friend was still among us? Did they lavish attention on their friend as they now lavish it on their grief?

We take for granted what is all around us, losing moments to hours, then hours to years, to inattention and neglect.

"I will see him next week sometime. I am busy with other things, and I don't have time for him today."

Only when we have lost them forever do some start to appreciate and value those we had with us all along. In such cases, our grief should be real, but it is grief for ourselves having wasted valuable parts of our time with others.

And what of the one who says they are inconsolable? None of their living, loving friends will do, because of the one who is gone.

A friend who puts the dead above the living deserves no friends among the living. Because if you know the true worth of your friends you will value their words of comfort.

And if you say you have no friends who understand you, then you have little understanding of yourself or others.

Do you think you are alone in feeling lonely, feeling sad, feeling lost? Do you think that none has suffered an unfairness or injury before you?

The conditions of mankind's existence are such that, though blessings are spread unevenly, suffering is widely shared. To think you are uniquely suffering is to risk adding arrogance to ignorance.

There are multiple ways to prepare yourself against the pain of loss of companionship:

- You can reflect on and savor the good moments as they are happening, and so build up a store of memories that will last as long as you do;

- You can build up reserves in your relationships, in the form of multiple friendships; and

- You can anticipate the end of all things, including your loved ones, not in dread and fear, but in simple acknowledgment that all things end.

Time you spend mindfully with your friends leaves a lasting impression.

You are not only listening but hearing. You are not only talking but being heard and understood. The laughter that arises spontaneously represents a shared joy.

You may revisit this treasure-house of memories at your leisure, when you are merely temporarily parted from your friends, or when they are permanently taken from us.

How would you have your friends remember *you*?

With this thought in mind, make it your habit to build memories of your current interactions so that you have good times to act as a bulwark against the bad.

When you are at peace with yourself, you make it easier for others to interact honestly with you.

You may teach without judging. You may observe without criticizing.

We think we want praise, but in our hearts, we know that flattery is a compliment that makes one uglier over time.

Be a good friend, and you will find friends.

Fortune can be fickle indeed, but having friends you can count on counts for a lot. You will then have companions to understand and share your feelings when one of you is taken out of order.

If you would treasure your times with true friends, you will every now and then permit yourself to imagine life without them.

Not to make yourself sad by hastening or even bringing about the loss, but to remind yourself never to assume too much. If you are aware that every parting could be your last, you will hold the embrace that much longer.

The casual "See you later," betrays an unthinking optimism that creates the conditions for bitter disappointment. If you never expect other than to see your loved ones again, of course, you will be grieved if they are taken away.

Better to think and to say "We may never meet again, dear friend. I am happy for the times we had together. Take care."

It is with sorrow, but not grief, that I bring this letter to a close.

I rejoice for the time we have spent together, dear reader, and you are never far from my thoughts and memories. I am happy to extend our time together through our correspondence.

For even though we do not meet, something is better than nothing, and in this case that something is everything to me.

Be well.

Chapter Eleven

On the Will To Live

The legal profession has found a way to work true magic: that is, they can speak for the dead

Today the sun is shining and everywhere Spring is in evidence. Fragrant blossoms perfume the air and please the eyes with vibrant bursts of color that stand out among rich fields of green. Life returns, refreshed and revitalized after its winter lull and pause!

And yet, not every sprig has sprouted. The blueberry bushes my wife and I transplanted have seen their numbers reduced by a fifth, bare stems reminding us that life is also precious and fickle.

Was it a nick of the shovel, a few too many rocks blocking the roots, or water that failed to flow when needed? The gardener and farmer take life the least for granted because they know what conditions it requires to flourish as well as how easily it can slip away.

Much of philosophy, dear reader, and certainly a great deal of Stoic writing, is concerned with what it means to live a good life. What are the pursuits that give life meaning, and how should we conduct ourselves during our lives?

The Stoics believed that a person should become a gardener tending their own well-ordered mind so they could live their lives according to reason. This meant applying reason to every sort of situation, positive or negative, and behaving according to reason rather than the unthinking passions of the moment.

Living well thus also meant contemplating the end of life and dying well. Have you noticed how many topics people today consider inappropriate for polite conversation?

Consider: We are all bound for one and the same destination. Though we usually delight in sharing every detail of our planned vacations, this is one pending trip that remains an open secret, known by all but unmentionable.

Yes, we're all traveling there together, but if you mention it, you are as welcome as the dog who drags a dead woodchuck into the living room. Better that you actually raise the dead than raise the specter of thinking of death and let zombies loose on our imaginations.

The Stoics understood that wanting things and fearing things prevents people from living in peace. Because wanting and fearing are conditions of the mind, the thought goes, mastering the mind provides the key to contentment.

If fear of death disrupts the good life, then it must be confronted. I fear that in modern society we have completely lost the lessons and the practices of the ancients and have turned things on their heads.

We have surrendered fully to the pursuit of more: More things, more life, more experiences. When we know from the evidence daily before our eyes that *more* is no guarantee of *better*.

We close our minds to things that are unpleasant to think of, as if merely shutting our eyes could make the danger disappear.

"Where does our willful blindness come from? Why have we forgotten that what is limited is precious, and quantity alone is no guarantee of quality?"

I put the blame at the feet of two of our oldest professions: First, doctors, about whom more in a moment; and second, those purveyors of hourly pleasure, selling themselves to the highest bidder without regard for the person purchasing their services.

I speak of lawyers, about whom also more in a moment, though you may prefer less of them.

Doctors have progressed far beyond the alchemy of their early days. Their collective progress in prolonging life has made some into mad scientists, pushing the boundaries of life extension outward, outward.

There is no part of the human body that we will not repair, cut out, or replace if it means the machine can be kept ticking. No part, that is, except the soul and the mind, which stubbornly resist being duplicated by our best 3-D printers.

"What," you say, "would you have our medical professionals forget their Hippocratic Oath? They are bound by millennia of ethics to not only 'do no harm or injustice' to their patients, but also not to administer poison though asked, or to suggest it be taken."

I say keep reading the Oath, my dear reader, for the following words are misinterpreted by many today:

> Into whatsoever houses I enter, I will help the sick, and I will abstain from all intentional wrong-doing and harm, especially from abusing the bodies of man or woman.

Does it really help the incapacitated or terminally ill to extend by any means their stay on earth for so long as our mad scientists can manage?

- Can it ever be intentionally wrong to shock a heart back into beating, after the manual massage of cardiopulmonary resuscitation has failed?

- Is it always a help to keep a body breathing by mechanical ventilator after the will to breathe no longer comes from within?

- Can it not be abuse to force feed a body by intravenous tube when all desire to eat has fled?

We ourselves might make a different decision were it our own body lying on the table, but the patient who cannot make a decision at all is assumed to always want more: Keep the fluids in my body flowing, hook me up to every machine, spare no expense in my maintenance!

Though the patient may have been a little lax in their own preventative care, we assume that they mean for others to move mountains to now make up for their neglect.

But how inconsistent we are when it comes to choosing the manner of our deaths! The one who is mute is assumed to ask for every aid. Yet the ones who have their faculties intact and their individual agency at hand put their powers to killing themselves and others with abandon.

Consider that most of the deaths in the U.S. today count our own behavior as primary or contributing causes: Heart disease, respiratory diseases, stroke, and diabetes.

It is not blaming the patient to note that a healthy weight and diet, and an active lifestyle, help prevent or mitigate many chronic conditions.

Cancer is near the top of death's choice of weapons, and while it is an indiscriminate killer, some versions are certainly courted by their victims, if not downright invited in to dance.

(And this does not even count the intentional deaths, those actively sought out, of which abortion would be the silver medalist on the podium were we to include it in the statistics for causes of death. We do not count abortion because the unborn do not count. I am not arguing the point about when life begins. I observe merely that murder, suicide, and execution represent but small figures compared to what happens to the unborn, who themselves are least able to express their wishes.)

How and why did this come to pass, dear reader? Why did we need government accountants to invent the quality-adjusted life year or QALY to tell us that we can determine the economic value of medical interventions by measuring both the quality and the quantity of life lived?

That a year lived in perfect health is worth more than one lived in pain and ill health, and indeed that some health states can be considered "worse than dead"?

Well, let me speculate on a possible reason.

If the medical profession has transcended alchemy to arrive at a practice more resembling science, the legal profession has found a way to work true magic: That is, they can speak for the dead.

To that short list of things that can be guaranteed in life (death and taxes), we can add a third: Lawsuits. No accident, no death, no act, no inaction, no treatment, but that a lawyer will be standing by to take the case.

A tort claim has only a few ingredients: Duty, breach, cause, and harm.

- Doctors more than most professionals owe a duty to their patients. Did we not just recite sections of the Hippocratic Oath, proof of what we intuitively understand?

- If the patient suffers an adverse outcome in a doctor's care, a lawyer can easily argue all the other elements of negligence: There must have been some failure (breach), and without it (cause) my client would not have died (harm).

Aristotle could have been describing the plight of doctors practicing modern medicine when he said:

> There is only one way to avoid criticism: Do nothing, say nothing, and be nothing.

This condition leads to predictable outcomes: A strong bias to seek the preservation of life at all costs. I may raise the costs of your care exponentially, but that is less expensive to me than getting sued for failing to pursue a possible treatment. So, you will be kept alive whether you want it or not.

At least in part, it is lawyers speaking for the dead who drive such interventions. But when patients are free to speak for themselves, they are considerably less concerned about extending life in all circumstances.

The explosion of living wills and advance directives is proof that laypersons know what professionals do not: We do not want to live forever if it means our quality of life is ignored.

Everyone draws the line differently. Ease my pain with palliative care, but do not perform extraordinary measures. Do not resuscitate, intubate, or ventilate.

No matter how much people close their eyes to the consequences of their daily decisions and conveniently ignore that they will one day have to pay the bill for their lavish expenditures, still I think many instinctively know that their end can be of their choosing.

The will to live does not always serve you best by driving you to seek more.

You may find that you achieve a better life by virtue of contemplating the end of your life and working backward from that point to living a meaningful life.

Be well.

Chapter Twelve

On Our Duty To Live

While we have breath in the body, we must not give up. Not because we fear death, nothing so mundane. But because we can do good in the world by living

You have tested positive for COVID, dear reader, and surely this is unwelcome news! Although be thankful that you have experienced thus far no more than a headache and a fever that abated after 24 hours.

It is true that many have contracted the virus without even knowing it and only discover later that they have the antibodies coursing through their veins. But others are laid low out of proportion to any pre-condition or co-morbidity, and of these, some have perished.

We have lost family, friends, and strangers to this discriminating killer. We think we are gaining the upper hand with our vaccines, but the mystery of why some are so afflicted while others remain unaffected is unsolved.

We who remain among the living are left to ponder the mystery of life as much as that of death. The latter is inevitable, it is just a question of time, what will carry you off and not whether. A good life, on the other hand, is something that some never attain no matter how long they live.

It is not the affliction of disease that necessarily prevents one from living a meaningful life according to reason. More often it is afflictions of the mind that leave the untrained stricken. And yet it is the mind that has the power to diminish, if not to fully heal, many an illness of body and soul.

The mind can transport us to worlds far removed from our present discomfort and pain. A moving song arouses a deep stirring within our breast, a captivating movie can make us forget our common cares for a few hours.

For me, it is the written word that most easily and most completely steals me away. I forget to eat, the hours slip by like minutes, and I become a master builder of cathedrals in the sky.

These castles are airy, but still, they have substance in my mind, and I am as convinced by the solidity of their walls as if I were rapping the cold stone against my knuckles. In these states, corporeal concerns lose essence and dissipate.

My hangover upon returning to reality is to realize I am human, ridiculous in my wants and desires, fragile and easy to damage. The gradual replication errors in my personal computer code compound and cumulate until I am but a single free radical away from cancer finding its origin in a once healthy cell.

Despite our fragility, in fact I would say *because* of it, we have a duty to persevere. For if we are vulnerable despite all the armor we have learned to take up and deploy in response to countless challenges, how much do our fellow travelers suffer, who are less protected and do not even know why they suffer?

Confucius tells us that a child who honors their parents will demonstrate filial piety. Specifically, he says:

> There is filial piety when parents are spared all anxiety about their children except when they happen to fall sick.

Do we think it is only us who suffer when we are ill and take no cure? Our family, our friends, and most of all our parents, are each given to suffer when we stumble about blindly in pain, in addiction, and in misery.

So, to start we shall be dutiful children to our parents and honor their sacrifices in bringing us into the world and teaching us to the best of their ability.

We shall do this by not giving them cause to be anxious about our condition. If we are unhealthy, we shall accept the help that is offered, we shall seek out the cures that are available, and we shall above all *help ourselves*.

Every person has in them the ability to aid or hinder their cure.

"What patient does not willingly, gladly, take the medicine that would heal them?" you ask.

An astonishingly large number of the unwell, dear reader, reject advice, defy treatment, and punish themselves with further decay. For the sake of our parents, we must be model patients. For encouragement, call to mind the words of the Buddha, who tells us:

> You yourself, as much as anybody in the entire universe, deserve your love and affection.

This is just the start. For what kind of friend are we if we incapacitate ourselves of the ability to be of support to them? For surely, they suffer just as we do.

If we are of sound mind and healthy body, we can assist them in their difficult times. Not because that means they are in a position to help us when we need a helping hand, but simply because that is what it means to be a friend: To give freely and willingly what you are able when you are able.

And if we must heal ourselves to help our friends, those few carefully cultivated from among thousands, how much more potential good can we do if we make ourselves available to the many?

They are none of them asking for our help, true. They do not even know we exist. But we know that *they* exist, and we know that they suffer, as surely as our friends and family do. Are they not our sisters and brothers in humanity?

What does it say if I let this brother fall by the trail and leave that sister hungry and thirsty because I have turned away and not spent the time to know them? If we but spoke a few sentences, we would know the truth of our shared burdens and our shared humanity.

The well-ordered mind following reason is content in itself, but this does not mean that it is cut off from the rest of humankind or that it seeks isolation.

The gurus who secrete themselves away in caves may be sufficient to themselves, but they are insufficient for any purpose other than serving as examples.

To some, they are an example of how to attain lasting peace. If that peace comes at the cost of sharing the burdens of humanity, I say they are rather an example of how to make selfishness a virtue. Everyone can help someone, but to help *only* yourself is to help no one.

Thus, we have a duty to live, dear reader, to will ourselves well when we are ill. While we have breath in the body, we must not give up.

Not because we fear death, nothing so mundane. But because we can do good in the world by living; we can make the world a better place by our presence.

We do not diminish ourselves by giving of ourselves, we only increase the stock of goodness in the world. I end with the kind words of the Buddha once more today, for his wisdom still rings true:

> Thousands of candles can be lighted from a single candle, and the life of the candle will not be shortened. Happiness never decreases by being shared.

Be well.

Chapter Thirteen

On Training To Improve

The side effects of not only being physically fit, but training to become and remain physically fit, are certainly real

The best thing you can say about the physical fitness craze, the best thing, is that inadvertently some will come to greater peace of mind by virtue of their training.

The side effects of not only being physically fit but training to become and remain physically fit, are certainly real. This is the case even though these benefits are rarely the original purpose for one's taking up the training.

"What are these inadvertent benefits of pursuing a course of physical fitness?" you ask.

Here are some examples that come to my mind. First, we learn how to form habits by observing that the things we repeatedly do become easier after just a short interval of repetition. How valuable to discover that we are not only or even primarily creatures of will, but creatures of habit!

The expenditure of will is only necessary to start us off. Once well begun we will continue on our course like a Newtonian particle continues in its direction unless acted upon by another force.

Next, we learn how to overcome adversity by enduring the inevitable strains we encounter in our physical pursuits. We learn that emerging victorious makes us yet more capable.

- Lifting weights puts stress on our muscles, creating small tears and cellular destruction that, upon healing, grow back stronger.

- Running and sprinting wears out our legs, but in return builds our ability to process oxygen and improves the heart's efficiency for all the remaining time we are at rest.

- Bicycling long distances taxes our tender behinds as much as it toughens our capacity for boredom.

- Swimming teaches us our skin is largely impervious to water, and that if we can only keep our mouths shut at the right times and in the right rhythm, we can be surrounded by otherwise fatal environments and emerge unharmed.

- Stretching and yoga remind us that our bodies are also machines and that it is both necessary and wonderful to periodically pause the abuse we inflict in order to lovingly maintain and care for them.

Finally, in pursuing a measured course of physical fitness, we greatly enhance our chances of living our lives free from avoidable ailments.

No diet or exercise can protect us from all dangers, though many convince themselves otherwise, but there are countless self-imposed chains of disease and ill health that the healthy specimen has broken and cast aside.

Do you ask me now if it is also a good thing that healthy habits may also lead to longer lives? Here I am more reserved in my praise, dear reader. A longer life can be a blessing, true, but living long by no means ensures that one lives well.

For all the benefits I have just listed, there are many things much less flattering that we must lay at the feet of a focus on physical fitness.

For one, how many mistake fitness itself for the end, rather than a means to an end? For another, the positive reinforcement generated by a focus on the body means it risks becoming one's sole focus. This in turn prevents attention to the much more pressing task of training the mind.

If we are constantly struggling to be physically fit, how many more struggle to be *mentally* fit when they do not even know that as much training is necessary for the mind, if not more, to stay healthy?

If we spent a tenth of the time obsessing about our state of mind as we did the numbers on our fitness tracker, we could be confident in saying all were on their way to well-ordered minds. But just as the pool is not the best environment for deep conversation, the modern-day environments we immerse ourselves in are not conducive to the habit of reflection.

Consider first what is on offer to the budding athlete in pursuit of a healthy body. The cyclist has a range of bicycles on display in ever lighter and more exotic materials, at prices ranging from the expensive to the shocking to the unconscionable. Compared to this, the helmet, shoes, lighting, lock, padded shorts, and reflective jacket are but pricy insults, annoying but far from the greatest harm.

The runner secretly laughs because they need nothing more than the open road and a pair of sneakers, right? Nike is having the last laugh here when they ring in the sales from lightweight sneakers that combine carbon plates, foam, and micro-weave into a package so light that they are worth their weight in gold.

And this is to say nothing of water-wicking socks, functional shorts, and odor-repelling microbial-infused shirts. Oh, it's cold today! Another jacket or two will ease your discomfort. What's that? Rain, you say? No worries, wear this hat and that jacket, and you're right as rain.

Sunny tomorrow? These prescription sunglasses will wrap around your head and block wind and stray light; look we have lenses for bright days, for foggy days, for forest paths, and even for nighttime journeys. Wrap your head around all the costs the runner faces, dear reader, and you will no longer pity the biker.

I myself would be embarrassed to tell you how much I have spent on successive generations of GPS trackers from the likes of Polar and Garmin. I can regale with you far more details than merely my precise location! My heart rate, steps, speed, and cadence.

Do you want to know the altitude, how long I slept and how deeply, the interval between my heartbeats, or whatever the delightfully named VO2Max will tell you about me? Before I've figured out the hundreds of functions on my current watch of wonder, another has come along with even more features, at an even greater price.

Yet for all the thousands I've spent on watches now collecting dust and not data, I would spend all this and more if someone offered a device that could tell me not just where I was on the earth, but why I was there. Can Garmin tell me if the direction I am heading is the right one, or am I just running in circles?

I could go on in this vein, but because I know your thoughts and I am kind, I will not.

Let me observe instead that among the thousands of offerings focused on the body's function, I suppose we should take heart that there has emerged a handful dedicated to what is within our heads.

Headspace comes to mind, with its laudatory mission of helping cultivate the practice of mindfulness. The ills being treated here are not those of the body, but rather things like sleep, stress, loneliness, regret, anxiety, and more.

Though it is too soon to say whether their offering is mere pabulum or manna for the mind, I am encouraged simply by the fact that this ancient art of training exists in a new form that makes it appealing to the masses.

In this instance, I welcome the madness of crowds and the folly of following fads. Even though it may be uncritical mob behavior that drives the growth in mindfulness practice, still it is the practice of the mind. Can we not expect practitioners to harvest inadvertent benefits regardless of their motivations?

Every day remind yourself that your most important function for living is your mind, and your body is more a vessel for carrying it about.

When you have the hierarchy of things in the right order, you will find it easier to devote the time to training your mind and not just your body.

Be well.

Chapter Fourteen

On the Utility in Catastrophe

People fall too readily into the habit of taking their lives for granted and this in turn leads them away from living their lives meaningfully and well

Many rail against the dark turn our media has taken. It seems they delight in arousing our anger and our emotions. They monetize our fear by keeping us hooked to our screens.

I tell you that rather than cursing the media, the modern philosopher should be giving them thanks. We shall thank them for these daily reminders of our frailty as humans in an unforgiving world.

If we kept a statistician by our side, we would know to walk more carefully under the branches of the trees in our neighborhood than we would think to duck our heads in worry about space debris from a Chinese rocket falling to earth.

If we were as facile with numbers as we are comfortable conjuring images in our heads, we would more eagerly step into an airplane than we would hop in our cars for the drive to work each morning. But things that fall from the sky are so much more interesting!

We cannot look away, and so they capture our imagination and make hostages of our reason.

But for just a moment, my dear reader, let us welcome the media whipping our irrationality to new heights.

- A shark has mistaken a surfer for a seal and taken a bite? Delightful!

- A lightning bolt has determined that the shortest route to ground lies through a hiker's head? Fascinating!

- A person has found a novel way to misuse a product and so slices, eviscerates, or defenestrates themselves? Most excellent!

Now it is not my aim to mock misfortune or tragedy, for though rare these instances are very real, not least to their chomped, electrified, and impaled victims. I take no delight in the suffering of others.

"So why," you ask, "did you just say we should welcome the news of these events?"

The explanation is this. People fall too readily into the habit of taking their lives for granted and this in turn leads them away from living their lives meaningfully and well.

If the misfortune of others serves to jolt us from our sleepwalking, then each of these dark clouds does indeed hold a silver lining.

The scope of human suffering is broad, and we need not limit our contemplation to these instances of isolated injury. The COVID pandemic is a powerful reminder that we are surrounded by pathogens and that sometimes the things we don't think about are wreaking unseen harm before they burst into view.

An earthquake triggers a tsunami that floods a thousand miles of coastline, dragging hundreds of thousands to their debris-choked watery deaths. This happened more than once in history, and it could happen again. Giant volcanoes lie dormant until, one day, they don't.

The earth, the seas, and even the air, all contain the seeds of our destruction, for all that we could not live without them.

None of us is safe from the fate that awaits all people. No matter the fortress we erect to keep out all risks, danger lurks within. A twisted ankle on a flight of stairs, a lumpy bit of bread choking off the air in a tight passage, or a tiny clot ending up wedged in the wrong vein, and the end is near to us all.

I guarantee you are up to the task of merely meeting your death. Untold billions before you have done so, of every temperament and ability. Do you think you will somehow fail to succumb when the time comes? Have no worries on that account.

Your gift in being forewarned is as follows: To be reminded of our ultimate fate is to be given the chance to become master of it. Not to prevent the outcome, for that is not the province of any person, but to be ready for it.

What then? Do you complain that life is unfair? That some have long lives and others are cut down in their prime?

Better you learn to live meaningfully for the shortest of times than you live a long and unknowing life. The relative lives of people are all so tiny on the grand scope of things that to worry about a year, a decade, or even a century is to miss the forest for the trees.

Even the mountains are ground down by the passage of time. Nothing made of matter will endure forever. Will you reduce your existence to one of suffering because of fears that one day your suffering will end?

Your salvation lies in the acceptance of the inevitable. When you accept that you will have an end, note that you are not hastening to a premature end. Nor do you need to welcome a thing to be unfazed by its appearance.

Though you cannot control what nature has in store for you, you can control what you think of it. And this you accomplish by thinking about it.

As you contemplate, do not listen to what foolish people say about what things are worth. Though many listen to the incessant noise, few hear or take away the right tune.

The media will give you their daily reminders without fail, but you must never forget they are not trying to help you. Though they try to lead you astray by telling you to worry, you will have no problem dismissing their false fearmongering and taking away the true lesson.

The recitation of tragedy makes you stronger, not weaker, when it falls on ears attuned to reason.

Be well.

Chapter Fifteen

On the Length of Life

If the ticking of the clock spurs us to a frenzy of activity it should not be to prolong our lives but to start living them meaningfully

I seem to have gotten you to swallow the greater portion of my earlier mail, but you have spit out my suggestion that ill health is no barrier to the happiness of a wise person.

"We are far removed from ancient Greece and Rome, where death and destruction lay in wait around every corner," you say. "If they had great cause to reconcile themselves to nasty deaths, that is no longer the expectation or reality for people living in modern times."

We do live much longer lives, I grant you, and are much less likely to be cast into slavery or exile or put to premature death by a tyrant's hand. Too, we have conquered many of the ailments and diseases that plagued our ancestors.

But though we have vanquished tuberculosis, AIDS, and measles in most places, still there are countless means by which we are escorted from the world's stage.

And now that the play numbers several more Acts for most of us, how should we think about those who depart in the early Acts versus those who linger long past intermission to the final curtain call?

I am reminded of a remark attributed to Abraham Lincoln, and for our purposes, it does not matter whether he actually said it or not.

In a discussion about the proportion of the torso and legs to the body, Lincoln was asked to comment on the proper length of a person's legs. His reply: "Long enough to reach from his body to the ground."

It is a gift to be witty when speaking of profound things, dear reader. I make claim to neither wit nor profundity but only truth when I tell you that a person's life should be as long as it lasts.

Is the world a better place when we extend the lives of wicked people? Would we have wanted more of Stalin, Mussolini, or Pol Pot? We need not make examples only of mass murderers to see the validity of this point.

"But this is no argument in favor of cutting short the lives of the good," you say.

True, and you know by now what I will say back to you, be patient with me a moment more.

We hold that the highest attainment a person can reach is to master their reason and live according to the judgment of their well-ordered mind. This wise person knows what is valuable and what is not and acts accordingly.

They are not troubled by superficial things but see beneath the surface. That which is in their control, including their judgment, decisions, and actions, they do control. That which is beyond their control, such as fate, fortune, and external things, they do not let disturb their emotions.

The wise leave these things in peace so that their reason may be left in peace. And because they know their death is inevitable the wise person is not burdened when it comes.

If they are not bothered, who are we to be bothered on their behalf? If we were wise ourselves, we would come to the same conclusion.

"So far you have dealt with the extremes — the evil and the good. What of the great middle, who are neither irredeemable nor perfect?"

I will reward your patience with this answer: The great majority of us knowing that our time is limited seek to extend life when what we should be seeking is greater understanding.

Would you rather live a hundred years in confusion and pain or a week in contented contemplation, knowing the meaning of sufficient?

If the ticking of the clock spurs us to a frenzy of activity it should not be to prolong our lives but to start living them meaningfully.

So I will amend my saying above to be this: People's lives should be as long as it takes for them to start living.

As soon as they have achieved this milestone, they will be satisfied with the length of their lives no matter how much longer they play out their parts.

Be well.

Chapter Sixteen

On Mourning the Dead

When compassion turns into indulgence that does not reflect well on either the recipient or the giver

I had occasion to advise a student who had lost his young wife to cancer. He was looking for condolences but had rendered himself inconsolable, dear reader, impervious to every wise word and helping hand.

There is a point beyond which showing patience and understanding no longer demonstrates compassion but rather turns into indulgence that reflects well on neither the recipient nor the giver.

Thus it was that I told my student the following.

I have been urging you and your fellow students to be mindful at all times, which implies two conditions: That you first be aware of the course of your thoughts, and that you then direct your thoughts to the present moment.

Do not lose yourself for fear of what the future holds and do not dwell on past regrets. This is but the advice to the novice, who has little control over their mind. You are in need of stronger medicine, and because I trust you are ready for a deeper lesson, I will pull back the curtain and expand this thought.

We remind ourselves to live in the moment because most people do not manage to live at all. Whether consumed by anger and resentment over their bad luck or impelled by urges they feel strongly but scarcely understand, by casting about in their thoughts they are cast adrift in rivers of discontent.

You are in such a sea of sadness right now that you do not see it is made of your own false tears.

"False tears," you say. "Do you dare question that my grief is genuine?"

No doubt you had true cause for grief. The loss of your beloved spouse so unexpectedly created a great shock. But in giving such free reign to your grief you have now made a habit of grieving.

What, did you think only pleasures could be made into vices? No, people are just as easily given to turning their worst torments into guilty pleasures.

Whether a sweet indulgence or a personal torture, the root of the vice is the same: Surrendering reason to the free flow of emotions, giving up control, and giving in to the torrent.

This is not true passion, merely the loss of reason. You should take no solace in the loss of your reason, for now, you have not only lost your wife, but possession of your very mind as well.

If you had your wits about you as much as you had your tear-stained handkerchief, you would see more clearly that it is better for your tears to fall quietly and naturally while you are composed.

Just as you should not add to your present troubles by worrying about future troubles, or disturb your present peace by recalling past battles, so you should not amplify your grief by adding to it with lavish displays of sorrow.

Look at you! Weeping and wailing and moping about, as if you are the only person who has ever suffered a loss.

Do you think for a moment that you honor your spouse with your carrying-on? Would she be proud of your displays or turn away in embarrassment?

You like to ride your motorcycle to and from class every day through our crowded city streets. Let's say it was you who was carried off early by a sudden encounter with a city bus. Would you wish for your wife to spend a year in sackcloth and ashes before shutting herself into a nunnery for the rest of her life? Shall her life end because yours ended?

You do your spouse a disservice and demonstrate only selfishness when you dwell without end on what you have lost rather than what you have had.

Your wife has gone to the fate that awaits us all. Did you think that she was immortal, and that death did not have her on the list?

Or perhaps it is that you cannot get beyond the thought that her life could have been longer? Certainly, it could have been, but do you go so far as to say that it *should* have been longer?

Remember, her life could also have been shorter, and it could have been more painful. All over the world, children die of starvation, preventable illness, and war. The cancer wards are filled with infants, but you in your grief rail against the world for striking down an adult in her prime.

Everyone who has ever lived has suffered loss. Some succumb completely and take their own lives. This is the ultimate tragedy because it compounds the ill fate of the world and creates unnecessary suffering rather than alleviating it, which is our highest calling.

Countless more find ways every day to live with their loss. Every type of person can do it, whether young or old, whether ignorant or learned, and has done it, and in every type of situation.

Consider that some 150,000 people die every day. Imagine if this led to hundreds of thousands more people removing themselves from a life of their own volition, forcing their semi-animated bodies through the day with sad faces and drooping shoulders. The earth would soon be filled with zombies. And yet, somehow this does not happen.

Even as thousands are newly thrust into grief this very day, as many more find their way back into the warmth and light of the living. Though it seems impossible to you now, you will survive your wife's death, and you will survive your grieving.

Not only will *you* survive, but your memories will survive as well.

You can begin to relieve your sorrow by calling to mind the good times you shared with your wife. What you had together, Fortune cannot take from your memories: The challenges, triumphs, laughter, tears, and so many silly moments that only you two shared.

If you are forced to bury your happy remembrances, then truly you have buried more than your wife.

To be able to remember your wife with the proper spirit, and truly honor her memory, it is time to leave off mourning and rejoin the living.

Be well.

Pragmatic Wisdom
Vol. 4

Stoic Lessons on Learning (Teachers and Students)

James Bellerjeau

A Fine Idea

Contents

1. On the Stealth Philosopher   185
2. On Sharing Wisdom   189
3. On True and False Philosophy   193
4. On Easy Lessons   197
5. On Instagram-Worthy Quotes   201
6. On a Good Talk   203
7. On Drinking Deeply   205
8. On Words and Meaning   209
9. On Your New Blog   213
10. On Good Examples   215
11. On Continuing Education   217
12. On the Best Course of Study   221
13. On How To Study Philosophy   227
14. On Precepts (Sayings)   231
15. On a Learning Mind   237
16. On New Students   243

Chapter One

On the Stealth Philosopher

Nothing turns a sharp ear deaf more quickly than the listener sensing you feel superior to them

Greetings dear reader!

I take heart in the fact that you are daily working to improve yourself. The path to greatness is not traveled in one giant leap. It is the accumulation of many miles that require a lifetime of walking.

But although the journey is a thousand miles, your task each day is the same: Make sure you take at least a single step.

Do not let your progress go to your head, however, and by no means should you preen your development before your fellow travelers. Nothing turns a sharp ear deaf more quickly than the listener sensing you feel superior to them.

Perhaps you have heard the phrase "pacing and leading" and wondered what it meant. It's simply this. If you mean to influence another to change, you first must come into harmony with them: I hear your words, I understand your situation, I feel your pain.

It is not just on the mental plane that you seek to harmonize. You may breach the gates of their resistance by observing and subtly adopting the posture, emotions, and mannerisms of your audience. It is only when the gates have been unlocked, let alone flung open, that your words can find entry.

Once the resistance of your audience's minds has been loosened by your pacing, then, and only then, do you have a chance to lead.

You lead by *showing* the way, and not by *forcing* anyone along the path. The moment your pupils feel pushed, they will rear up like stubborn donkeys and go no further. He treads the path most surely when it is a path of his own choosing.

Numerous other ways in which you may spook the horse: Either through an overly aggressive delivery or a manner of dress inconsistent with your message.

Just as we would buy no suit from a disheveled tailor, take fitness lessons from an unfit instructor, or follow the health advice of a smoking doctor, so will your audience dismiss even your brightest observations if you deliver them from an inappropriate vessel. If you wish your fine wine to be enjoyed to the fullest, serve it from a crystal decanter.

Although we struggle to discern others' true intentions and inner thoughts, we have no such difficulty judging their appearance. True, appearance is irrelevant to the truth of your words, but for your words to work, you first must be heard.

Nor should you make the opposite mistake of dressing yourself too ornately, for this too will strike your audience falsely. If your audience is one that is comfortable in jeans, why then so must you be if you hope to have them hear you.

And if to another group casual Friday means not wearing the pin-striped vests of their three-piece suits, then you may break out your suit and tie. Know your audience first by fitting in with them, and they will know the truth of your words.

Here for your daily improvement is an idea that will give you companionship on many a quiet night's contemplation. The Buddha advises us to let go of both grasping and aversion.

- Cease to desire, and your monkey mind will be calmed.

- Cease to push away things you dislike, and likewise, you will calm your troubled spirit.

"But how," you ask, "can avoiding two polar opposites create the same effect?"

In this way, my dear reader: Though they seem like opposites, they are in fact the same. Just as gravity causes the feather and the cannonball to fall at the same rate, so grasping and aversion both find the same cause in our fear.

In the case of grasping, we fear not getting what we desire (or losing that which we have acquired). In the case of aversion, we fear being confronted with that which is hateful or painful.

The fear is rooted in another cause, namely not centering your mind in the present. It is only in the future that we may lose what we currently possess or be harmed by that which may afflict us.

To be able to see into the future the consequences of our actions is humankind's greatest advantage. But this foresight comes at the cost of carrying back haunts and demons that bedevil us.

Banish worries about tomorrow to where they belong — the future! They have no place in your daily meditation.

Be well.

Chapter Two

On Sharing Wisdom

Wisdom shared is wisdom doubled, and nothing pleases me more than adding to the store of wisdom in the world

Greetings!

I feel, dear reader, that I am not only continuously improving, but have become improved.

I do not yet, however, fool myself with the fantasy that I need no further refinement. There are many among us who could benefit from less flab or flirting with fame and firmer muscles.

That I see my own failings with fresh eyes does not depress me. I take it as a sign that my perception is sharpening. And if these thoughts are just placebos, am I not yet healthier for their consumption?

It is with this optimism that I am encouraged even further to respond to your questions. I see in you the same desire to improve, not least in your acknowledgment of doubt. I too doubted, and a problem shared is a problem halved.

How you would rejoice to know how much I feel I have come to understand, and how this wisdom grows daily. "Share this wisdom with me," I hear you already, and I tell you I do so gladly.

Wisdom shared is wisdom doubled, and nothing pleases me more than adding to the store of wisdom in the world.

If bad news is an orphan, good news has many parents. Let the truth be fruitful and multiply and let any who wish stake a claim to parentage.

You do not lack sources of truth. Thanks to the internet, the wisdom of all ages is but a keystroke away. Why then do so many fail to gain wisdom from the source that flows endlessly at their feet?

You do not understand water if you will not wade into the river. When your feet stand on pebbles smoothed by the eons of water passing over them, you may gain firsthand a feeling of the truth that a lifetime spent reading will not impart.

Saying is not enough, only doing. Reading is not enough, only doing. Do not do as I *say*, do as I *do*.

And now I both say and do thusly: Remember to follow systems, not goals. That is to say, adopt simple habits that move you in the right direction, rather than focusing on the desired destination.

If you want to lose weight, rather than setting a goal of losing ten pounds, remove the unhealthy snacks from your house and buy fruits and vegetables instead. When you are hungry and have only healthy options to hand you are more likely to choose correctly.

In this way, you increase your chances of success regardless of which shores you wanted to wash up on. Knowing where you want to go helps set a direction, true. But a direction alone brings you no closer to your goal. (You will find Scott Adams a most able teacher if you want to know more about systems versus goals.)

Many daydream of starting a business, becoming wealthy, or achieving high office. How much more useful to know what steps you need to take on your journey.

Researching these steps is not difficult, and many who have gone before you have shared their steps. Consider Cal Newport or Tim Ferris if you want a point to jump from. Taking daily steps along the path of continuous improvement will render your ultimate destination irrelevant, even as it increases your chances of arriving there.

I leave you with this small thought of the day, which gave me pleasure when thinking of you. It is this phrase from Ronald Reagan, who understood that a single step, no matter how small, will help so long as it is a step in the right direction:

We can't help everyone, but everyone can help someone.

Be well.

Chapter Three

On True and False Philosophy

Remember that philosophy is neither just for show nor for other people's benefit

I suspect I don't need to convince you, dear reader, that the unexamined life is unlikely to be guided by wisdom.

A person may be blessed by Fortune, and to all outward appearances successful. But if they themselves do not contemplate the purpose of their existence, what separates them from well-tended beasts of burden in our fields and pastures? We can pity them as worse off than the impoverished pilgrims taking their very first steps along the path of meaning.

The more you consider the reasons for the right actions, the more enlightened you will become. And though your work takes you a lifetime, still you are better for each day's toil than those living in ignorant luxury. Their supposed happiness relies on luck alone and can be taken from them without notice.

You do not need to put on a show for me to make me understand your progress is no mere performance. And though I know your intentions are good, remember that philosophy is neither just for show nor for other people's benefit. It is personal and for you.

Philosophy is not just words but must drive your thoughts and actions. Although you may think you have learned to walk the path, be careful that in your confidence you do not raise your eyes to the horizon and thus lose your way. Just as your feet must stay grounded, so too should your thoughts.

A well-ordered mind is at constant risk of being thrown out of equilibrium. Each day brings countless opportunities to test your foundation. If any test is not met with success, whether through the failure of resolve or through simple inattention, you give up ground previously hard-won.

Your opponents peddling alternative philosophies are many and will include the physicist, the deist, and the atheist.

- The physicist tells you that "Everything that is and will be is determined by fixed rules that govern the interaction of all particles. Show me the matter existing a moment after the Big Bang, and I will tell you the action of every atom for eternity."

- The deist cries "Nonsense! All we are and will be is in God's hands, and only God determines the fate of the Universe and all its beings."

- And quietly the atheist is heard to mutter, "There is no god, there are no universal rules, there is only now, and I am not sure what that means."

I ask you dear reader, what meaning exists in a collision of quarks and gluons? Should meaning be found in surrendering intellect to blind faith?

Whether the future is foreordained or in the hands of an all-powerful referee, or rather we are careening along in a game of chance, only philosophy provides a framework to give our lives meaning.

And though some or all hypotheses may hold portions of the true nature of reality, we are all still bound to the mortal plain. Thus, the more we draw our attention away from the invisible, whether vast or tiny and focus the locus of control on ourselves and our thoughts, the closer we can come to a meaningful life.

In case your mind has wandered in search of what additional treasure my letter holds, you need stray no further. For I have been to China on your behalf and have brought back this gem from Lao Tzu:

> Be content with what you have, rejoice in the way things are. When you realize there is nothing lacking, the whole world belongs to you.

ON TRUE AND FALSE PHILOSOPHY

Consider the differences between true desires (those consistent with nature) and false desires (those going against nature).

- True desires originate within you and are satisfied within you.
- False desires originate externally, and your attempts to satisfy them are external to you.

You are hungry, you eat, and your body signals when you are satiated, provided you are listening. You exercise your muscles, you burn energy and your muscles tire, and you will stop when you have had enough. These are true desires.

Contrast now the desire for money or fame or possessions. How many do you know who, upon gaining a million dollars, did not find their appetite whetted for even more? Having lined up an imposing line of zeros, there is always room for one more.

And the seeker of fame is never satisfied, for there is always another who has more followers, more likes, and simply more. When you look to external things for your happiness, each purchase offers but a crumb against your insatiable hunger.

You can one-click order until your cart is filled to overflowing, but you will hollow yourself out trying to fill a bottomless chasm.

The British philosopher Bertrand Russell understood the difference between true and false philosophy. He stated it thusly:

> It is preoccupation with possessions, more than anything else, that prevents men from living freely and nobly.

Be well.

Chapter Four

On Easy Lessons

Everywhere we turn, we are confronted with the incredible shrinking attention span

You have mentioned to me twice now that the study of philosophy is out of vogue for most people, and that the written word is so antique as to be virtually forgotten.

If we are not on Facebook, X, or Instagram, or better yet posting a weekly Spotify podcast or YouTube video, then we might as well put on our orthopedic shoes and sweater vest and spend the afternoons playing Bingo at the senior home.

Everywhere we turn, we are confronted with the incredible shrinking attention span.

- Who has the time to read entire books when Blinkist can give you the gist in a blink?

- Why watch a movie in a theater when you can stream 30-minute episodes on any device wherever you are?

- And who has thirty minutes to watch a full episode, when fifteen-second diversions are available nonstop at the flick of a finger?

You can scarcely finish a thought before the mind has wandered, flitting about like a hummingbird on the non-stop search for nectar.

"In such an environment," you say, "surely it is folly to expect to find an attentive audience willing to sit and do the hard work of reading and thinking. Hadn't we best adapt our message for the audience's abilities?"

It's true, we could chew our message to cud and spit it out for a slack-jawed crowd to mindlessly slurp. Though we would surely extend our reach to the broadest audience in this way, my dear reader, we would also dilute our message until it lost its meaning.

Do you teach an athlete to run a marathon by strolling around the block? Or to lift a great weight by putting feathers on one's forearms? No, and nor do we train the mind when we give it such light fare.

Little effort means little progress. It is ruminating on deep thoughts that generates growth, not consuming half-digested musings.

I don't suppose the glitterati will let this challenge go unanswered. They will pile up the charges against us and make the case thusly: "If you can't express your ideas simply in ways an average person can understand, you don't understand them yourself."

This we may hear from a Hollywood starlet whose claim to fame is a nub nose and a symmetrical face that is as much the result of gifted plastic surgery as genetics. I can see why they prefer the simpleton's version, but the arrows they shoot at us never hit their mark, because they cannot hit what they do not know to aim at.

Our critics do not surrender, but rather they turn their weapons on our audience: "The Stoics' medicine is bitter, and their course of recovery long and hard. Come to our side, and we will make everything easy for you: The one-hour workday, the no-discipline diet, and the no-sacrifice path to success!"

This is appealing fare, no doubt, and it will attract the masses as surely as it fails to nourish them. The only guarantee the consumer of such light sustenance can be sure of is that another snack will be available for purchase just as soon as this one disappears from your monthly credit card statement.

Deep down, do we not know when we are being sold nostrums and snake oil? We are willing dupes in being dazzled by packaging and bamboozled by dust-jacked blurbs. Show me a popular self-help author, and I will show you someone who has chosen to sell surface appeal instead of depth, and platitudes over purpose.

The greater the renown among the public, the less likely you are to have served before you gourmet food. For the masses want cheap and tasty meals, and you deliver these in quantity by following mass-production principles.

There is one type of reading that I give you my blessing, indeed my urging, to avoid at all costs: That is self-help books of almost any kind.

"What?" you wonder. "Am I to discard the advice of experts altogether? And how ironic that you who are so keen on dispensing wisdom forbid my seeking it from others."

What we are discussing in these letters, my dear reader, are truths and wisdom that belong to no expert, but are the common good of mankind. Furthermore, we are picking them up not as finished goods but must adapt, amend, and apply our lessons in a personal context.

Your self-help expert generally comes in two flavors: The scholar who has studied tables of figures until they tease or torture out statistical significance, and the business executive who explains their success in hindsight and with a healthy dose of selective memory.

As to the first, whether squeezed between unprovable hypotheses and the repeatability crisis, you are likely as well served by consulting your palm reader as you are the academic under pressure to publish.

And as to expecting the average executive to have sufficient self-reflection to understand the role factors beyond luck played in their fortune, let's just say you will get as useful advice from the one who explains how they picked the numbers for the winning lottery ticket.

In freeing you of this burden, I have greatly eased your load, for there are now whole aisles in the bookstore you may profitably avoid. In return, I ask you to stop and consider this:

> Whenever you find yourself on the side of the majority, it is time to pause and reflect.

The majority are often not wrong, of course, but they are not right just by virtue of being many.

"What philosopher uttered these words?" you ask.

It was the American humorist and fantabulist Mark Twain. Having long catered to the masses in aid of keeping his coffers stocked, the man also known as Samuel Clemens in his private time knew well this lesson: That to reach the greatest audience you must appeal to the least common denominator.

Better that we count our students on one hand than sell out our principles for profit.

Be well.

Chapter Five

On Instagram-Worthy Quotes

You mustn't take the headline for the whole of the message but rather read on

What has become of my closing quotes, you wonder, where I shared wisdom collected from sages across the ages. Am I no longer able to reinforce each letter with the lessons duly noted from earlier masters?

Fear not, my store of pithy sayings has not been depleted.

The Stoics alone numbered many who became adept at condensing their knowledge into rich kernels, making them easy to pass on and share. One sees their influence across the intervening centuries, in students as diverse as Shakespeare, C.S. Lewis, and Steve Jobs.

The Stoics, in turn, represent but a fraction of notable thinkers who have grappled with great truths. Thus, from sources without end, we have a rich menu of maxims to choose from.

Moreover, for any single idea, you can call upon ten or twenty formulations, each of which either reiterates or reformulates a central theme.

The sayings we collect and repeat do serve laudable purposes: They whet our appetites to know more, they refresh our memory of what we have already studied, and they provide a glimpse through an opened window of what truths lie beyond.

But just as the container is not the content, the maxim is not the full message, only a key for interpreting the map. Though one may memorize a thousand sayings, and repeat them back in any setting, are they any better than a trained parrot?

A chatbot may respond to any of a hundred programmed questions, but are you having a meaningful interaction? Alexa on your countertop has become your daily conversationalist, but if you probe beneath the surface will you find anything of substance?

Thus, I caution you, my dear reader, that to know why an idea is worthy of study at all, you need to digest more than Instagram-worthy morsels. Such light fare may be eagerly sought by the masses, but not the sincere student.

You mustn't take the headline for the whole of the message but rather read on. Read widely and deeply.

I want you to walk the grounds that gave root to an idea, wallow in the soil that nourished it, and be drenched by the summer storms that gave it strength. If you tend to the garden of ideas in this way, you will know not only how the fruits there came to ripen, but you will enjoy an abundant harvest.

Now consider this: No matter how strong the seed stock you start with, would you be a mere tender of another's crop, or will you add something new to the storehouse of humankind's bounty?

When you are the master of your garden, you can cross-pollinate ideas and bring whole new lineages of thought into being.

I think that although you may start out with what others thought, you need to end up with what you think.

Be well.

Chapter Six

On a Good Talk

Give me persons of any age who have made their own choice to learn, not because anyone compels them to, but because they believe it will bring them something of value

If there is a better way to communicate with another person than by face-to-face conversation, I do not know it.

Our letters are certainly valuable, for when I write to you I picture you in my mind and it is as if I am speaking with you directly. And a letter from you is a bright spot in my day, in which I feel like I can hear the voice of an old friend.

What then should we think of the various ways in which today's teacher reaches out to pupils?

At one end we have the MOOC, or massive open online course. Any can join (open), and thousands do (massive), and all interactions take place remotely (online). One great voice can reach the masses, and I suppose we can be thankful for the democratization of learning.

But though each has supposed access to the master, I expect only a fraction feel truly addressed, because they are being talked *at* not talked *to*. As a result, while many begin such courses, few complete them. Have we really brought learning to the masses, or only given them a glimpse but left them wanting?

If the MOOC suffers from students lacking commitment, should we expect a better outcome when we apply a selection process? That is when we admit only students who have met some sort of qualification?

This may increase the chance that our words will land on attentive ears, but I am not yet satisfied.

- Consider how many students are present out of obligation rather than thirst for knowledge.
- They were compelled to complete their grade school, though they would have preferred to do anything but learn.
- Many are similarly prodded along to college because they are told they need a degree for success in life.

Do these children any more willingly roll from their beds, shoulder their backpacks, and fill morning lecture halls?

Give me persons of any age who have made their own choice to learn, not because anyone compels them to, but because they believe it will bring them something of value.

With such students, we can talk. Not talk at, or even talk to, but talk *with*. The best lecturer does not just lecture but also listens.

The best class is one in which the professor learns something from the students, all while the students are learning. It is hard, it is rare, and it is special when it happens.

The larger the group, the greater the inhibition on speaking one's mind. This is because we fear looking foolish more than we fear remaining ignorant.

Have you noticed how often a large group will sit in silence until one brave soul says they do not understand? Suddenly there is a chorus of voices affirming, "I have the same question!"

Treat each interaction, my dear reader, whether with five, with twenty, or with a multitude, as a conversation with a single earnest person, and you have a chance of being understood by all.

Be well.

Chapter Seven

On Drinking Deeply

Think of a summary as but a sip, nourishing if it comes after a full meal, but leaving you empty if you have consumed nothing before it

You have requested that I outline for you the main teachings of philosophy that we are discussing, and I am happy to do so. A summary of key points is surely useful if it is in the hands of one who has intimate experience with what is being summarized.

But what of the one who wishes merely to memorize the list, and confuses the aphorism for the underlying wisdom?

A nail is useful to hold two pieces of wood together and fix a point between them. But if your toolbox is filled only with nails, you will be an impoverished carpenter.

Better the one who knows why this piece of wood and not another, why this length, and how these beams support the weight of the structure. And better still the one who can tell you what it is that they are building.

If you would be a capable builder, you must learn the complete skills of the trade. It is not enough to strap on the toolbelt, because all this does is put you in proximity to dangerous implements.

We do not let lawyers loose with but a book of quotes or give doctors access to our bodies if they've had access to no more than a season of Dr. House.

Serious work requires serious study, and a summary is best in the hands of the accomplished student and not the novice. Think of a summary as but a sip, nourishing if it comes after a full meal, but leaving you empty if you have consumed nothing before it.

You are an accomplished student, dear reader, because you are comfortable drawing directly from the sources of wisdom. When you read the writing of the great philosophers who have labored for our benefit before us, you are drinking deeply from wells that never run dry.

You also know that by slowing down your pace, you advance your progress. Rather than flitting from one thought to the next like a bee on an endless hunt for pollen, you can dwell in one place until your needs are met.

To know the difference between needs and wants is to start to bend your will to obtain the one and avoid the other. What most people seek most avidly, you avoid assiduously.

The greatest risk is getting what you want too quickly. If you are met with early success, in your studies, in your career, or in relationships, you have no cause to question what you are doing.

The established path — finish your studies, earn money to care for yourself and loved ones, and strive to be a person worthy of love and respect — exists for a reason, and you do not better yourself by being contrarian for the sake of it.

But nor should you blindly accept the fare put in front of you. Taste what is on offer and decide for yourself which parts are to your liking.

Know that what you consume daily will become your habit, and left unobserved your habit will become your vice.

Many take pleasure not only in the vice itself but in surrendering to the vice. Surrendering means you have made your decision and no longer need to think about what you want, but only to pursue it.

And because thinking for oneself is the hardest thing, it is no surprise that so many wish to be done with it as soon as possible.

But to give in to wants because it is easy is to expose yourself to a life of hardship. If losing access to a vice will make you sad or mad, you are mad not to cut it from your life.

I say excise the want, not the thing. You can still enjoy all that you eat and drink and have, so long as you will not miss them when you do not have them.

Always observe what you are doing and ensure that you are doing it of your own choosing. In this way, your habits become the summary of your prior deep thinking and not evidence of your absence of thought.

Be well.

Chapter Eight

On Words and Meaning

A gifted thinker turns words into more than words by adding meaning. This particular alchemy comes about when we go beyond the surface and address what is of lasting value

You say that you are overwhelmed by the number of books there are to read. Your bookshelves are overflowing, your Kindle is full, and there are not enough hours in the day to read a fraction of the homework you've assigned to yourself.

Do not assume that reading more titles will deepen your understanding of more subjects. And do not think that reading faster will hasten your progress to any destination other than confusion.

The more a person brags about being widely read, the greater the chances they are a shallow thinker. When you flit from one book to the next, sampling great writers across time, you pick up fleeting impressions of the places you visit, no more.

If you want to get a true sense of a city, you must linger in its streets, mingle with its citizens, and match your pace to its rhythms. Better you spend a month in one place than you book a whirlwind tour with twenty stops.

"I understand," you say, "and I would rather you gave me your thoughts directly than shorten my reading list."

Nothing would give me greater pleasure, my dear reader, than to see you again and have this conversation in person. The social distancing of the pandemic era may have kept us healthy in body, but the isolation is making us ill in spirit.

The Zoom meeting and Teams call are but thin comfort compared to the hearty embrace of a hale companion. I yearn for the day when I can add my vaccine passport to my traveling kit and once more point my boots on the road in your direction.

Until then, you ask me to send you my thoughts in the next best form, these letters. I do not flatter myself that you prefer my words to those of the bestsellers scattered around you because you think I am creating great fare.

But compared to wilted greens, day-old bread, and thin gruel, any meal prepared freshly will seem fine.

I would have you think of me not as the master of the kitchen, but as a dedicated sous chef: learned but still learning, always ready for a lesson from the greats.

What every great cook knows is that they do not own the secret to good taste. Everyone who puts a knife to the cutting board is entitled to experiment and improve.

But let us make sure we spend time on substantive improvements. I may probe and explore a topic from all sides, but I do not fool myself that I am describing ten different things when I am using ten different words.

A pinch of salt, a dash of pepper, a sprig of parsley: The seasoning does not make a new dish. This is one of the risks with sayings, and why I have cautioned you not to mistake the summary for the full idea.

The saying should call up in your mind a chorus of voices, each containing a few notes and bars of the larger composition. Just as the printed recipe is far from the finished meal, the saying is but an index entry, pointing to the page where the recipe is described in detail.

And though you may know what steps to follow, you must still collect the ingredients and perform your transformation upon them.

What separates the gifted chef from the uninspired is not the components they start with. Give two cooks equal amounts of rice, beans, herbs, and butter, and be amazed at how varied the results will be.

A gifted thinker turns words into more than words by adding meaning. This particular alchemy comes about when we go beyond the surface and address what is of lasting value:

- that a person is not more valuable by virtue of having valuables;

- that a person thinks clearly when they come to the same conclusion despite all others changing their minds, and only adapts their view in light of new facts not new opinions;

- that a person is wealthy in proportion to the things they can let go;

- that a person is happy when living in accordance with their nature, who is unshaken by what happens externally; and

- a person gains a more well-ordered mind when they realize the greatest harms are the ones we inflict upon ourselves.

It is clear that the recipe for a good life is available to all, but preparing it well is not the work of amateurs.

The Irish poet Oscar Wilde had this in mind when he said:

> To live is the rarest thing in the world. Most people exist, that is all.

If you would be accomplished in this effort, I commend to you the words of the Indian lawyer Mahatma Gandhi, who counseled:

> Live as if you were to die tomorrow. Learn as if you were to live forever.

It is the serious student who takes every opportunity to be about their studies.

If you spend your time in reading and contemplation, you will not miss your life by bending to your books but will instead find it.

Be well.

Chapter Nine

On Your New Blog

Acquire new knowledge while thinking over the old, and you may become a teacher of others

I see you have taken my recent words to heart, dear reader, and put your own words to paper in the hope of giving them meaning.

I meant to take a quick look at the new blog that you have started on the side, with the intention of making a thorough study later. But I was drawn in, and I can't say against my will, for I was glad to remain immersed in your thoughts.

When I came back to my senses, I was amazed to see that the afternoon was gone, and the sun had already set. The dog needed walking, the other animals clamored to be fed, and I had missed my office hours that day. Judging from the Post-it notes now coloring the surface of my door, there is no shortage of students looking for guidance who also turned away with their needs unmet today.

Students of the good life could scarcely do better than to consume your writing themselves. It seems another master has entered our midst, and your voice rings out clearly among the greats.

How pleased I am! Not just at your progress, for what teacher does not rejoice at the accomplished student, but that you are breaking new ground and charting new territory. I see in your blog entries what I was trying to describe as the signs of understanding: You are not just reformulating what you have heard but finding new insights.

I am called to mind the words of that great Chinese philosopher Confucius, who said:

> Acquire new knowledge while thinking over the old, and you may become a teacher of others.

I had to share these first impressions at once, but you deserve a studied response. I will give you my thoughts in more detail after they have had time to marinate and mature.

And I promise to be a true friend and tell you no lies. It is sometimes cruel to be kind, and I would not spare you the rod if your course needs correction.

But if I find you have strayed, I will be a little more lenient than Confucius was when he said:

> If I raise one corner for someone and he cannot come back with the other three, I do not go on.

I will grant you the second corner, dear reader, for I wish you to continue on in this way.

When you share genuine insight with others, you learn something of yourself, even as they learn something of you.

Be well.

Chapter Ten

On Good Examples

The best way to become wealthy is to become rich in your mind. Plunder the wisdom of the ages and take into your ownership your self-possession

We do not lack for knowledge of what to do, we lack the will to do it.

The collective wisdom of humanity lays revealed before us. We need not even leave our homes to browse these volumes, for they are never farther than an internet search away.

Do not give yourself the excuse, dear reader, that you do not know the path when you fail to seek it. Many have gone before you and you need but follow in their footsteps.

For myself, though I may sit alone on a bench with my face to the sun, I am in the presence of many teachers:

- the lessons of Confucius are before my eyes as if I sat in his classroom;

- the words of Cicero ring out as if I was in the forum to hear them delivered live;

- when I call to mind Seneca's letters to Lucilius, I feel they are written directly to me; and

- though Marcus Aurelius was recording his personal thoughts, it is as though they are playing out in my own head.

No matter where I am and no matter what I am doing, I have these examples always before me.

I can almost see them gathered around me like force ghosts. It helps me to imagine they are watching me just as I am watching them.

In this way, I know not only *what* to do, I feel myself encouraged daily to take the proper steps to *do* what I ought to do.

The only riches you can be guaranteed to possess are those that are contained within you.

External things come and go, and their pursuit will distract you from things that matter.

The best way to become wealthy is to become rich in your mind. Plunder the wisdom of the ages and take into your ownership your self-possession.

When your thoughts have thus become well-ordered by following the good examples of others, then you become a good example yourself, able to pass on your riches to future generations in ways that no inheritance tax can diminish.

Be well.

Chapter Eleven

On Continuing Education

I myself try to be an earnest student. Though I am far removed from my formal school days, I am never far from a book or an idea

I put to you last the burden of constant vigilance, of watching your mind lest it become infected with viruses and weaknesses that would sap your reason. I told you that this daily toil cannot be avoided because the threats to your ordered mind are themselves unceasing and unrelenting.

I have more than just bitter news on offer, dear reader, and today I will give you a message that is sweeter, though it too is about serious things.

Just as people are creatures of habit and we become what we repeatedly do, so your mind becomes more skilled with practice at spotting and blocking the viruses that bombard you. With your daily habit of reflecting upon and reinforcing your reason, you will readily spot traps and dead ends.

This is not to say that you become unthinking and take for granted what you have learned, but that the lessons spring more easily to your mind and to your defense when needed.

But do not rest on your accomplishments, my dear reader, for you are never further than one step from a fall. Our friend Confucius advises us to

> Pursue the study of virtue as though you could never reach your goal, and were afraid of losing the ground already gained

and surely this is sound advice. Even though you may gain confidence in the subjects of your daily meditation, are you confident you have learned everything that may be of use to you?

Let us hear again the voice of Confucius, who made no claim to wisdom for himself, but once more praised the virtue of the student:

> In me, knowledge is not innate. I am but one who loves antiquity, and is earnest in the study of it.

I myself try to be an earnest student. Though I am far removed from my formal school days, I am never far from a book or an idea.

If passions and desires are missiles and bullets being fired constantly at our vulnerable reason, ideas and beliefs are the shields that protect us. I would rather carry a thousand shields about my person than I should find myself missing the one that could have protected me from a cruel blow!

So I suit myself for school as diligently as the parent preparing their child for kindergarten, reflective band about their neck, pack upon their back, and mid-day snack at the ready.

"Look how foolish he is to be marching back to school with the smallest of children," the ignorant will mock. I should be so lucky to always have such feeble-minded critics.

I fully admit to knowing but a fraction of all that I could and all that I would. The criticisms of the empty-headed are more a reflection upon them than upon me. I dismiss them as easily as I do the impatient honking of the commuter at the schoolchildren's crosswalk who is eager to get to their work cell so they do not need to be confronted with the prison they've made of their minds.

Here's something I've realized in my later years that those who are students only in their youth may never learn. The toil seems greater which never varies and is repeated over and over.

Sisyphus could have been made to perform any punishment, but Zeus set him to push a boulder endlessly up a hill. How like Sisyphus are people in their pursuit of money and objects, always the same distance from their goals no matter how far they have come, doomed to struggle without end and without ever nearing satisfaction.

How different the task laid before the willing lifelong student! We have before us a rich buffet of delicacies whose recipes have been created, experimented upon, and improved across ages. This month we are dining on Chinese food, next month it is European fare that best suits our palates, and later we may enjoy the heat and spice of India. Is it a fusion of tastes you are after? No problem, for every combination is available for the taking.

When you are feeling full, by all means, take some time for digestion. Did that last dish not agree with you so much? Put it to the side for now. I wouldn't discard it, even though it is not to my taste, because I remember two things: It appealed to someone in time and it would be interesting to know why; and even if I do not enjoy the meal the first time I try it, perhaps I will find it to be an acquired taste or that it is improved when consumed with other flavors.

We each try many things in our pursuit of happiness and meaning. The usual burdens and cares we pick up as we age make us heavier and wear us down. By contrast, the meals we consume in knowledge and learning make us lighter the more we eat. Let us therefore put work into the task of ordering our minds. If we can stick with this effort, I feel sure we will be rewarded.

For every degree that our perception sharpens, we see that there is more to be seen. For everything that we think we have come to know and understand, we should be looking about in delight because there is so much more that we do not.

The wisest person is the one who is least confident of the extent of their wisdom. To learn, to study, to engage with great minds: This is work but no burden, this is effort but no toil.

If we have compassion for humankind, let us make it our mission to help more people realize that while material things offer meager and fleeting rewards, reason's rewards are abundant.

It seems only proper to let Confucius close for me today dear reader. He has been my faithful companion throughout and can reinforce today's learnings in his own words:

I used to spend whole days without food and whole nights without sleep, in order to meditate. But I made no progress. Study, I found, was better. It is not easy to find a man who after three years of self-cultivation has not reached happiness.

Be well.

Chapter Twelve

On the Best Course of Study

If you would not have your children tear down the foundations that hold up society, do not send them into the factories that labor explicitly for that purpose

You want me to tell you the best course of study for a young person, for an older person, or for any person for that matter.

You may expect, as I did when I first applied myself to the task of answering your question, that a clear answer exists.

- For example, the only truly useful course of study is the one that trains the mind to be well-ordered and follow reason.
- That the only sincere students are those who learn to look within and follow the precepts of philosophy.

There is something to this, but I do not think we should be satisfied with a quick answer. Just as the philosopher would, let us look below the surface to see what further insight we can glean.

I would argue that the serpent in the Garden of Eden was the first in a long line of philosophers who used clever logic and sophistry to support a line of argument that leads to conclusions that are either of little use to their students or downright harmful.

In any event, what Adam and Eve gained by eating from the Tree of Knowledge was not wisdom but self-awareness. They became aware of their nakedness and the nature of good and evil.

How bitter that the first human consequence of their newfound awareness was for Adam and Eve to seek to shirk responsibility for their actions: Adam blames his eating the fruit on Eve, and Eve blames her eating the fruit on the serpent.

God curses all three of them. Eve's curse is painful childbirth and subjugation to her husband while Adam is cursed to a lifetime of hard labor followed by death. Thus did the first humans fall and suffer ejection from paradise.

The first children did not fare much better. Cain is jealous that his brother Abel's sacrifices were favored more by God. Cain murders Abel, for which he is condemned to a life of wandering.

"What does any of this have to do with my question?" I can hear you wondering.

Well, dear reader, in my own wandering I am working my way to the first point, which is this: Before setting yourself on the path of seeking knowledge, be aware that knowledge is dangerous. Its acquisition comes with the burdens of awareness and responsibility that cannot simply be laid aside.

One of the most fundamental things humans became aware of is that there are differences between people. Thus, Eve was subject to the rule of Adam, and Cain sees that Abel's sacrifices were better received by God.

From the very beginning, the human ability to reason brought with it the drawing of distinctions between humans. Almost everything we do in our lives, including the courses of study we choose and the attendant careers we put ourselves on the path to pursuing, serves to delineate these distinctions more sharply.

Do you see now why some gurus have retreated from society into their solitary mountain caves? To be among the company of other people is to be constantly reminded of our differences, and for many, like Cain, this is not a source of joy.

And yet, people are intensely social in the sense that most wither and suffer miserably when they are deprived of interaction with their fellow humans. The worst punishment you can inflict on a person is not physical torture but solitary confinement.

So, the hermit's cave is habitable by only a tiny minority and does not offer suitable accommodation for the vast majority of humankind. What to do then? How to organize ourselves so that we can co-exist without literally killing each other by virtue of perceiving differences between ourselves?

With this context in mind, I think you will more readily accept that one of the great purposes of education is to socialize people into getting along. We are seeking foremost to teach conformity to the rules of society because the alternatives are anarchy and warfare.

Culture and acculturation are the aim, from the first day of kindergarten onwards. Though it may be the veneer we use to cover the core mission, the acquisition of knowledge is secondary.

I believe most founders of schools and universities genuinely wanted to better the condition of humankind.

Whether it was their intention from the start to shape generations of students in the mold of useful conformists, this has been the effect. And I do not say this is wrong, dear reader.

For modern society to work at all we need to accept a set of common values and common conditions. Even though much of what we take for granted is quite arbitrary, the common suspension of disbelief is what makes cooperation among competitive, aggressive, and emotional people possible.

Education at every level bends itself to the task of bending minds within lines of acceptable thought and guidelines of acceptable behavior. Conformity of thought is an incredibly powerful tool to shape the culture of society.

And herein lies a great danger. The very tools of education that humankind developed to keep us from each other's throats can also be used to turn society to other purposes.

In the past few decades, we have seen the steady growth and subsequent march of postmodernism across much of higher education.

Postmodernists would tear away the common blinders we have collectively put across our eyes to expose a different underlying reality. Not for the sake of any objective truth but in the naked pursuit of power. To a postmodernist, structures in society are questions of what ideologies create political and economic power, and who controls those ideologies.

In effect, I have been arguing from the same premise that they do: Our whole system of education is a structure designed to direct society in a desired direction.

The as-yet irreconcilable flaw in all our systems is that we have not been able to eradicate human differences. Without exception, every society we know generates hierarchies and this is by no means limited to the human realm.

In hierarchies, there are winners and losers, the powerful and the weak, the happy and the dissatisfied. Cain is long since dead and gone, but his spirit lives on within each of us. When we detect a difference, murderous envy is never far from the surface, and never so safely hidden that we can relax our guard.

I submit that postmodernists see themselves as the inherently weak and unhappy, the losers under the modern rules of life, at least in their own minds. Surely it must be so, for why else would they propound theories that have as their effect the *complete destruction* of modern society as we currently know it?

Do you think I exaggerate? Consider that the targets of postmodernist criticism include objective reality and truth, human nature and morality, reason, science and social progress, and even language. What sort of society will we have once we have cast all these to the curb?

Make no mistake: We are in a battle for the future of human society, for the very soul of humankind.

By assuming that schools and universities are doing today what they did a century ago, we have let loose predators amongst our children. We are surprised to see our children turn into predators themselves, tearing at the very throat of society on what seems to be the slightest provocation. Is the answer to a perceived unfairness to tear everything down?

As we look upon the rubble in shock, I say we should not waste time in trying to lay blame, as in "Why didn't we see this sooner? Why wasn't anyone paying attention?" The damage is done, and the question now is one of survival.

Thus, I come at last to the first answer to your question on the best course of study for those of all ages: It is not to be found in any modern school or university.

Worse, by subjecting yourself to their ministrations, you risk making yourself a tool in the destruction of society. Would you be an unwitting soldier in this army?

Now I am not advocating that we remain ignorant, nor that we remove ourselves from the fight. The fight is coming to the willing and unwilling alike. Your only choice is the manner in which you will enter the battle.

Do you send your own children to be warriors for the enemy? If you would not have them tear down the foundations that hold up society, do not send them into the factories that labor explicitly for that purpose.

"Do you really mean to suggest that we must home-school our children?" you ask, "Not everyone has the luxuries of time or money to do this, and what does the average person know of teaching all that is necessary for modern life?"

These are the wrong questions, dear reader, and I despair that people will open their eyes in time to see. There is something worse than trying one's best and doing a poor job, and that is others trying their best to do an evil thing.

- Is it better that you leave your car sitting un-serviced in your driveway or that you take it to a mechanic you know will pour salt in the tank and cut the wires?
- Are you not wiser to take your health into your own hands than to visit the doctor who will prescribe you poison?

Our salvation lies in independence of thought and action because this is incredibly dangerous to the stability of an ideology.

This is why the mob reacts so strongly to having its orthodoxy challenged. Cancel culture is nothing more than the impulse to destroy what is deemed to be an attack on the desired view.

For almost all of humanity, I would have said conformity to the mainstream view was the safest course. But when the current view is that society shall be destroyed, our only course is to reclaim the moral high ground by refusing to submit.

Thus, the best course of study is to see first to your own education and then that of others.

Be well.

Chapter Thirteen

On How To Study Philosophy

Philosophy means the love of wisdom and consequently is made up of the efforts you put into attaining wisdom

So, having urged you to be about your own studies, can I be surprised when you ask me for guidance about how and in in what direction?

No, although I urged you not to put your mind in the care of those who would weaponize you for their own purposes, I would have you weaponize your mind in defense of yourself. And I suppose you will not be surprised when I tell you that the lessons you need to learn most ardently are those of philosophy.

I have previously urged you to read broadly and widely. This is because you do not know where and how inspiration will strike. It comes to people unevenly and at different times, and what works for one may be useless for another.

The best way to increase your chances of success, at least initially, is to make many tries at the prize. If one lottery ticket gives you but a tiny chance, then a hundred or a thousand tickets will multiply your odds.

But your odds will remain forever slight if you do not lay a certain groundwork; otherwise, your reading will be aimless and fruitless, like buying lottery tickets for last week's drawing.

Wisdom is what you are seeking, my dear reader, the highest attainment of the well-ordered mind in pursuit of reason. Philosophy means the love of wisdom and consequently is made up of the efforts you put into attaining wisdom.

I have talked with you many times about virtues and vices, about first- and second-order goods or pursuits, and about the many things that lead people astray from the path of reason. Although these distinctions give rise to much confusion, what is clear is that philosophers are on a path seeking wisdom through philosophy.

Philosophy does not follow a single path but offers multiple branches.

- We talk of moral philosophy, which is concerned with the thinking, motivation, and actions of people.

- Natural philosophy takes up our observations of the universe we find ourselves in and everything in it. In the meantime, this branch has diverged into the many roads that lead to the hard sciences.

- Finally, we have logical philosophy, which addresses how humans make sense of the universe through words and expressions, and how to build logical arguments from unbroken chains of reasoning. We most often turn to logical philosophy to identify falsehoods, for these are more abundant and easier to identify than eternal truths.

I urge you to build your foundation in moral philosophy, and within it to focus on the most critical question of how to discern what is truly valuable and all the things that are not.

Your motives are only partly under your control and will steer you to wrong action if left unchecked, but they can be brought under the domain of reason. For you to apply right reason at all you need to know what is worth pursuing.

I repeat myself to you often, dear reader, because these basic lessons bear repeating. Without this clear understanding of the relative value of things, all else you pursue will be to false purposes and likely wasted effort.

- You should understand that bravery is one of the ways to overcome fear, but that fear itself is a construct of the mind.

- You should know the value and correct application of loyalty, temperance, and kindness.

- You will never waste your time if you are spending it studying how to live your life simply, modestly, and with self-restraint.

ON HOW TO STUDY PHILOSOPHY

Although knowledge of the things that are valuable is the cornerstone on which your good life will be built, your tower will not raise itself towards the sky unaided. You create the structure of your life by taking actions consistent with your values.

Each time you act unthinkingly, you have missed an opportunity to lift a stone and cement it into place. Each time you act inconsistently, you are a sloppy builder, sometimes creating a smooth surface by accident but more often leaving sharp edges that you will need to return to later for repair.

And if you act against your values, you are tearing down your substance and creating destruction around you, though at first, you may be the only one to sense it.

Do you feel that I am preaching to you again, dear reader? I know the only one whose words will have lasting effect are your own, so I call upon you to be your own constant cheerleader if not a stern policeman.

Until you bring your thinking into order and direct your actions consistently with your thinking, you will have to resign yourself to my lessons. I will not stop talking until you have put a stop to your desires, for it is your desires that lead you from the path every time.

Once you can test your wishes and reliably return the answer that you have enough, so will my words cease — you will have had enough of them because they are ingrained in your being.

In sum, you study not to learn more things but to learn what things are valuable.

You think about what you have studied to prepare yourself to apply the learnings to your particular situation. And though no exam is administered in this course, still you test yourself in every situation where you are called upon to make a choice about how to act and how to feel about your actions.

You will know you are making progress in your studies if the wise decision is clear to you, even though it still costs you constant vigilance to control your motivation and constant effort to control your actions. This is enough to be on the path to wisdom and headed in the right direction.

Be well.

Chapter Fourteen

On Precepts (Sayings)

The next best thing to having good examples by your side is to have precepts never far from mind

You know that I have at times made comments critical of psychology. I should be as critical in my comments on philosophy, dear reader, for the root cause of the problem in both cases is the nature of people.

In both fields, our mistakes in both theory and practice come from assuming that two people in the same situation will behave in the same way, or that even a single person will act similarly when the same situation is repeated.

Psychology at least has gained popular attention and broad appeal while Stoic philosophy remains the dusty preserve of the solitary academic.

Why the difference? Both are after all concerned with the workings of the mind and with understanding the motivations behind our actions. They spring from the same deep-seated sense of wondering, "If only we could understand why we do what we do, could we find a way to be enduringly happy?"

If we begin with similar topics and we pursue similar aims, the conclusions of the two fields and our corresponding prescriptions to adherents surely differ. Psychology tells us that nothing is our fault, while philosophy tells us that everything is.

The psychologist will say that we are creatures formed as a result of our environments, starting with our childhood experiences and traumas and continuing on through to the inputs and stimuli we receive every day.

- The path to happiness lies in first making sense of our pasts and then in carefully controlling our environments to ensure we are confronted only with surroundings that lift us up.

- At a minimum, we shall avoid people and situations that bring us down.

The philosopher says that we are creatures formed by our minds and that the path to happiness lies in ordering our minds to follow reason in any environment.

- People should not seek to control their circumstances but to control their thinking about circumstances.

- We do not flee from hardship. Rather we see that overcoming hard times can be more beneficial to wellbeing than being surrounded with ease and luxury.

Is it any wonder that philosophy molders while psychology thrives?

Which doctors are more eagerly greeted by their patients? The ones who say sternly "You need to make some serious lifestyle changes because the path you're heading down is going to lead to inevitable sadness, sickness, and decay."

Or the ones who whip out their prescription pads with a smile, saying "Good news! You currently show signs of A, B, and C, and in a few years left untreated, you will almost certainly develop X and Y. But I can prescribe you this small army of pills, taken twice daily with meals, and you'll be right as rain."

Do you doubt that most people would rather take a pill that merely conceals their symptoms than undertake a course of treatment that will result in a lasting cure but only if they put in serious effort?

I say for all their wisdom, philosophers have fundamentally misunderstood human nature if they think their bitter medicine will be easily swallowed.

Is this the reason that sayings and precepts are in such widespread use when we talk of philosophy to the masses?

- If our whole treatment is too much for the patient to take at one time, perhaps we can dole out our medicine in bite-sized pieces.

- Taken individually, the maxims of philosophy are lighter fare, and easier to consume, remember, and repeat.

And so now we come to the question of whether these treatments are any real help against the underlying maladies humankind suffers from, or whether we too are quacks purveying snake oil to unwitting rubes at the country fair.

When we dispense philosophical precepts, do we only smooth over symptoms and leave our mortally ill patients not only uncured but unaware that they are still terminal?

We can approach our answer from two sides, top-down and bottom-up.

Starting first from the lofty heights of the philosopher who has achieved wisdom.

- This person knows that reason is the only virtue and that following the judgment of their well-ordered mind is the path to happiness.

- Such a person has no need for maxims because they need but consult their reason to know the true value of all things in every situation.

- Their course of action is not prescribed by others because they are the physician of their own soul at all times.

The point of sayings is not to cure the philosopher who has attained reason, but to help raise up all others who are not yet safely underway.

Let us therefore consider the situation from the bottom up, from the perspective of the condition we all find ourselves in much of the time, which is that of needing help.

To one who needs help seeing, to say nothing of acting, does a simple saying provide valuable guidance by lighting the way?

I assume for our discussion, dear reader, that our patients are desirous of seeing their way out of suffering and troubles. I say this knowing all too well that there are none so blind as those who do not want to see. But for the willfully blind neither precept, nor theory, nor practice in any discipline will bear lasting fruit. So, I limit myself to the case of the willing student with an attentive ear.

For such students, sayings are a sweet starter that whets the appetite. Not fully satisfying in themselves but providing encouragement to consume more.

We should all be encouraged to think about useful topics and be given a helpful nudge in the right direction. The hardest part of many tasks is to start, and if the saying prompts us into motion, then it has already served a useful purpose.

Once started, we benefit from support along the way. Give me a tip on how to improve my running form while I am running, and I am delighted to hear it. Tell me how to conserve energy, improve my endurance, stand straighter, step quicker — there is no end to the advice on many small things that I will gladly take on if I have the slightest sense it will help me in my current pursuit.

Though neither a new running shoe with a carbon sole, nor a T-shirt with sweat-wicking fabric, nor a new electrolyte drink will make me into a champion by themselves, they each give me a helpful push to continue. And if that push is only in my mind, but prompts me to start, then is that not where the proper motivation to undertake any great deed ultimately begins?

A saying will not do the hard work for you. It can only offer support.

But though sayings are not complete, and we ourselves have to lift and put one foot in front of the other, who does not welcome support at every stage? Whether you're just starting out, or nearing the finish line, you still appreciate the clapping and calls of encouragement during the race.

It is no doubt most beneficial to have good examples in the form of other people, personal teachers as it were, to show us the way.

The next best thing to having good examples by your side is to have precepts never far from mind. These are the written condensation of the best examples of people across time.

We no longer have access to Plato and Socrates or to the painted porch of the Stoics, but we have access to their sayings. If it helps you to think on the wisdom behind the words, then imagine someone saying them aloud to you, and having a conversation with them in your head.

Learning to follow reason more often than emotion is a race we must run slowly and steadily. I always say that it is not your speed that matters but simply that you continue to progress. Your steps will fall more lightly the more you practice.

The more you are reminded to practice, for example by keeping a saying close to hand, the more you reinforce and stay your course.

Will a life lived purely by sayings result in your becoming wise in all things? Or is more required, for example, the study of doctrines, or theories, underlying our philosophy? I will take up this topic another time.

For now, I want to sound a note of caution in case I have made the path to progress sound easy to find and trivial to maintain.

Look around, dear reader, and ask yourself how comfortable you feel that humankind is safely out of range from the barbarism we have descended to over and over throughout history. Take these words of Seneca from 2,000 years ago, and ask if he could not have been writing today:

> There are many who set fire to cities ... no one withstood their attack; but they themselves could not withstand desire for power and the impulse to cruelty; at the time when they seemed to be hounding others, they were themselves hounded. Do you believe that the man was in his senses who could begin by devasting Greece, the land where he received his education?

Replace "Greece" with "the United States" and you have your description of modern critical theory, Antifa, BLM, and anti-Zionists.

When Seneca reminds us that the path to happiness is never found in making others unhappy, he admonishes us to heal ourselves before looking to change the world.

When we are surrounded by burning and chaos, we should avoid the flames and consume the good advice that philosophy so abundantly offers in the form of sayings.

Be well.

Chapter Fifteen

On a Learning Mind

When you are told by experts what to think you may become a believer, but you will not become a thinker

Have you ever considered what makes for a successful student, dear reader? I am talking now about a traditional college or university student of any subject, and not just the study of philosophy.

Back when people were interested in at least predicting such things, to say nothing of understanding them, they devised a method in the form of the standardized test.

The very names behind the tests' abbreviations reveal their erstwhile purpose: Scholastic Aptitude Test and American College Testing. Each year aspiring high school students across the U.S. would sit down to the SAT or ACT exams and seek to demonstrate that they had sufficient understanding of reading, writing, math, and reasoning to succeed in higher education.

Admissions officers gave great weight to standardized test scores because they were highly correlated to students' ability to successfully complete a traditional university education. More than any transcript of impressive-looking grades or carefully concocted but unrepresentative essays, for almost a hundred years the SAT provided a stark, objective assessment of your relative readiness.

"You are writing about standardized testing in the past tense," you observe. "Aren't the tests still administered and used in college admissions?"

Though our college days are behind us, they are indelibly etched in memory. You would be wrong to think, dear reader, that your college experience shares anything beyond the name with what students today experience.

More than 900 institutions of higher learning had already made the switch to so-called "test-optional" admissions prior to the pandemic. COVID-19 gave an excuse for many of the remaining universities, including all the Ivy League and many of the top liberal arts colleges, to drop the SAT/ACT testing requirement.

What has driven this rapid and widespread change? Aren't universities still interested in knowing which students are prepared for the rigors of higher education?

I have told you before that divining motivation is not easy, but we can default to observing actions and inferring intentions along the way. Let us look at the actions of the players involved in university education and see what inferences we may draw.

"What players do you mean," you ask.

I am thinking of universities themselves, including their professors and administrators; the people paying for the cost of education; and the prospective students themselves.

Consider first the university ecosystem, which I consider to be a professional machine. Having spent years toiling in professional service firms of lawyers, and decades more employing them alongside accountants, tax specialists, bankers, and others, believe me when I tell you I can recognize some of the features of the professional model.

At the very top, you have the owners or equity partners, to whom residual profits flow. They number the least and earn the most. Naturally, competition is fierce to become a full partner, or in the case of the university, a tenured professor.

The partner/professor is supported directly by an army of striving hopefuls, let us call them associates or adjunct professors. The leverage ratio differs from setting to setting, but the common feature is that there are many more people seeking promotion than will ultimately be elevated.

Whether it is 10–1, 7–1, or some other number is irrelevant. What matters is that the competition for advancement is fierce.

As a result, the associate/adjunct is the modern equivalent of the Roman slave, theoretically on a path to purchasing their freedom but until then toiling away for little more than their daily ration of bread and water.

Do they teach the classics with joy in their hearts? No, the bitterness of envy, the despair of fighting the system, and the anger at the unfairness of it all, oozes forth from their lessons, though you will find them nowhere on the syllabus.

The self-destructiveness of critical theory, defining every relationship in terms of relative power, springs directly from the bent backs and bent minds of failed academics.

- If material success is found in the world of business, then the businessperson must be achieving their success by oppressing others who are weaker.
- If one group has enjoyed more successful outcomes in life, it must be because they have taken advantage of others who are further down on the ladder.

How can these adjuncts and professors think otherwise, when the evidence is all around them?

If the university environment has grown petty with such poisonous thoughts, what explains the growth in university admissions? What student would willingly thrust themselves into this maw of pity and self-hate?

Well, the message that the world is an unforgiving, competitive place begins long before college, dear reader. From the moment of one's birth society sends you signals, first through your parents but soon enough directly.

"More wealth and possessions are the way to go. You want to be successful and wealthy, don't you? You need a college degree to make it in the world, now more than ever."

Children take on ideology all too readily, for it is their nature to be impressionable. They make the best recruits for armies because they are the easiest to brainwash.

So, the question becomes not whether to go to college, but which college, and how do I get into the "best" one I can?

Universities have done a masterful job of creating perceived scarcity — that is, they are selling something hard to get, when in fact the opposite is true. The credit for this grand marketing job goes to the university administrator.

Though the administrator is a bureaucrat, as far removed from the molding of fresh minds as the cook staff in the cafeteria, they are so much more valuable than even the teachers.

"Why is this," you ask.

Because they feed the machine with new recruits and keep the money flowing. At many universities, the number of administrators has grown to equal or exceed the number of tenured professors. Where once we considered the number of students per class to be indicative of the quality of teaching, we now ask how many support staff there are to grease the wheels of the university machine.

This flow of money is our chance to finally understand what has happened to universities, and why they have so readily jettisoned testing.

When a bank is exposed to the credit risk of their debtor, they will carefully scrutinize the business plan and ability to repay. When a lender carries no risk because the loan is guaranteed, the business model shifts completely. Now the concern is not creditworthiness, but volume.

In the interests of promoting higher education for more Americans, the Federal government guarantees student loans.

The incentives for universities are clear: More loans, in greater amounts, drive greater profits. In just the last fifteen years, the amount of student loan debt in the U.S. has more than *tripled* to over $1.7 trillion.

Now do you see why standardized testing had to go, with its nasty suggestion that some students were more suited for higher learning than others? Is it now much easier to understand why universities seem to care little anymore for imparting knowledge but spread only spite and social envy?

Do the otherwise lavish expenditures on five-star dining, world-class sports arenas, and soft-pillowed safe spaces now make sense? When the learning itself was once the ultimate measure of a university's worth, can we be surprised that it has now become an afterthought?

"This is so short-sighted," you say. "And it is unsustainable. Don't universities see that they are sowing the seeds of their own destruction? That at most in one or two generations, the students so ill-treated will wreak ruin on society?"

At their most fundamental, dear reader, I believe humans are good at learning short-term lessons and poor at divining long-term consequences.

A short-term incentive to make money will outweigh long-term risks every time. The business cycle of boom and bust would not otherwise exist and persist as it does. Despite the wracking financial crises we let loose every 10 to 20 years like clockwork, the next generation either never learned or self-servedly forgets the lessons of the previous generation.

At last, we come to the students themselves and the conditions for a learning mind.

A successful student is least likely to be nurtured where dogma exists, by which I mean unquestioned acceptance of conventional wisdom. When you are told by experts what to think you may become a believer, but you will not become a thinker.

The reaction of many youths has been to simply ignore the voices of their elders because they have rightly perceived their elders are no wiser about so many things.

But from this promising start, many youths have drawn a terribly mistaken conclusion: That they already know everything they need to know about themselves and about how the world works.

I tell you the only successful student is one who keeps a learning and open mind. That sounds like a definition by definition, but what I mean is this: If you are convinced you know everything, you cannot learn anything.

- If you do not question, you will not learn.

- If you do not doubt, you will not progress.

- If you do not listen, you will not hear. You do not need to listen uncritically, but you do need to listen.

And as you are listening, you will need to develop the second condition of the learning mind. This is to learn to live with uncertainty and doubt.

Some of your cherished ideas will be challenged! You may be wrong about things you felt strongly about. You may discover that some things you took as fact were just narrative. That the narratives you have been fed since birth have been created to serve purposes that may not serve your purposes.

Upon deeper reflection, you may find nuance and perspective that your youthful ideology was entirely unaware of.

It is in the times of greatest uncertainty and doubt that the learning mind makes the greatest progress. You will not find this progress in a safe space.

Allow yourself to become uncomfortable so that you may become learned, and you will be on the path to wisdom.

Be well.

Chapter Sixteen

On New Students

Philosophy always welcomes new students

I am happy to hear that your conversation with the wealthy and now questioning parent has gone well. It is usually all but impossible to be objectively heard when discussing how someone is raising their children.

It is a testament to your powers of persuasion that you managed to get them past the point of doubt to the desire for a change. Philosophy always welcomes new students, and we hope this parent is taking the first steps on the path to wisdom.

The desire for change is certainly a necessary precondition for progress. But it is just as certainly insufficient to carry the new student far.

Your friend comes to you in a desperate state because they have been too successful in life.

"Too successful? What do you mean? Should their proven track record at overcoming obstacles not also help them pursue a different path now?"

You have only temporarily caused your friend to question the wisdom of their choices, dear reader. Consider the forces arrayed against your further progress: Their family, their other friends, and all of society.

Then there is their own mind, which we know is an unreliable partner unless honed by the most rigorous of training. They will think back on all they have done; all they have accomplished. In their old life, they were the master, the unquestioned conqueror. Now they are the novice, starting all over from the bottom of the hill.

No doubt your friend means well. You have flamed the nagging discontent into a discomfort they no longer feel they can ignore. But if it was an excess of luxury that brought them to this pass, they will also be sorely tempted to let their past luxuries lull them back into submission.

After a break from fine things, they will find their entreaties all the more alluring. They presently think they cannot live with their vices, but they will soon realize they cannot live without them.

By all means, encourage your student to continue, and be a role model as much as you are an active teacher. But let's see for how long their actions match their resolve before we welcome a new pilgrim in our midst.

Be well.

Pragmatic Wisdom
Vol. 5

Stoic Principles

James Bellerjeau

A Fine Idea

Contents

1. On Friendship and Philosophy — 247
2. On Like Minds — 249
3. On Stoic Virtues — 251
4. On the Greatest Good — 255
5. On the Rule of Law — 259
6. On Internal Versus External Value — 263
7. On Generosity and Gratefulness — 271
8. On Inspiration and Progress — 275
9. On Doctrines (Theory) — 279
10. On Counting on Chance — 283
11. On Making Plans — 287
12. On Thoughts and Actions — 293
13. On Your Associations — 299
14. On Clever People — 303
15. On Divining Virtue — 305
16. On Reason of the Well-Ordered Mind — 311

Chapter One

On Friendship and Philosophy

You are sufficient in yourself if you do not need friends for your happiness, but you need not go so far as to not want them

As I mentioned to you in a previous letter, not needing things is a way to maintain an unshakable foundation. But to say you do not need something is not to say that you will shun it if offered. So it is with friendship.

You are sufficient in yourself, and for this reason, you need no external affirmation for your happiness. But you can still desire an exchange with colleagues and interaction with the world.

Though you lose no sleep over losing all contact, that does not mean you seek isolation. You do not need millions of dollars to be happy, but that does not mean you would turn down a bonus.

My payment to you is this: You are sufficient in yourself if you do not *need* friends for your happiness, but you need not go so far as to not *want* them.

Friendship is, in any event, never far from your reach. If your desire is genuine to share, to help, to give of yourself, you will find friendship.

If, rather, you look to your friends for what they can do for you, expect the same from them. In this way, how you approach your friendships serves as a regular test of your principles.

If you are seeking friendships from any motive other than your own generosity, you may well find fortune-seekers among your fellow man. But you cannot be surprised when such friends vanish as quickly as they came if your fortunes should take a turn.

The loaded spendthrift never lacks companions, but when the flow of money ceases, only crickets remain.

Approach your friend-making with the seriousness it deserves. Is this one for whom I would sacrifice everything? If you are spurred on by noble emotions, then it is only just that you proceed. Such a friendship is worth wanting because you are not left wanting as a result of the desire.

This, my dear reader, is how we correctly understand what it means to be self-sufficient but to still want friends. Though you have everything you need within you at all times, it is natural to appreciate friends.

Mandela and McCain in their cells were left undiminished by their years of imprisonment. All they possessed was their self-possession. And having demonstrated their self-sufficiency beyond any doubt, do we doubt their joy at rejoining the company of man?

I have talked today about the value of friendship, and the difference between needing and wanting something.

To pay another installment onto my account I leave you with these insights on what is truly valuable. Scottish author Robert Louis Stevenson showed that he understood the value of friendship when he said:

> A friend is a gift you give yourself.

Be well.

Chapter Two

On Like Minds

The coward looks on and says all is good; it is the hero who says your ship is veering off course. Watch carefully your instinct to reward the first one and punish the second

I am a constant cheerleader for you to be devoted to your studies, and you see me on the sidelines always urging you on. I want to see you win your self-possession because I will be the winner as a result.

This is because a friend is not always your friend, while a true friend will be true to you.

"But," you ask, "aren't you speaking in riddles?"

What most people seek out for friends, dear reader, are those who make them feel good. When such companions hold up a mirror to you, it shows no flaws, only virtues.

If in your self-reflection you see only perfection, you are not prompted to move or improve. Bad habits are left in place, and flaws are politely ignored like a fart in a crowded elevator. Let others stink in silence if this is what their friendship brings you.

Now a true friend will not flinch from the whip hand or shy away from dirty work. They do not avert their gaze from ugly truths. Having looked upon a flaw, they take the further step of exposing it to your view.

A friend who risks your ire by looking you straight in the eye is a treasure beyond price! They make themselves uncomfortable so that you may have a compass to correct your direction.

The coward looks on and says all is good; it is the hero who says your ship is veering off course. Watch carefully your instinct to reward the first one and punish the second.

I want you to be a true friend, so I get the benefit of all the lessons I have lavished upon you. Though you owe a debt to no one but yourself, for my tuition is given freely, still I wish to be the beneficiary of your progress.

How will you know if you are making progress? Here are some signs:

- if you can more easily recognize the difference between needs and wants;
- if you can feel your desire for wants diminish daily;
- if you spend more time being thankful for what you have than in distress about what you do not have;
- if you do not look externally for your satisfaction but find and nurture its source within.

When your mind is well-ordered, and we are of like minds, our efforts do not cease but rather turn to more profitable pursuits.

The learner is like a drowning swimmer, whose head only breaks the surface when pulled up by the teacher. You gasp great lungfuls of air but are soon submerged again without a helping hand.

But when you have learned to keep your head above water, both you and the teacher can safely swim to shore under your own power.

Be well.

Chapter Three

On Stoic Virtues

Today I want to talk with you about the Stoic virtues, and how to value the pursuits that people seek

The outward appearance of a person tells you nothing of their inner value.

Consider Stephen Hawking who, though immobilized in his wheelchair, roved the limits of the universe and greatly expanded human understanding. Would you say his broken body was worth less than the perfect specimens gracing this year's fashion week?

And when their perfect figures have become disfigured from the passage of time, will you then consider them to be worth less than when they were parading down the catwalk?

Today I want to talk with you about the Stoic virtues, and how to value the pursuits that people seek. This is not only not a trivial question, dear reader, it is the only question that matters. The lack of clear answers drives people to distraction, and to seek happiness in things that can never deliver it to them.

So, what then should be a person's highest pursuit? How do they best live their lives? Let me describe what the Stoics believed.

The Stoics tried to distinguish between different types of pursuits and counted the first order as those that we should actively seek out: Joy, peace, victory, good children, the welfare of our country.

Then there are second-order conditions that we do not seek out, but which we call upon as needs arise: Bearing up well in cases of suffering and severe illness.

And finally, there are conditions about which we are indifferent, which are not in our control, including our physical stature.

The Stoics believed that virtue based upon reason, the well-ordered mind you have seen me write about so much, is the highest state a person can achieve. To control the mind and your response to circumstances is the greatest good, and this is what the wise person seeks to attain.

There is an important consequence of putting reason at the pinnacle and I would spend some time with it to make sure you follow.

The virtuous result of a well-ordered mind applying reason is the same *regardless of the circumstances*. That is, whether you are enjoying a positive pursuit in a measured way for the right reasons, or enduring a hardship for the right reasons, you are applying the same reason with the same result.

Thus, there is no difference between the Stoics' first- and second-order pursuits, even though the circumstances of the person differ greatly.

"Do you mean to say," you ask, "that there is no difference between pleasant and unpleasant things, and that we should value them equally?"

As regards virtues, dear reader, all that differs between them is the circumstances in which they are revealed. Because we regard reason as the ultimate virtue, then a hard circumstance cannot make the virtue less valuable; a joyous circumstance cannot make the virtue more valuable.

The virtue itself comes from doing things consistently, directly, and with reason. You cannot be more right than being right in your conduct, and the circumstances only change your behavior, not the reason for your behavior.

I sense you are resisting so let me make the point another way. The virtuous act is one that you do *willingly*. If you are reluctant, hesitant, afraid, or otherwise resistant, you are not behaving entirely of your own will. You will be confused, you will have doubts.

Thus, you are not behaving willingly, and your act is not the virtuous one of the well-ordered mind. When you are following reason, you will handle a beneficial tailwind or a serious hurdle in the same way, willingly.

There is of course a difference between pleasant and difficult circumstances, between joy and pain, and we are good at recognizing the differences.

Where we are able to choose, we will choose joy and avoid pain. The value in dealing virtuously with either, however, is the same. Virtue is the master of the emotions that otherwise threaten to submerge us, whether it be under waves of pleasure or waves of pain.

It is not just the external circumstance of the moment that virtue allows us to overcome. Reason also brushes off external consequence. That is, though all may criticize you, condemn you, or cast you out, the wise person does the virtuous deed all the same. The right course of action is the same regardless of the praise or blame of others that is forthcoming.

Reason also overcomes differences among individuals, as I noted above. Whether you are as rich as Jeff Bezos, or as poor as the migrants making their way across the border river with their few possessions held above the water in sacks, the virtue of your actions is not higher or lower because of your belongings.

In the same way, it does not matter whether the person is tall or short, handsome or ugly, healthy or ill. All the things that vary according to good luck and bad luck cannot affect virtue: Possessions, money, the person, their position. These all come and go, unevenly distributed and alternatively given and taken away.

Consider friendship, which is one of the things that Stoics saw as desirable. Would you value a friend more for being rich than poor, for being tall and handsome instead of short and ugly?

Would you say they are your friend so long as they hold an important position, and turn your back on them once they've left office? This would not be true friendship, because friendship looks to what is within.

Or consider one's children. What parent says they love their children differently based on their height or hair color? That because this one has the gift of gab, while the other is shy and retiring, they should be ranked in another order?

To sum up, my dear reader, virtue does not depend on circumstance, either of the person, or of the situation, including whether the act is pleasant or unpleasant.

The virtue we seek, reason and the well-ordered mind, is the same in all circumstances. Feeling joy with self-control and suffering pain with self-control are the same.

Yes, we desire the first and admire the second. To think that they are of different value, though, means you are placing value on external things and not intrinsic ones, on the clothes and not the person dressed in them.

The external things that the masses pursue provide fleeting and empty pleasure. The things that bring them anxiety are similarly just shadows, not worthy of fear.

With reason, you can master your emotions and senses. Your senses do not know what is virtuous, they merely take in what is given. Only the mind is able to recall the past, to look forward to the future, to reflect on the meaning of the moment, and ultimately the purpose of life.

It is reason that allows us to judge the good or evil of things.

The greatest good a person can possess is to conduct oneself according to what comes, in accordance with reason. Whether you are seeking out a positive pursuit or enduring a negative situation, you have equal opportunity to apply your reason.

We prefer that our bodies are strong and healthy, and that we take delight in the things we have. We would rather not suffer ill health or serious setbacks, but the value in them comes from enduring them willingly, with a calm mind.

I say if you must choose, remember that rising to a challenge can be a greater test than not letting yourself get carried away with good fortune.

Thus, we should desire to be strong in adversity even more than we should bear good fortune with equanimity.

Be well.

Chapter Four

On the Greatest Good

The greater your desired change, the larger will be the necessary expenditure of your personal resources

I taught my course on Common Law Contracts today, and because I couldn't make it to Switzerland this time, my class attended via Zoom. Do I fool myself that their faces were as eager as when they cannot hide because they are sitting in front of me in the classroom?

Though I am delivering the same message that I have many times before, are my messages as clear as when I can look into the pupils of my pupils' eyes? A conversation face-to-face gives countless imperceptible cues, and body language relays agreement, confusion, impatience, boredom, and more.

On the screen, I must have greater faith that though I cannot see my students seeing me, still they listen and hear me. I have learned to trust the power of imagination by writing these letters to you, my dear reader. I can now call you to mind as easily as if I am speaking to you directly.

I hope you will take it as a compliment then, and not as a sign that you need further instruction, when I tell you that I enroll you virtually in all my Zoom classes so that I can speak directly to you for the benefit of all the others. In return for your service, I will reward you today by discussing what is the greatest good that we can attain, and why.

If the world were an easier place for humankind, perhaps we would not need the lessons of philosophy so much. But why is it so difficult for the lessons to take hold? Just because the world is hard, does that mean the solution must be hard as well?

Fortune is fickle and scatters benefits unevenly, which means that some encounter only good luck while others seem to have only bad. If you wish to more reliably change the course of things, it seems clear that you will need to expend effort. The greater your desired change, the larger will be the necessary expenditure of your personal resources. Nature rewards us only grudgingly, after we have paid our respects by paying our dues.

We sacrifice now for the chance of future benefit. And before you bemoan that you hate the phrase "No pain, no gain," consider how much worse it would be to suffer the fate that many otherwise do: "Pain *and no gain*." Because pain is in store for us all, it is a matter of how much we will feel and not whether we will feel it.

The question, then, is how to best prepare ourselves for inevitable setbacks, disappointment, and pain. This is, I believe, the prize held out to us by philosophy, the thing that we should seek above else. It comes in the form of a well-ordered mind, living according to reason.

The Stoics called the supreme good I am describing as that which is honorable. They felt this virtue was found in true and consistent judgment about the nature of things.

While I can accept this as the core of the answer, dear reader, it does not feel complete. Do you become inert upon learning to accept that which you cannot avoid? Do you cease to desire to do anything when you have ceased to desire specific things? Are you indifferent to suffering to the extent that you do not seek out pleasure?

If we do not become uncaring, then why not, and what are the principles guiding us? For me what's missing so far from our discussion is the ultimate aim or direction of the person who is in the pursuit of mastering themselves by mastering their mind.

The Stoics gave a great deal of attention to cultivating the well-ordered mind because we are surrounded by temptations that lead us astray and fears that paralyze us. Seneca himself in describing his progress to Lucilius says:

> When will it be our privilege, after all the passions have been subdued and brought under our own control, to utter the words 'I

have conquered!' Do you ask me whom I have conquered? ... greed, ambition, and the fear of death that has conquered the conquerors of the world.

The Stoics are celebrated precisely because successfully navigating their path is an achievement. The understandable response by many to the unfairness and pain of the world is to pursue pleasure and to give in to impulse. If life is hard, why shouldn't we seek enjoyment wherever and whenever we can find it? Isn't that at least better than meekly suffering whatever evils arise in the world?

You have heard my answer to this before, and I will not repeat it here, other than to simply say you have control over your reactions more than what happens externally, so focus on the former to be better prepared for anything arising in the latter.

Knowing that hardship and evil exist so abundantly in the world, humans have struggled to find meaning in life and to make meaning of their lives.

Although others have made suggestions across the ages, there is a modern-day thinker among us who in my view has found a significant piece of the puzzle. He is Canadian psychologist Jordan Peterson. Peterson has given much thought to the question of how humankind might respond to the conditions of the harsh world we find ourselves in.

I can only recommend to you his book *12 Rules For Life, An Antidote To Chaos*. No, I have not mislaid my general aversion to self-help books, but every now and then even a landfill yields up a treasure. I am not so dogmatic as to refuse to acknowledge genius in insight, even though it springs from a dubious source.

Peterson starts as the Stoics do, with instructions for us to first heal ourselves. I leave his detailed guidance to your own good study. Knowing though that we each have the capacity to make the world worse and to hurt others, he goes on to say we should make our ultimate aim the *alleviation of unnecessary pain and suffering*. He says

> Make that an axiom: to the best of my ability, I will act in a manner that leads to the alleviation of unnecessary pain and suffering.

This then can be our aim, our direction, the thing that gets us up off the couch and out the door.

While we are working to make ourselves better and insulate ourselves against the pain of life, can we not also help make the world a better place? We can do this now, even though we are not yet and may never be perfect ourselves.

I believe everyone can make a contribution in their own way. Some will heal the sick, others will protect the weak or bring certainty to the enforcement of laws. Others will provide food, care for the infirm and elderly, and invent new technologies. How many ways there are for us to ease the suffering of our fellow humans and improve the lot of humanity!

When I look across time now with this fresh thought in mind, I see that indeed others have also arrived at the same answer. To close this letter, but I trust not the thought from your contemplation, I will call upon two fellow travelers to continue to inspire us. First, and although it makes me sad to think of her fate, I am happy that Anne Frank's words live on:

> How wonderful it is that nobody need wait a single moment before starting to improve the world.

And finally, to give us comfort that we can find personal meaning in easing others' suffering, that the effort is worth the sacrifice, let us listen to the Dalai Lama when he says:

> If you want others to be happy, practice compassion. If you want to be happy, practice compassion.

Be well.

Chapter Five

On the Rule of Law

The rule of law is a gift beyond price that should be defended at all costs

There is a public virtue that is as important for the modern philosopher as the private virtue I have been encouraging you to cultivate. Although we remind ourselves to place no value in external things, still we operate in the external world.

"What is this public good," you ask, "and why is it of benefit to the philosopher?" I will tell you, dear reader, so that you may give it the proper respect and through your actions also reinforce it: It is the rule of law.

We can think of the rule of law as the reason of a well-ordered mind applied to the body politic on a society-wide scale. Just as we individuals know, or rather we should know and must continually remind ourselves, that our actions have predictable consequences, so the rule of law gives us certainty that defined actions will have guaranteed results:

- If we enter into a binding contract in which I am to lease an apartment from you, then I may be sure that I will have quiet enjoyment of it as of the agreed date for the agreed sum, or I will have a remedy that I can reliably enforce.

- Property that belongs to a person, the fruit of their personal labor, cannot be taken from them by any other person without due process of law.

- The state will protect your person from physical harm by another, and though it is more powerful than every citizen, the state will not prevent even the weakest from speaking their mind freely.

Though some of our fellow citizens accept these blessings without a thought, the philosopher knows to praise them above all else. For it is the rule of law and its governing of external things that gives us the freedom to focus on internal things.

When we know that our person and our property are secure from assault, we ourselves become the only person who can create a real threat to our happiness. When we know that we can not only think freely but talk freely, this allows us to share our learnings and let wisdom grow in any individual where it has taken root.

"But aren't the benefits of the rule of law as you've described available to all?"

Indeed, they are, at least within the same society where the rule of law is applied. But though a commodity is equally distributed, it will be prized most highly by those who have contemplated its worth.

How ironic that we only come to appreciate the worth of something after it has been taken from us.

- A sailor cast adrift will appreciate the sight of shore more heartily than those who walk the same streets daily.

- A starving man will approach the buffet with an appetite not shared by his well-fed fellow diners.

- Citizens of a country at war will relish a quiet morning uninterrupted by martial cries far more than those who have only known peace.

Wallowing in our peace and prosperity, too many have forgotten that our condition is not the default in human history, and that our riches have been hard fought for and hard won.

"Are you saying that suffering is the precondition for appreciation," you ask, "and do you suggest that philosophers are the only ones who have suffered?"

Give me a moment, my dear reader! I am about the explanation, and I need you to be a patient traveling companion as I make my way. Do not rush me through the waypoints just because you think you have sighted our ultimate destination. To travel well is to experience the journey and not just to arrive. Keep faithfully with me on the journey and I promise you will not look back and consider our stops to have been wasted time.

Here is what I mean to say when I say that one must recognize the true value of a thing to properly appreciate it. The citizens in the wealthiest and most secure countries have become so preoccupied with possessions and status that they risk losing everything of value they have gained by seeking things of little value.

Consider the Western obsession with income inequality. Many wring their hands and wail that the top 1% have more wealth than they need, when everyone in society has seen their standard of living rise above that of kings a few generations ago.

Truly we are blind when we can see only that our neighbor has a crumb more than us. We lose sight of the fact that we ourselves have mountains more than just about every other person alive today, let alone across the sweep of history.

The situation is more dire than you would at first think. When people argue that the wealthy should not be allowed to keep the harvest they have brought in, that it shall be forcibly wrested from them and redistributed, not to the needy but to the mere wanting, we are pouring powerful acid on one of the pillars of the rule of law.

This corrosive once applied inevitably spills over onto the other pillars: Their speech is offensive and serves no purpose, what harm is there in censoring it; certain persons have received power and prestige out of proportion to their numbers, shall we not redistribute positions and status more equitably?

Though they are separated by just two letters, *equity* and *equality* could not operate at more opposite ends of humankind. Because you cannot make some plants grow as high as others, the only way to create parity when seeking *equity* is to cut all down to the same size.

It is true that the condition otherwise guaranteed by the rule of law, *equality* of treatment in all things, means some will take to the conditions of the soil and thrive, while others languish. But do we tear up the entire field, plow it under and salt the earth, because some seeds are strewn on rocky ground or are shaded by their neighbors' faster growth?

I can see the scythes, pitchforks, and plows none too far, dear reader, lit up by the glow of the mobs' torches. The hunger for more is insatiable and knows no reason. It will burn and destroy what it cannot possess, for spite also knows no reason.

Thus I tell you that the rule of law is a gift beyond price that should be defended at all costs. If philosophers see the truth in this it is our duty to spread the word.

Every person who comes to see that taking things to oneself does not add to the stock of joy in the world but only adds to its misery, is one member of the mob quietly slipping away, one less building torched. It is our sacred duty to protect and preserve the rule of law so that more may become rich in internal reason.

Be well.

Chapter Six

On Internal Versus External Value

If you take a step, even a tiny step, in the direction of your choosing, you will have improved your situation over that of yesterday

I do not chasten you, dear reader, though it seems you have taken my latest letter to this effect. Believe me when I tell you that I see in you a trusted, fellow traveler, whose eyes and ears are open and receptive.

When I become dogmatic and exhort you, it is not because I think you do not hear or are stubborn, but because I am driven to passion by the strength of the thought. I rejoice that I can share these thoughts with you, and through you, many others will hear you speak.

I have made the case that external things are not to be valued and that true value is found within. The well-ordered mind following the precepts of reason is self-sufficient, which is the only possession that is worth pursuing.

If we are to have any hope of gaining adherents, we must make this case persuasively. Just because I repeat a point does not make it true. So let me try to rephrase the argument, to reframe it so that we see its contours in a different light.

Before the average person can be convinced to look within, we must first convince them that the external things they have been taught to value are but poor facsimiles offering false promises of lasting contentment.

Let us start our proposition to our fellow travelers by asking them a few questions:

"Are you happy, my friend, are you content? Are your wants satisfied and your fears quelled?"

If our conversational partner answers "Yes, I have everything I need. I am peaceful and untroubled," then our position is no longer that of the prosecutor, but the attentive student. Let us listen to this wise person explain how they have found contentment, and probe whether it is built on a lasting base, or is the result of good Fortune alone.

In any event, I have little worry that we will spend too many hours in such pleasant conversation. The answer to our question will more frequently be a version of the following, "Well no, not yet. How could I be? I am troubled by a boss who micromanages me, a spouse who misunderstands me, and ungrateful children who do not appreciate the sacrifices I have made for them.

"And can you believe I found out my co-worker makes more than me, even though I have as much experience as he does? Hey, did I tell you about the vacation we have planned this summer? We're renting a cottage on Cape Cod ..." And so on, you may insert your own variation of the theme.

Everywhere we go we observe that everyone we meet is beset with expectations. Expectations of how their life is supposed to go, how their career is supposed to progress, and how their material wealth and possessions are meant to grow.

They are beset by worries: That they will not meet their true love, they will not land their dream job, that they will not be rich or famous. They are plagued by fears. What if they or their loved ones fall ill, or they fall prey to identity thieves, or heaven forbid that a disgruntled soul turns to violence and they are caught in a mass shooting?

You can almost read the anxious thoughts running across their anguished faces: "A COVID mutation might carry off my parents. Ooh, what if *I* become a COVID long-hauler? Wait, is that a Boeing 737 MAX you expect me to board? Hmmm, the car is no safe haven either. Don't we have to drive through downtown, and what if we are car-jacked?" I tell you, dear reader, there is no hell to match the ones people create in their imaginations.

Having asked our hypothetical partners to describe their current state of mind, we trust that they will acknowledge when they are not satisfied. What is the next step in your conversational journey?

Well, I know from experience one potential path you may safely avoid. Waste no time telling a person that they should be happy because they have objectively more than (take your pick): A poor child in India, all of the people in Africa, the unfree inhabitants of China, the downtrodden South Americans, or indeed any or all of humanity that existed throughout history.

So long as a single person in sight of your friend's eye has a speck more than they do, their discontent is simply not to be reasoned away by logic. If we assume Jeff Bezos is watching Tesla's share price in fear of Elon Musk overtaking him as the world's wealthiest person, what hope is there of the average person being satisfied when their neighbor has more than them?

The only person you may safely compare a person to is themselves. In your conversation with them, you may first call before their mind a danger I have pointed out to you previously: Creeping expectations.

Remember the millionaires of the UBS survey who, at each level of wealth, felt that a third more money than they had at that moment would be just about enough? Never mind that the carrot is tied firmly to a stick that is always out of reach by design. Satisfaction is like social distancing in the pandemic of desire: The two conditions are never to approach within spitting distance of each other.

When you suggest that a person compare themselves to none other than themselves, you can also offer them one of the keys to the kingdom of happiness: Continuous improvement. For there is true magic in this formula.

If you take a step, even a tiny step, in the direction of your choosing, you will have improved your situation over that of yesterday. Do you want to exercise more? Simply park a few spaces further away in the lot and take the stairs instead of the elevator and you are a success for the day.

Now instead of your goal receding to the horizon the faster you pursue it, you will be stealthily advancing without arousing notice. Does it matter that you sneak in the back door so long as you have successfully invaded the building you were seeking to conquer?

With the seed of this thought planted and hopefully germinating, you can ask your interlocutor the next hypothetical question: "If you can travel a distance by taking incremental steps in the same direction, is there any reason to think you cannot apply this same method to your personal happiness?"

Gently, gently, dear reader, let us not spook the horse, though they have been docile enough this far. This is a delicate turn we are now navigating. I suggest you start incrementally yourself, a gentle nudge in the direction of letting go of past grievances.

We all carry many burdens and worries with us. It is human nature for us to pick up and hold close everything that we come into contact with, without regard to whether this hoarding helps or hinders us. Many of our burdens relate to the concerns of today and as many more to the uncertain promises of tomorrow. Could it be that we can safely give up dragging along with us the baggage of yesterday?

Most of us can readily see that there is a difference between the things we can influence and plan for versus things firmly rooted in the past. The past is beyond influence, beyond change. Is there really any benefit to turning events over again and again in our minds, like Smeagol turning the One Ring over and over in his skeletal hands?

A simple habit you can offer up for service here is the deep breath. Not to calm oneself, though it will also have that effect, but to use the breath as a gentle vehicle to carry off a troublesome memory. Breathe in deeply and on your exhale let the breath carry away a worry, a resentment, or a grudge with it.

These are ugly, heavy things in our minds, but breath can carry them away like the lightest of feathers if only we open the windows of our minds to let them out. I do not suggest trying to clean every cobweb from every corner in one sitting. Let continuous improvement be your guide here as well.

Today I will be content if I shed a single burden of the past. And if the burden is too heavy to be shed in a single breath, still you may blow a part of it away. A bit is gone today, a bit tomorrow, and soon what seemed unbearable has broken up into fragments and faded.

At this point, dear reader, you are well-advised to give your friend a break from your lessons, though I do not give you a reprieve yet from mine today. For though you are advising them to empty their head of worries, you have thus far only filled their head with exotic and exciting ideas. Let these ideas sit in quiet and calm for a while, lest you crowd them out by trying to stuff more into a vessel of limited size.

To be clear, I am not calling your friend or anyone stupid when suggesting that their minds are limited. We each can comfortably consume only so much in a single setting. We must give some time for digestion lest we gorge ourselves and risk losing the whole meal as the body vomits it out entirely.

After some interval of time, you can inquire again, "How are you, my dear friend? Have you thought about what we discussed, and have you been able to relieve yourself of any past burdens?"

What happy news it will be to hear of their progress because no progress is too slight! Better a single step in a purposeful direction than a thousand miles spent in aimless wandering.

And if there is no progress that too is no harm. For it gives you a natural point to resume your conversation. For now, let me assume your words have borne fruit and there has been at least one such positive step. How do you guide your fellow traveler at this stage?

I would say that to *plan* for your future is not at all the same as to *worry* about your future. When you worry, you are turning over fears in your mind, much like you earlier turned over burdens of past problems.

How to deal with these unhelpful dwellers in our minds? I say unveil your fears, make them known to yourself, and write them down in every detail! This will shed light on what you have to deal with and, rather than making your worries worse, you will lessen their impact as follows: Looking over your list of fears, you will quickly see that there are many you can do something about, and some that you can do nothing about. Having identified which are which, you can now direct your efforts to the former and forget the latter.

"How can I forget a fear of something I am powerless to prevent?" your friend may ask. I say turn the question on its head and ask, "How can you *not* forget it, and banish it completely from your thoughts?"

In response to the puzzlement this may elicit, you must explain that it is futile to make yourself unhappy today because you may be unhappy tomorrow. It is folly to make yourself ill by thinking that you may one day fall ill. An asteroid may strike the Earth! Do you dig a great hole and cover yourself in dirt such that the work is already done when the rock arrives from the heavens?

Most of the bother we cause ourselves when we worry about the future comes from contemplating our fears in an undifferentiated mass. When we call them out by name and rank them, we become the general directing which way they shall go. And I say march the ones we have no control over out of your sight and out of your mind.

If you wish, let your breath carry them off in a similar fashion, one at a time. Soon you are left with just the hard-core fears of your own making. This is where our instinct to plan is put to legitimate use.

Here is how you plan for conquering fears on topics that are within your control. After you have listed your fears, simply list a few things you can do to start to address them.

- If you are worried about advancing in your career, there are steps you can take. You will make these steps both more effective and more likely to come to pass by writing them out. The act of writing stimulates thinking, which generates ideas, which will give impulse to action.

- Are you worried about being lonely in love? Know that you are not alone in this worry and that for every single girl, there is a single boy similarly yearning, along with every other kind of pairing the heart yearns for. How will you find each other? You will not find a partner in your solitary worries, but in the steps you take to meet your fears by meeting others. One of those meetings will bring you face-to-face with your partner.

- Say you are worried about saving enough for retirement. Here too, there are steps you can take. You may not identify all the steps in one sitting, but that matters not. You will have changed your frame of reference from a person worried about events to one working on managing them, and this makes all the difference.

And do you know something wonderful? Tiny steps made consistently in a direction of your choosing will also carry you along in confronting your fears too. Continuous improvement is a wonder drug that cures many ills and advances many causes. Let it be your secret weapon that you flourish in all manner of human endeavors.

No doubt you will think it is a wonder that I have at last come to the end of today's letter. I hope I have not exhausted you, though I sense your stomach is bloated from the meal, for we have not exhausted the topic yet. Digest well, dear reader, that we may enjoy another meal together soon.

Be well.

Chapter Seven

On Generosity and Gratefulness

Though a person first does you a favor and then commits a harm, you should value the former greater than the latter

Today I want to offer up some sayings at the start rather than waiting until the end. These are made not as installment payments on my account but as gifts freely given. You will understand why by the time you are done reading this mail, if you do not know already:

> It is more blessed to give than to receive.

These words are attributed to that most generous of givers, Jesus, who ultimately gave his own life for the benefit of humankind.

Was anyone met with greater ungratefulness than Jesus Christ? (Maybe Donald Trump, if it is not blasphemous of me to suggest?) Was anyone more deliberately misunderstood? Why was his message so threatening to those in power?

I might have some thoughts on these questions at a later time, but I am inclined to begin our travels more on the worldly plane. Surely the Roman Emperor Marcus Aurelius was someone who had cause to expect his every word to be carefully attended to and understood. He controlled mighty armies and dispensed untold wealth and privilege.

But do you know what he taught himself to remember each morning, dear reader? We can look inside his mind to share in his thoughts:

> Begin each day by telling yourself: today I shall be meeting with interference, ingratitude, insolence, disloyalty, ill-will, and selfishness — all of them due to the offenders' ignorance of what is good or evil.

How wise Marcus Aurelius was and how generous.

"What," you say, "how do you see either wisdom or generosity in this mantra?"

It is doubly clear to me. In the first case, he is wise in acknowledging the world as it truly is, not as he wishes it would be, even though the real world is often frustrating, scary, and dangerous.

In the second case, and even more impressively in my view, Marcus Aurelius imputes no ill motive to those who would do him wrong but rather ascribes their actions to ignorance. Surely this is a deliberate act of generosity.

"But do we not fool ourselves when letting evil doers off the hook by assuming they harm us accidentally? If we are praising someone for clear seeing, do we not need to clearly see and acknowledge that the interfering, ungrateful, and selfish are sometimes acting knowingly?"

We know people act deliberately, true, but this does not mean we must assume they are acting to deliberately do us harm. They may not be aware of the impact of their words or actions. They may believe they are accomplishing a greater good, for themselves or others, in opposing us.

What Marcus Aurelius is saying is that if these persons were wise and understood the true value of things, they would not act the way they do. So even though they act deliberately, they act from ignorance.

"Now you are confusing me," you say. "Shouldn't we weigh an act of generosity against an act of evil taking into account who does it and in what circumstance? If I do my friend a favor this week, and he does not repay me, can I not acknowledge the scales are tipped out of balance?"

The way to lift the fog, my dear reader, and see things clearly when everything seems relative, is to pick the proper frame of reference. The frame of reference through which we view events is that of the well-ordered mind pursuing reason.

We are seeking first to create the conditions for satisfaction and joy within ourselves so that we may ultimately create benefits for others. We seek to alleviate unnecessary suffering, and at a minimum to not contribute to the world's stock of suffering, which is abundant enough without our adding to it.

Taking this perspective, we can discern some important lessons. Though a person first does you a favor and then commits a harm, you should value the former greater than the latter.

On the favor, we should strive to be grateful for the fact that we have received something, rather than merely valuing the thing itself. Material wants can never be satisfied by acquiring more material things. Greediness for things is the root cause of ungratefulness. No sooner have I received something than I am looking for the next thing, so do not value that which I have just been given.

If we are not to be unthinkingly ungrateful ourselves, we must properly value the generosity giving rise to the favor. We harm ourselves when we do not appreciate what we already have and that which we are given.

"But now," you ask, "what of the harm done to us by others? Even if we accept that the harm is done from ignorance, are we not still harmed?"

What, will you keep a detailed list of petty grievances like Raymond Babbitt in Rain Man, tracking every hurtful word uttered by his brother Charlie? Will we tot up the slights and insults of the day, and determine by nightfall whether we are three insults to the negative, or one compliment in plus?

An insult delivered to a wise man causes no harm. On the contrary, we welcome the input! Either our accuser is right, in which case they have done us a favor by holding up a mirror to our faults, or they are wrong, and they have only harmed themselves by uttering foolishness.

And consider this further. Do we improve our relationship with a would-be enemy by treating them as such? Do we improve their state of mind when we respond in kind to their insults? Do we try not only to keep an enemy but nurture their enmity?

The Buddha answers this correctly when he says:

> Overcome anger by peacefulness: overcome evil by good.
> Overcome the mean by generosity; and the man who lies by truth.

Contrast what happens when you treasure each act of kindness with the greatest gratefulness. Imagine that you forgive and forget every supposed injury that could do only psychological and not physical harm to you. Be moved by your own generous spirit to help others.

In this frame of mind, benefits will accrue to you out of proportion to what you have given to others. By being the most generous of friends, the most helpful of neighbors, and the most forgiving of debaters, you will not only disarm and win over your fiercest critics but also find favors rebounding to your benefit.

All this is but secondary because the greatest benefit is to yourself: You will be both satisfied and at peace.

Be well.

Chapter Eight

On Inspiration and Progress

Ask yourself why so many fail to make the transition from good ideas to good actions, from good thoughts to good deeds

Somewhere between inspiration and progress lies the magic that makes things happen.

"What is this magic," you ask? It is action.

We start with an idea, perhaps we have a goal we are trying to achieve. As yet we are in the realm of the mind. Well and good, for we praise the virtue of reason and a well-ordered mind above all else. But to see progress we must move from our thoughts and engage in actions.

"This is a trivial insight at best," I hear you saying.

Perhaps so for it is indeed easily said. But ask yourself why so many fail to make the transition from good ideas to good actions, from good thoughts to good deeds.

I realize I did not finish the good deed in my earlier letter describing my day to you. I left off before lunchtime even.

The addition that has most enriched my time post-full-time employment has been spending more meaningful time with my wife. We have taken up the habit of walking.

For hours we roam the paths around our house, to the extent that it makes my running seem like strolling. We have walked the treads off several pairs of shoes already, and we are eager to push our legs and our soles further.

As far and widely as we wander our conversations roam even wider: Life, love, politics; family, friends, strangers; COVID, vaccines, and healthcare; good examples, bad examples, how to moderate extremes. How to keep relationships with friends at a distance, how to support far-away family, and how best to encourage our children's development.

Ultimately all topics come back to practical questions of what to do with our time and how to live our lives. If you wonder at my appetite for philosophical conversation, dear reader, it is because I have come into the habit of daily practice with such positive reinforcement.

As enjoyable as the walks and conversations are, there comes a time when talking ends and we must implement our decisions.

People hesitate not because they lack decisiveness. It is because they fear the consequences of their decisions.

If you deliberate you are being careful and thoughtful. As soon as you act you open yourself up to criticism: Was it the right time to act, was this the right decision, did you implement it in the right way? We would rather be paralyzed and do nothing than take action and be seen to have decided wrongly.

"What will free us from deliberation purgatory and get us moving again from our paralysis of indecision," you ask?

My counsel is for you to continue talking but this time engage in some soothing self-talk. If you have applied your well-ordered thinking and are deciding for the right reasons, tell yourself that you have done well no matter the short-term outcome.

Though your plans go immediately awry, that is not the benchmark you will measure yourself against, no matter what others think or say. You will remind yourself that steady movement in a consistent direction will bring you great distances if only you are steady in your application.

Course corrections are so much easier if you are already moving, so get about the business of moving in the direction of your choosing.

That Renaissance polymath Leonardo da Vinci is said to have said as much with these words:

> I have been impressed with the urgency of doing. Knowing is not enough; we must apply. Being willing is not enough; we must do.

I would add to his wisdom an exhortation from the Buddha, who is otherwise so gentle in his expectations:

> There are only two mistakes one can make along the road to truth: not going all the way and not starting.

We must start living our lives, my dear reader, by acting them out in full measure. Otherwise, what are we waiting for?

Whether we are ready to go all the way I cannot say. But I am already walking the path of wisdom, and the further I progress the more I see. I see you clearly in my company, and I would have you continue on in this fashion.

Do you ask how to speed your own progress? I have a thought for you that you can put into action at your convenience.

I talked to you recently about the companions we have always at our sides, sharing the road with us as they inspire us with their wisdom across the ages.

To ensure you stay headed in a true direction, make it your daily habit to not only spend time with these companions but to make their wisdom your own. Synthesize the best lessons you have found as viewed through your own particular lens.

And take the final step to commit your understanding to paper, if not for the benefit of posterity, then at least to send to me. You will deepen and refine your knowledge by first seeking to mine it from within the confines of your head and then by sharing it with another.

Fear not that you are working ground well-trodden by earlier treasure hunters. There will never be a time when everything is known and all mysteries are discovered. Make your own contribution.

In this way, you will make lasting progress no matter what fruits your labors bear.

Be well.

Chapter Nine

On Doctrines (Theory)

The ultimate aim of living well is to understand the value behind our circumstances and then take deliberate actions in line with reason

Has it been deliberate on my part to keep you in a state of longing when I told you I would delay taking up the question of the importance of doctrines in philosophy? Was I trying to test your patience and give you a chance to practice your virtue in accepting situations as they are rather than as we wish them to be?

Part of the wisdom in philosophy is to know the true value of things. If you only knew what a torrent of words you would unleash by insisting on an answer, you would be more careful about asking, dear reader!

Before you start wishing that I leave off before I have begun, I will take up the question where we left off, which is whether a well-ordered mind and right reason can be brought about by precepts alone, or whether more is needed.

I hope I left you with the impression that precepts are helpful in many cases. Today I must acknowledge that precepts are not sufficient or successful in all cases.

You will recall that I spoke of the need for receptive ears and willing students. Many people are deep into their illusions about what things they should pursue because almost everything in society is pushing them in a different direction.

Though they are well-meaning, they are hardly likely to be improved by a saying alone, because it is too heavy a burden to lift, too great a height to climb.

Consider that from the moment we are thrust into the world we are surrounded by material things. Humankind's facility for drawing distinctions between things is unparalleled, and what was once a necessary survival skill has become the root of many problems.

Sharp discernment was surely helpful to early humans in navigating a dangerous and unforgiving world.

- Does that sound presage danger, or is it just the wind?
- Am I safe sleeping in this cave with a sturdy wall behind me and a warm fire at my feet, or shall I nap out under the stars?
- Do I prefer to eat this familiar plant, or will I dine on that new fungus?

Not only did we need to learn to tell good from bad in almost every setting, but the consequences of choosing wrongly had immediate and often fatal consequences. Nature provided us with the ultimate reinforcement about how we should behave regarding material things by killing us for misjudging.

What has happened since the early days? We have largely tamed nature. For most of us, the closest we will get to a dangerous animal is on our TV screens. Some pay lavish sums to be transported in jeeps on safaris so they may be exposed to wild animals in their natural habitat.

No, the only things now stalking modern humans are our desires and our fears. For when I say we have tamed nature, did you think I meant we have tamed our natures? When I said we are far from dangerous and wild animals, do you think I have forgotten that the most dangerous animals are humans and that we are most dangerous to ourselves?

Today because we are under no threat of privation but rather drowning in abundance, we draw distinctions between luxuries. We drive ourselves to distraction by pursuing a more expensive house or car, and Nature is not there to correct our faulty judgment.

We kill ourselves gradually with greed, jealousy, and all the other vices. The punishment is too far removed from our actions for us to take heed of how we have gone astray.

To be well-meaning and still commit mistakes out of ignorance is at least understandable, considering the circumstances of modern life. I say the ultimate aim of living well is to understand the value behind our circumstances and then take deliberate actions in line with reason.

Yes, taking correct actions simply as a result of following a precept is helpful, for it is better than making your life worse through mistakes. But this is still far from wisdom.

Thus, we must concern ourselves with the doctrines that underpin our philosophy if we are to move from sometimes making the right decision to knowing *why* it was the right decision. Only then do we have a hope of escaping our self-constructed prisons and being dragged back down into despair by circumstance.

Because following the reason of a well-ordered mind is the goal we seek, it matters not just what actions we take but the reason behind our actions. What judgment gave rise to the decision to act thusly?

From this perspective, we give no credit to the accidental act of goodness, and we give much greater condemnation to the knowing act of harm. In both cases your state of mind as you are choosing what to do is critical.

Consider this the first doctrine of Stoic philosophy that we would offer to lift our heavy burden from us. It is the vehicle by which we will first know and then master our own natures.

In our relations with others, the doctrine I would have you follow is to behave as if there are no others, only yourself. I am not preaching selfishness, but rather unity.

- Would you so eagerly harm another if you believed you were in fact harming yourself?

- Would you lie, cheat, or steal, if you were the victim of each of these crimes?

- In making the world a worse place by feeding envy and resentment, are you not fouling your own habitat and making the world worse for yourself?

Now let's return to material things, which as I noted, we are confronted with at every turn. How shall we make use of them? What things shall we pursue?

We must consider each thing separately and place a value on it accordingly. You should know why you value some things more highly than others.

We should not listen to what people say about things, but consider the substance, the purpose, and the impact of both the seeking and the obtaining of things. Above all, your opinions of things should be the result of your own thinking.

You are lost if you surrender your judgment to that of the masses because they are fickle and see only the surface which is ever-changing.

I could say more, but in this case, I will concede what I suspect you are now thinking: Sometimes less is more.

My conclusion is this, dear reader. Precepts are a helpful, but not sufficient, contribution to living a good life. The doctrines of our philosophy provide the framework in which the precepts find their application.

Without the framework, there is no order, no reason behind our decisions. And since finding our reason is the purpose of the endeavor, it is necessary to pick up the theory behind the practice to properly put the precepts into practice.

Be well.

Chapter Ten

On Counting on Chance

The external world provides the canvas on which our lives play out, but we provide both color and picture

The only thing you can count on is that you cannot count on chance.

For once, dear reader, I have delivered to you the conclusion at the start of my missive. I take a chance that you will read further, for you can learn nothing more profound than what I have just written.

But if you decide to stay with me for a little while, perhaps I can explain why I think this and, equally important, what it means for you.

If you build your peace of mind on the foundation of your mind, then it is yours for so long as you have your wits about you.

The gifts of nature and of Fortune are not ours to command. This we know from cool intellect and hot experience. If you stake your happiness on external things, you are tying it to matters outside your control.

This does not mean that you cannot take happiness from external things, but only if your happiness does not depend on them.

Furthermore, we make errors in judgment about external things. The external world provides the canvas on which our lives play out, but we provide both color and picture.

- A foolish person determined to make themselves unhappy can sulk amidst the splendor and cry bitter tears of deprivation though they lack no material thing.

- They can take good Fortune unremarked and curse their luck for not getting more.

A wise person takes what is given and builds it into the greatest good:

- In privation they find endurance, in abundance they find moderation.
- When confronted with obstacles, they see opportunities to overcome them.
- Though the future is uncertain, they are not uncertain in their minds, for they know they will deal with all that comes.
- And bad luck is no bad thing because they have prepared themselves for worse. "Is this all I have to contend with?" they will say with a smile, "I was expecting much worse."

Left unchecked, our natures turn to worry about the unknown. But does it make any sense to make yourself unhappy now because you may be unhappy in the future?

Channel your natural uncertainty by guiding your thoughts to the *worst* that can happen, so you are ready for whatever happens. You need not disturb your peace by contemplating all the ways your luck can turn for the worse. Rather, build your confidence in your own resilience by remembering that you can endure and overcome any situation.

Your well-ordered mind cannot be taken from you against your will.

All that we value: Property, relationships, and life itself, is of a temporary nature.

- We may lose a friend or a treasured possession, but we need not lose them from memory. We enjoyed them for only moments it seems. Let us enjoy them permanently in our minds.
- We can lose what we have, but we can never lose what we have had.

Regret is the thief of appreciation, my dear reader. Protect your mind from it as carefully as you would guard your password vault!

If you doubt that you can overcome any obstacle, take comfort not only from all that you have already achieved but also from the good examples you can see around you.

- The courageous acts in the face of great danger.
- The generous gifts of time and money are given freely by others to ease the burdens of many.
- The patient teacher who never stops trying to light the spark in eager young minds.

Do you think these ordinary heroes never knew doubt? Do you think they sprang from a different stock than the rest of the human race?

The seeds of greatness are within us at all times. In fact, they are never more than a single deed away from springing into being.

For all that chance toys with us and seems to thwart our plans, it also gives us unexpected moments to rise above the ordinary.

It is our circumstances that provide us the opportunities, and it is our choice to do great things. I have no doubt that you will choose wisely when your opportunities arise.

Be well.

Chapter Eleven

On Making Plans

The fact that you may not achieve all that you plan for is reason only to be prepared for failure, not failing to plan and refusing to try

If I have asked you to remember anything, it is that we cannot control our fates. Fortune gives and Fortune takes away, from health to wealth to life itself.

Because we do not have the ability to control much that will happen to us, the Stoic philosophy is to focus on what you can control. This, we say, starts with our thoughts.

- We may not be able to control the weather, but we can use our reason to determine that we will not be downcast because it is overcast and that we will not weep bitter tears because it rains.

- Following the chain of logic to its ultimate conclusion, we will not weep at the end of our own lives or prevent fear from living our lives.

If we do not need specific conditions for happiness, dear reader, and we concede that the future is uncertain, does this same logic dictate that it is futile to plan for the future?

I could give you a hundred examples of well-laid plans gone awry, and you could give me a hundred of your own in return. Friends cut down at the peak of their powers, others deserving but never achieving success. The healthiest-seeming companion carried off at a stroke.

To put it bluntly, you could die today so why worry about tomorrow?

I think there are two reasons to be less strict than the Stoics, even though we agree with the starting proposition that only death is certain, and everything else is subject to the whims of chance.

But are we so fragile that we cannot live with uncertainty? Does the fact that tomorrow will be different from today in unpredictable ways offer up hope as much as it does despair?

Luck comes in many flavors, and good luck, great luck, and the best of luck are among those in abundant evidence. When we say that Fate can be cruel, are we being too harsh in our judgment if we do not also admit that Fate can be kind?

So yes, I do not need my luck to turn for the better to be able to live a good life, but I am open to the possibility that I will be lucky in some things.

And just as I will not permit the bad luck I am sure to receive ruin me, nor will I be undone by the favors of Fortune that come my way. I will use the same well-ordered reason to place the proper value on external things. Just as I do not fear death, I do not shun success, good luck, and prosperity.

"But you have not answered the question," you object, "and are only talking about dealing with events outside our control, whether they be good or bad."

You are right, dear reader and I appreciate your keeping me on track. The question was whether to plan for the future, knowing that it is unpredictable. I needed to lay this additional foundation for my answer, but I am now ready to continue.

You would readily concede, I think, that people can make their situations *worse* by their actions. Would you be so stingy as to refuse them the ability to make things better?

And if we can make situations both better and worse, surely there is no rationale to strive for anything but the best, is there? The fact that you may not achieve all that you plan for is reason only to be prepared for failure, not failing to plan and refusing to try.

Knowing that we can make things worse by inaction as much as by our actions, I say it is our duty to plan for the future and to do our best in all things.

Particularly when we raise our eyes from ourselves and remember that we have an influence on those around us, we should be spurred to action. Provided we have helped ourselves by coming into possession of our well-ordered minds, we can help countless others and make the world a better place.

Who has the potential to do more good in the world: The monk who shuts themselves in a cave and achieves perfect peace of mind, or the flawed but striving amateur who directs their efforts to aiding the broader society of which they are a part?

"You have convinced me on the first point," you say, "that uncertainty itself is no reason to retreat into inaction. But you said there were two reasons to be less strict than the Stoics. Have I missed the second?"

Nothing escapes your attention, though mine obviously wanders. The second reason is that we live in vastly different times than those of 2,000 years ago.

To read Seneca, Aurelius, and Plutarch is to read of unending human hardship: Torture, exile, the gladiator games, plots, murder, sickness, and suicide. And this was not the fate of just the ancients.

After the fall of Rome there followed a thousand years of darkness before the embers of enlightenment rekindled. In the middle of the 17th century, Thomas Hobbes spoke truly when he described the natural state of humankind without a political community:

> continual fear, and danger of violent death; and the life of man, solitary, poor, nasty, brutish, and short.

It was not my point to depress you here but to lift your spirits, so let me get back on track.

The condition for the great majority of people alive today could not be more different than that of our ill-treated ancestors. Most of us can expect to live much longer lives, free of disease, and free of the predations of our fellow people that plagued humanity for so long.

Am I so bold as to say we have conquered chance? Not at all, and you know me better. We are still subject to all the same whims of Fate, but with one important difference, which is that our odds are so much better.

Here is where we must take the statistician and actuary to our sides. To be a Roman emperor was a most dangerous wish. They had a better than 60% chance of being murdered on the job. Today a person living in the U.S. has something like a 1 in 20,000 chance of being murdered in a given year.

Certainly not nothing, but better than an emperor. Reading the tea leaves by using the distributions of large numbers, our actuaries prepare life tables telling us our probability of death by age. What a wonderful and revealing table it is.

- Let's say you have reached the age of 39, which is the average age reached by the great mass of humanity across time. Today, your odds of dying in your 39th year are just 0.2%, half that if you are female.

- You can take a full two further decades before your odds of dying in a year reach double digits: at 59, your chances rise to 10%, 6% for females.

- And you can add yet another twenty years before you are facing the coin toss that Roman emperors would have gladly taken because it was an improvement on their odds: at 79, you have a 52% chance of dying that year, 38% if you are female.

Writing these figures to you, I am forced to conclude that your only legitimate modern complaint is to be born male, at least when it comes to longevity and risk of death.

Why even the centenarian has but one chance in three of dying, the same chance a Roman emperor had of surviving their reign. No, we are not in a position to complain about our portion of life.

So, to recap the argument and conclude before I have too greatly increased the risk that you stop reading.

- We have excellent chances of living long lives. Those lives are still beset with uncertainty, but it is not the kind that our ancestors faced.

- We can do both good and harm by our actions, and the only choice following the right reason is to seek to do good.

- If we plan for the future, we may see our plans thwarted but we may also see them succeed. The greatest good can be accomplished by setting great plans.

Thus, it is our duty to plan for the future.

Be well.

Chapter Twelve

On Thoughts and Actions

Although the external world almost certainly will judge you by the outcome of your actions, you must focus on the reasons for your actions

I have not been too busy to answer your question, dear reader. I just did not want to, at least not yet. People use the excuse of circumstances to pass off blame for their own decisions, but I will not do so.

We do not control circumstances, true, but we are in full control of how we react to circumstances. So, when someone says they are too busy to do something, this means simply that they have set different priorities.

You wonder why I was hesitant to answer you when I have been so willing to expand on every question up to now. When I feel myself shying away from a topic, I have learned it comes from one of three causes:

- either I do not understand it yet and so feel I have nothing useful to say; or

- I think I understand it, but I do not like the direction my thoughts are leading; or

- regardless of my understanding, I do not like the topic.

"What sorts of questions fall into this latter category," you ask.

They are questions the answers to which serve only to amuse and not to enlighten. In other words, the topic is a diversion, and learning about it may bring you some knowledge but will not bring you further along the path to wisdom.

In remembering that I have much to learn myself, however, I can be of a more generous spirit in this instance. Perhaps your question is one that will bring wisdom, and it is merely my own blindness that prevents me from seeing the way.

So, you have asked if the operation of the well-ordered mind, namely our thoughts, is itself equivalent to the actions we take or whether one is superior to the other.

This is not a "which came first" chicken and egg situation, but more a "can one exist without the other" situation.

- We know people can act with bad intention and so cause harm on purpose.

- And we know they can act with good intentions and create a good outcome on purpose.

- I think the more interesting category of actions comes about when people act without seemingly good or bad intentions and so appear to cause harm or good accidentally or unknowingly.

In the world of business, we tend to judge actions by their effects. If your action harmed me, then I do not need to wonder about your motivation because the important thing is I have been harmed. If a situation benefits me, I do not need to question whether it was intended to be beneficial because I still profit from it.

We have been helped or hurt, and can we identify the cause? Having identified the action, we do not spend much time guessing at the motive.

But to the extent we feel it necessary to judge motivations in business, we are comfortable to infer motives from actions. Sometimes we want to understand motives to be better prepared for future actions.

We are guided in the direction of looking at the impact of actions because antitrust laws prevent us from talking to competitors. And is it really necessary to ask a competitor if they wished to gain market share when they lowered their prices? Moreover, if we did ask them, would we be responsible businesspersons if we trusted their answer?

I am reminded of the wise words of Confucius when he said

> At first, my way of dealing with others was to listen to their words and to take their actions upon trust. Now, my way is to listen to what they say and then to watch what they do.

People lie, they mislead, and more charitably, they sometimes do not understand their motivations themselves.

Let us leave the world of business and enter the realm of law. In criminal law the question of motives is paramount. The action is given, the only question is one of intent. What was the defendant's state of mind when they committed the crime?

We treat someone who accidentally killed a person very differently from someone who did it in a fit of rage, and differently yet again if they planned the foul deed. But is the legal world really so different from that of business?

To start with, how many defendants are telling the truth when we observe almost all of them insisting they did not commit the crime? I cannot believe our police or prosecutors are so inept that they never manage to identify the responsible perpetrator even some of the time.

Can they make mistakes? Most definitely for they are only human. But it strains credulity to assume they are mistaken all of the time, every time. So, the logical conclusion is that defendants lie to protect themselves. Our system is such that we do not have to help lay out the rope for our hangman, and this is good and proper.

What is the court and jury to do? We fall back on the weight of the evidence. A case proved by circumstantial evidence is nothing more than inferring motives from actions.

The prosecution seeks to establish that the defendant took certain actions. The judge instructs the jury that they are entitled to infer the defendant took them with a specific intention. The defendant will not tell us their mind, so we read their mind by inferring their motivation from their actions.

Finally, we come to the crux of the question. We know it is possible to say one thing and mean another. Is it possible to *think* one way and *act* another?

It is possible to think an evil thought but nonetheless act another way. Every child forced to apologize to their sibling at the end of an unresolved squabble is familiar with this situation.

But how about the consequences of acting in pursuit of a virtuous thought that is the product of a well-ordered mind? Can such an act be of equal value to the reasoned thought?

"But wait," you say, "There is no guarantee that your action will achieve the intended result. Though your intentions are pure, you can still make things worse. There's a reason for the saying 'The road to hell is paved with good intentions'."

It is indisputably true that actions may not have the desired outcome. But this is the same thing as saying we do not control external circumstances. We control our thoughts, and we control our judgment of things, but we do not fully control external things.

The good Samaritan sees a person lying on the sidewalk and seeks to aid them. In their attempts to help, a blood clot is dislodged, and the person has a stroke and dies. Was the attempted aid an evil because it had a bad outcome?

I maintain that you are responsible for your thoughts first, and your actions second. You should seek to take action in a way that represents your best effort, consistent with your thoughts. So long as your judgment is reasoned, the good or bad outcome of your actions does not make your thoughts greater or less worthy.

Moreover, because your actions can go awry and lead to consequences inconsistent with your thoughts, your thoughts are necessarily superior to your actions. The philosopher having attained the wisdom of a well-ordered mind must not let the outcome of their actions undermine the foundation of their thoughts.

Thus, I tell you that although the external world almost certainly will judge you by the outcome of your actions, you must focus on the reasons for your actions, and this alone.

I have to thank you, dear reader, for insisting that I answer your question. For now, I feel I have come to understand these words of Seneca, which I will pass on as my payment in return for your unexpected favor:

> No one, I think, rates higher or is more consecrated to virtue than he who has lost his reputation for being a good man in order to keep from losing the approval of his conscience.

Be well.

Chapter Thirteen

On Your Associations

If you wish to have a better understanding of the world, spend time in the company of people who demonstrate their depth of perception and see beyond the surface of things

I gather I depressed you in my letter presenting such a scathing indictment of our institutions of higher learning. The places that once nurtured the greatest thinkers for generations are now creating pampered disgruntled anarchists.

Moreover, these fallen intellectuals are bankrupting the country as they simultaneously enrich themselves and impoverish the minds they have been paid to better. Hmmm, now I am depressing myself in summarizing this sad state of affairs.

But my aim today is not to depress you, but rather to lift your and my spirits by describing one sure way out of the darkness and back into the light.

If we assume that there is a genuine desire for learning and self-improvement, and I believe this is always the case, is there a better path for eager students to follow? There is, and I can describe it more succinctly than I did make my case against the universities: Surround yourself with wise people who want the best for you.

We are more directly influenced by our peers than we know. Rather than being inadvertently molded into the shapes that society directs us, or that our circumstances offer up by default, use this fact to your advantage.

If you wish to be a happier person, spend time in the company of happy people. If you wish to become a sportier person, get yourself to the gym, run over to the track, and make friends with the most enthusiastic amateur athletes you know.

"Why should this be so," you ask, "And how does it work?"

Take first the simple explanation, dear reader, which also serves as a good reminder that we do not need to make everything so complicated. It works because it works! Even if I don't know why, I can still take advantage of this fact if I have observed it reliably working over and over again.

But I know you are a more demanding student so I will give you two further answers. The first I would describe as active interaction or mindful presence. That is, when you are with other people you can purposefully use them as your role models.

See how this one behaves and what it gets them. You do not have to repeat their mistakes personally to learn to avoid them. My advice here is to surround yourself with role models of your choosing and study them carefully so that you learn from the best examples possible.

That excellent scholar and teacher Confucius gave the advice in this fashion:

> If I am walking with two other men, each of them will serve as my teacher. I will pick out the good points of the one and imitate them, and the bad points of the other and correct them in myself.

I will also call upon Confucius to give the second of my answers. This vehicle is available to everyone, mindful or not, student or not, and it is powerful because it works unthinkingly. It is of course the power of habit, or as Confucius says:

> Men's natures are alike; it is their habits that carry them far apart.

To reinforce this point, and to show that modern thinkers have come to a similar conclusion, here is how Naval Ravikant describes the idea:

You are a combination of your habits and the people who you spend the most time with. Many distinctions between people who get happier as they get older and people who don't can be explained by what habits they have developed.

If you wish to have a better understanding of the world, spend time in the company of people who demonstrate their depth of perception and see beyond the surface of things.

And do not assume that I mean you must find these clear thinkers around the water cooler at work! Take into your arms a book by a great philosopher, and you will have made a worthy friend indeed. If you make it a daily habit to spend some time in thoughtful conversation with such partners, I have no doubt you will find yourself in a better frame of mind than if you just let another hour of TikTok videos scroll by.

As much as I value the company of the great thinkers across the ages, I do not counsel you to take up the habits of the hermit. Pay attention to the people you do spend time with, whether it means you linger at the water cooler with the most helpful or seek out their association in some other setting.

You are helped in the company of people who help you in *any way*, whether mentally, physically, or emotionally, on significant matters but also in small things.

"You have been telling me that the highest virtue is the reason that comes from a well-ordered mind," you say. "Having achieved reason, and knowing how to properly value everything I confront, what good does the association with other people do me? They cannot help me reason any better."

This is true, insofar as we expect two wise people to come to the same conclusion about the nature of things and the proper course of action. Even if you believe you have attained wisdom, I would counsel you to seek the company of other wise people, and I would again give you two reasons to do so.

First, I have found no one who is not helped by positive reinforcement. Even Confucius remained a student his whole life long, taking good lessons and bad lessons from those around him.

You may have found wisdom in many things but are you certain you have found it in all things? And if you are so bold as to say you have found wisdom in all things then I offer you my second reason.

It is that you have a duty to pass on your wisdom and to teach the willing students who come after you. Confucius was also a lifelong teacher, and the world is truly a better place for his example.

In my experience, the best teachers are simultaneously expert and beginner, experienced and novice, as open in dispensing wisdom as they are in receiving it from their students.

So, seek to have a dialogue with your students and don't just lecture to them. They will certainly learn from you, and you may just learn something from them that keeps you on the path to wisdom.

Be well.

Chapter Fourteen

On Clever People

You should seek to understand the deeper meaning and be aware that in the wrong hands, words can hide as much as they reveal

The world does not lack for clever people, dear reader. What we lack are wise people. It is a bit like the wealth-happiness dilemma we were discussing recently.

"How so," you ask.

In the sense that, like wealth, cleverness is easy to display while wisdom is something you have to seek out and discover. Most people reach for the first (wealth/cleverness), because there are many paths to obtain them, and assume it will automatically deliver the second (happiness/wisdom).

I observe that many find upon having attained the first they no longer feel the urge to pursue the second with the same vigor.

So it is with the study of philosophy. You yourself have been tempted by the quickness of sayings. They are brief, witty, and undeniably contain kernels of wisdom. To memorize them and repeat them at appropriate moments makes one seem clever.

To the uninformed, a well-placed saying can even seem profound. But you might as well call your trained parrot a philosopher if you think repeating sayings makes you wise.

The purpose of finding meaning and bringing reason to your well-ordered mind is not found in words, no matter how well you string them together. Your goal is to bring your actions in line with your reasoning.

You can learn more by observing a quiet and thoughtful person than you can by listening to the most voluble of speakers. We are distracted by surface appearances because they are the first things we see. You should seek to understand the deeper meaning and be aware that in the wrong hands, words can hide as much as they reveal.

The more physicists study smaller and smaller distances, the more they learn there are worlds within the tiniest particles. Everything we see and touch with our senses appears to be just the top layer of many more dimensions, compactified away from our current ability to perceive.

I find it fascinating how many truly staggering developments in science happened as a result of one person's thinking. The mind creates and the experiment merely provides evidence to support or disprove. So it is with your own thoughts and actions.

This is not to say that you should avoid the pleasure of words, my dear reader. I too would rather read an author who knows how to write well, not least because it is at least a hint they have learned to think well.

So long as you remember that wordplay is just that, play, you will give your other studies and your other teachers the attention they deserve.

Be well.

Chapter Fifteen

On Divining Virtue

If an analogy allows us to sneak by the defenses of our untrustworthy perception, confirmation bias, and wishful thinking, then it is a most useful comrade in arms

You have probably noticed, dear reader, what a great difference a salesperson can make to the atmosphere of a store.

We can all call to mind the cashier who seems to feel that their duties are beneath them and is sullen and surly as a result. Or the floor assistant who is alternatively bored and contemptuous by turns, who considers the browsing customer an inconvenience.

These emotional black holes seem to suck the joy and energy out of a room, co-workers and customers circling around the event horizon of their superdense discontent, from which no happiness emerges.

"What does this have to do with my question," you ask. "I wanted to learn how to tell which things are good and honorable."

The starting point is easy enough, in that you should pursue that which is honorable. An honorable action will always be a good action. Through our studies, we are seeking to train our minds to use well-ordered reason to determine the right conduct for the right reasons.

We have two principal means at our disposal to determine what is honorable, and they both start with observing the world around us.

- We can draw direct conclusions from what we see, and

- We can make analogies by considering comparable situations.

Both methods have advantages and disadvantages, and to know them in more detail is to use them more adroitly.

At first glance, direct observation seems the most useful tool for the budding philosopher. If I do X, then Y happens. Observe this more than once, say ten or a hundred times, and you can be reasonably certain something is going on, even if you do not know the mechanism.

And the beauty here is that you can call upon more than your personal experience. You have the combined lives of humanity across history to serve as your laboratory.

You see now, dear reader, why we talk so often about looking to others for good and bad examples. Every situation offers an opportunity to ask, "What were the consequences of this behavior, anticipated and unanticipated?"

With so much raw data to hand, you might wonder how it is that humankind has come to no firm conclusions as to the best courses of action. How is it that so many philosophers disagree, to say nothing of the great masses who are pulled first this way, then that, by competing advice that changes with the changing of the seasons?

Alas, our problems in relying on observation are manifold.

- Firstly, humans are not great observers. One of the more reliable findings of the social sciences is that our perceptions are faulty.

- Secondly, we are not objective observers. We seek out information that conforms to our current beliefs, even when we think we are being open-minded. Thus, unless we are vigilant, we do not put ourselves in a position where we could even observe the right examples.

- And the third problem is the most damning. It is that we filter our observations through our minds, at least when it comes to human affairs.

This means different people apply different meanings to the same situation. Worse, the same person applies a different meaning to the same situation depending on how they are feeling that day.

Hence, repeated observations do not necessarily lead to firmer conclusions, because we are unreliable, biased observers, and inconsistent in our thinking.

- If one person sees a billionaire making a sizeable donation to a charitable cause, they may consider them to have committed a most honorable act.

- Another person sees the same donation and considers the source, saying "This is ill-gotten money from selling opioids that create addiction. To accept it is to give cover for the crime."

- A third cannot get past the fact that billionaires exist at all and says "Income inequality is the worst problem facing humanity. Bill Gates is giving away just enough money to avoid facing the guillotine, no more."

Because our perception is flaky, and multiple observations can yield multiple conclusions, philosophers also make use of the second tool: Analogy.

We move from the specific situation to the general, in the hopes of finding universal principles. What we lose in detail we hope to gain in broader applicability.

Also, by moving to the realm of analogy we take ourselves away from observations that individuals will disagree over and specify situations we can agree upon.

The beauty of analogy is that you don't need agreement on every observation to accept the premise that there is some principle at work.

I tell you that money doesn't buy happiness, and you point to three wealthy friends who appear happy to you. I point to studies (and I have done so not long ago) saying there is a limit to what money can do, and how little you need to accomplish it.

Still, you will have a corner of your mind reserved stubbornly for the thought "I understand and I see this could be true for others, but it doesn't apply to me."

Let Jesus say, "It is easier for a camel to go through the eye of a needle than for a rich man to enter the kingdom of God," and you may be given pause. Not to immediately change your mind but a little space within which to think about the strength of your conviction.

Analogies help us see a topic from fresh angles. The underlying insight may be the same, but sometimes we are blocked from comprehending it directly.

It is as if the castle walls are well-defended, the drawbridge pulled high, but the back entrance remains unguarded. If an analogy allows us to sneak by the defenses of our untrustworthy perception, confirmation bias, and wishful thinking, then it is a most useful comrade in arms.

When I tell you that the mind is everything and that our thinking permits honorable action in every situation, some part of you resists. You want to respond with the obvious answer that some situations are objectively worse than others.

"Why should I be as happy getting smacked in the face with a brick as I am by the tickle of a feather?"

I do not know why the human mind resists so strongly the idea that the mind is itself the cause and the solution to many of our problems. Perhaps it is the instinct to shun responsibility because to accept responsibility is to accept ownership of the consequences.

So, philosophy approaches a topic head-on, suffers a defeat, and makes a temporary retreat. We see if there is another way past the tight defenses of the faulty thinking that plagues humankind.

If I ask you to imagine the surly shopkeeper and to picture this person vividly in your mind, you are more likely to be open to the idea that a person's bad attitude can influence not just themselves but also their surroundings.

I expect you can just as easily think now of their opposite: The person who seems delighted to be where they are and to be doing what they're doing. Helpful, attentive, and happy to answer questions. Same store, same day, separated perhaps by only a single department, but this person spreads light where the other only smothers it.

Does this analogy make it easier to believe we can shape our experiences with our thoughts? And if we credit the idea as possible, what new avenues does this open up for us to explore?

Here is one way to distinguish an optimist from a pessimist that may surprise you. The optimist looks to the negative, while the pessimist looks to the positive.

"What do you mean," you ask. "Isn't this the opposite of what the terms mean?"

Not at all, and I use the example to demonstrate once again the power of the mind.

- The optimist says "It could be worse," to convince themselves of how good their current circumstances are.

- The pessimist says "It could be better," to remind themselves of all they feel they lack.

What you believe will determine what you feel, and what you feel will determine your reality.

The honorable person uses their reason to apply judgment to all the situations life creates for them. They do not rail against Nature or Fortune but apply their reason to the circumstances they find themselves in.

An honorable person would never be a surly shopkeeper. An honorable person accepts their tasks as if they were their privilege and performs them diligently and happily.

We use a variety of words to describe aspects of virtue because they are revealed in different settings: Bravery, self-restraint, prudence, and justice. They are all merely different views of the same well-ordered reason applied to judgment in varying circumstances.

Though the situations may differ, the wise person displays consistency in judgment. Apply your perception to observing and emulating the wise person and you will be exercising virtue.

Be well.

Chapter Sixteen

On Reason of the Well-Ordered Mind

The well-ordered mind following reason is filled with happiness because it is not distracted by extraneous things or burdened with wrong opinions

> Public opinion has great power to wash away reason, like a dye, from the soul of man ... unless one is right well on his guard when he engages himself in things external, and is resolved to participate only in the things themselves, and not in the feelings attendant upon them.

These words come courtesy of Plutarch. I am relaxing my strictures against sayings today, dear reader.

You may rightly ask why when I have been so stern in warning you of seeking wisdom lightly. It is because you have been a diligent student and have put in the time and effort of serious study. I know now that when you read a saying from a wise person, the summary will stir up your own thoughts of the substance behind it.

You have developed your reason to such an extent that I trust you with the temptation of these sweet vices. For though I myself have to be strict in regulating pleasures, today I will only draw upon healthy sources.

Aside from Plutarch, I have a few other favorites. Here is our old friend Marcus Aurelius, talking to himself in words that we could profitably use ourselves:

> It is in your power whenever you shall choose to retire into yourself. For nowhere either with more quiet or more freedom does a man retire than into his own soul ... and I affirm that tranquility is nothing else than the good ordering of the mind.

No recitation of condensed wisdom would be complete for me without paying tribute to Seneca himself. By seeking to be true to himself and focusing on things he could control, he served as an example to countless who came after him.

Would that we become such shining examples ourselves, dear reader.

> Set yourself free for your own sake; gather and save your own time. While we are postponing, life speeds by.

We are conducting our studies for a purpose. If we have resolved not to be idle, and even in our free time to obtain some good for ourselves, then surely it is for the aim of living good lives.

Not in the future, or at some point when we will have attained a more perfect state. Right now, today and every day. We have but one life and what a shame it is to be living unhappy or, worse, to be living in a form of suspended animation.

What can bring about this state? It is the same thing that disturbs it, namely our minds.

We mistakenly place the blame on external things, but this is an illusion that we can penetrate by careful contemplation. Thus, our highest purpose is to order our minds so that we can follow reason in all things.

It is reason that distinguishes us from all other creatures. But for all that this makes us unique, we have much more in common with other creatures than differences. We are both driven by instincts, and our appetites serve to keep us alive. They are indispensable to life.

These same appetites become insatiable when they are given too free reign. That which is instilled in us to preserve us becomes the agent of our undoing if we are unable to control ourselves. Our reason is the means by which we exercise control over our instincts and our appetites.

Our desires give us the motivation to act and in acting we find meaning. Without meaning, we may as well be like animals. Our desires thus serve a critical purpose in giving our lives direction.

But our single-minded pursuits can also lead us astray. It is all too easy for us to mistake the attainment of a goal for the purpose of our actions. Living rightly is its own reward.

In contrast, for many achievement of that which they sought so desperately is its own form of punishment by bringing new troubles with it. Our reason is the means by which we keep our desires in check.

Our critics say that we take the joy out of life by mastering our appetites and our desires.

The exact opposite is true, dear reader. The well-ordered mind following reason is filled with happiness because it is not distracted by extraneous things or burdened with wrong opinions.

We do not eliminate appetites and desires but rather turn them to serve our purposes. No meal is so enjoyed as that consumed by a hungry person. It is not the composition of the food as such, but the composition of the mind, that allows for the greatest enjoyment.

So it is with all the things that we humans pursue with such avidity. We believe the thing itself will bring us satisfaction, but we are only satisfied when the mind is in the right condition.

If you sometimes felt I have given you new burdens by asking you to think and to study, you now know it was to free you of the burden of accepting what everyone else does. Never for the sake of being contrary alone, but for the sake of seeing a better way.

Some time ago I quoted the saying "a friend is a gift you give to yourself," and I feel I have been blessed by your friendship, dear reader.

In return, I tell you that the reason of a well-ordered mind is its own gift, and I sincerely wish that gift for you.

Be well.

Pragmatic Wisdom
Vol. 6

Stoic Lessons on Thinking Well

James Bellerjeau

A Fine Idea

Contents

1. On Anxiety — 317
2. On Consistency — 323
3. On Finding Joy in the Right Places — 327
4. On Conquering Fear — 331
5. On Admitting Mistakes — 335
6. On Traveling to Change — 339
7. On the Value of Work — 341
8. On Keeping Your Promise — 345
9. On Composure — 347
10. On Rumor and Fact — 349
11. On Role Models — 351
12. On Calm Amidst Bedlam — 355
13. On Outrunning Yourself — 359
14. On Joy and Enjoyment — 363
15. On Endurance — 367
16. On Adversity — 369
17. On Self-Care — 371
18. On Accepting the Inevitable — 375

Chapter One

On Anxiety

There are more things apt to worry us than there are to wound us; but we're harmed in our heads more than by anyone else's hand

I know you are ready for learning because you have already taken one of life's main lessons to heart.

> Fall seven times and stand up eight

So goes the Japanese proverb, and so also go the lives of the fortunate. It is our fate to fall, and only when it happens do we know how quickly we'll rise to our feet again.

You may think you are a trooper, able to withstand whatever fate throws at you. Think how reassuring it is to have your faith tested and come out judged a success.

The pandemic closed your workplace, cut you off from your friends, and kept you a prisoner in your house. Everything you didn't realize you took for granted was whisked away without notice, and in the stillness that remained you noticed that you remained.

Be thankful that you have been subjected to tests that you would never choose to submit to and come out victorious! This shows strength of character more than any course of study alone.

There are more things, dear reader, apt to worry us than there are to wound us; but we're harmed in our heads more than by anyone else's hand.

I know you will recall my prior teachings, that whatever happens to us is not unwanted if we are sufficient in ourselves. This is no doubt true, though I am writing here to advise you to be kinder to yourself.

Troubles will come to you without you wishing them, so don't trouble yourself before they do. The specters that disturb your dreams may slink by unseen, and in any event, they are not today knocking at your door.

Anxiety comes in four flavors:

- being bothered by things that are behind us,
- being bothered by things that should be beneath our notice,
- being bothered before any trouble is brewing, and
- being bothered by things that are no bane at all.

We agonize ourselves more thoroughly than a medieval torturer in the dungeons of our minds when we relive painful moments in our pasts over and over.

We also blow things out of proportion, dream disasters, and jump at shadows. Offense can be found any place one looks, if one goes looking for it. Those who have experienced real hardship are less likely to be troubled by trifles.

But let's leave aside differences of opinion about who is harmed the most by the least and focus on the remaining two anxieties: Worry about that which has not happened yet, and worry about that which should not worry you at all.

Everywhere you look, disaster looms. Social media, television talking heads, and politicians all proclaim: The heat death of the planet from man-made global warming is overdue, although you may be carried off by floodwaters before you can be burned alive.

Rogue regimes threaten our way of life, if not our very lives, be it Iran or North Korea, Russia, Venezuela, or the Middle East. Our livelihoods are under attack from afar by China, and closer to home our border with Mexico groans with South American immigrants.

Before you give in to existential despair, ask yourself this: "Does any of this affect what I am doing today, and am I any worse off in a tangible way? Or do I accept the prophesy of doom without any evidence that I am actually damned?"

If you wonder how to tell whether the trouble is real or imagined, you can use this rule of thumb: You are either affected right now or will be afflicted tomorrow, or both.

The right now is within your purview to assess and do not let another tell you that you suffer when plainly you do not. We will come to tomorrow soon enough, so first acknowledge that today is OK.

"But" you say, "tomorrow may be terrible if we don't act to prevent catastrophe now." I urge you to remember that history is heaped more with gloomy predictions that never came to pass than those accurately foretold.

The forests are dying, the oil is running out, the air is becoming unbreathable, crime waves will destroy cities. I do not say that bad things do not happen, oh no, but that prophesies of bad things are no good guide for what they will be or when they will arrive.

Some people take a thrill in being terrified. The more dire the outlook, the happier they are to hear of our terrible fortune.

But my dear reader, it is a mistake to take the media's frenzy for anything other than whipping up the masses for profit. Too many uncritically accept all that is critical without questioning the track record of the purveyors of doom.

Who dares question the "consensus" opinion when the fate awaiting "deniers" is not in doubt: Ostracism, if not exile? That the consensus may be based on little more than opinion itself matters not when its breathless repetition blows it into a castle in the sky.

When you remember that most prophesies of disaster do not come to pass, you make room for yourself to be happy today. Even if you will suffer later, you do not suffer now, so why do you make yourself sad with the anticipation of your sorrows?

If you wish, you could bask yourself entirely in worries, but what sort of existence would that be? Better to be a hopeless optimist than a hopeless pessimist. You are just as likely to have your comforting daydreams come to pass as your nightmares, for all the good that dwelling on either will do you.

Thus, consider bright thoughts alongside dour ones, and when unsure which will come to pass, pick the one that makes you feel better.

Even if you think the hill slopes downward, point yourself upwards, because you do not need to add your own momentum to its direction. Rather than letting yourself be carried along with the weeping crowd, take a single step to the side and orient yourself to the sun.

I commend this course to you lightly, because it is a slight solution. Let the next person say "I wish for the best."

You are infinitely firmer in your foundation by virtue of embracing the view "Let come what may. I am made stronger by my fortune because my reaction to my circumstance is more important than my current situation."

But I know I browbeat you without need, for you are beating your own path in the right direction.

To finish today, I will address a proclamation of supposed wisdom for you. Consider the saying

> Time you enjoy wasting is not wasted time

from Marthe Troly-Curtin. Lest you get overly fond of this thought, my dear reader, for it is surely appealing, remember that just as a great wall is built a single brick at a time, so too was Rome dismantled. Our lives are spent in building up or in breaking down, and we must choose a direction.

Or if you prefer to stay with the world of rock and roll, I cannot say it better than those latter-day philosophers Pink Floyd:

> Ticking away the moments that make up a dull day
> You fritter and waste the hours in an offhand way
> Kicking around on a piece of ground in your home town
> Waiting for someone or something to show you the way

ON ANXIETY

> Tired of lying in the sunshine, staying home to watch the rain
> You are young and life is long, and there is time to kill today
> And then, one day you find, ten years have got behind you
> No one told you when to run, you missed the starting gun

I know that you will not mind partaking in the font of wisdom wherever it may bubble up. For it is not the vessel that determines the value of a drink, but the contents themselves.

Be well.

Chapter Two

On Consistency

The way to identify a wise person is to observe the one who maintains consistency in the face of passions all around them

To be healthy, to be of sound mind and body, and to be facing a voluntary decision to call a halt to your current pursuits. I am happy for you, and as much for myself, if I have helped you arrive at this point of self-reflection.

I caution you, dear reader, that you cannot be a hypocrite. It is not enough to think good thoughts; you must transform thoughts into deeds. The lessons of philosophy are hard-won, and their proof is in the pudding.

Though you think your thoughts are pure, if your actions are compromised, your lessons will have availed you little.

- Consider the coach who exhorts the team: do as I *say*, not as I *do*. From what authority does he speak, and why should we listen?

- Consider the political party that uses every leverage and maneuver when it has the reins of power but bitterly decries their use by the other party when the electoral winds have shifted.

Why do we give such hypocrites a moment's consideration?

Knowing the nature of humankind, and how easily the weak can become the powerful, the drafters of the U.S. Constitution created many checks and balances on the unfettered exercises of power by a bare majority. We now see the guardrails recklessly dismantled in the raw pursuit of power.

None of our politicians doing the dirty work ask themselves why it was these limits were put in place, and what furies we unleash by their removal. We could forgive them for their folly, except that we are all fellow passengers in the bus they are steering ever closer towards the cliff's edge.

"Are you telling me to be a saint," you ask. "Am I never to place a wrong foot or risk being seen as a false student?"

I do not require that you be without fault, although indeed some are able to match every thought and deed. But nor can you be reckless. Credibility is built upon consistency.

Each time you say one thing and do another, you are a hypocrite. How many times can you wear this cloak if you expect others not to assume it is your habitual dress?

And particularly if you seek to hold others accountable for their sins while you sell yourself indulgences, don't be surprised if the bedrock of your beliefs is eroded.

Though all around you changes, you shall be consistent. Though all around you stays the same, if it goes against the proper wisdom you have learned, you shall be consistent.

Fads and trends come and go like wildfires burning through a dry landscape. They burn fiercely, whipped by great winds, threatening all whom fate has put in their path. But you know that the flames of fads burn out as quickly as they arise, with the difference being these flames burn only those who grasp them willingly.

- For many years it was business suits, suddenly khakis appeared, then came Patagonia vests, and now hoodies slouch into the boardroom.

- Pity the poor necktie, whose constricting embrace will grace no more necks. To chase fads is to lose consistency.

- Your closets will not groan with the weight of wardrobes you do not wear, for you will remember that your simple, durable clothing is functional, not ornamental.

You know I am fond of the Buddha, who has managed to capture great wisdom in a few words. I borrow today from his store, in the hopes of paying forward the debt:

> Even as a great rock is not shaken by the wind, the wise man is not shaken by praise or by blame.

The way to identify a wise person is to observe the one who maintains consistency in the face of passions all around them. What meaning does the praise of the masses bring? What lesson do you learn from the criticism of the ignorant?

You are as well served to assume that the croak of the crow is encouragement for your good deeds as you are to fear a seagull's droppings landing on your back are a warning.

What I am saying is this: Do not be tempted by sweet praise or pained by bitter criticism from anyone whose opinion and character you do not know and trust.

And as is my wont of late, I give you an additional gift to reinforce the notion I am trying to tease out:

> It is an invincible greatness of mind not to be elevated or dejected with good or ill fortune. A wise man is content with his lot, whatever it be — without wishing for what he has not.

You will recognize I dip once more into the deep well that is Seneca.

If you once learn to be happy with what you have and, as importantly, not sad about what you don't have, you will have arrived at a state of unassailable strength.

And once arriving at this peak, you will see that any step in another direction is inevitably a step downwards, making it easy to maintain your resolve.

Be well.

Chapter Three

On Finding Joy in the Right Places

Life is meant for living, and joy is a sign your life has found meaning, provided its source comes from within

You may expect from others that they write of the latest celebrity romance making the rounds in Hollywood, or perhaps the latest politician "flamed" by a late-night comedian for being caught in another lie.

Perhaps they shall compare notes on the sports teams currently in season and describe who has chased after a ball most adroitly.

Not me, and not today. Instead, I write something of lasting value, that will accrue to your benefit as well as mine.

And what is this thing of "lasting value" I hold out before you? It is this simple advice: To seek joy in the right places.

You do this first by fostering a sound mind. A well-ordered mind is both the pre-condition for all your further philosophical progress, as well as the ultimate outcome.

When you are self-sufficient, you know that your satisfaction cannot come from strangers bearing gifts. Though you believe you are likely to always be on the receiving end of life's bounty — through a combination of your talents, your hard work, and your prior successes — nothing external is guaranteed.

Your happiness, dear reader, is your highest aim, and you aim best when you direct your gaze within. Learn to be happy with who you are, where you are, and what you have, and you have learned the recipe for joy.

"Am I not to take pleasure in anything the world has to offer? Why else have we been gifted with our various senses if not to savor a fine meal, linger over a lovely sunset, or dwell in the delight of well-played music?"

I do not counsel you to be a curmudgeon, taking pleasure only in denying others theirs. Nor should you take up the scourge of the ascetic.

Life is meant for living, and joy is a sign your life has found meaning, provided its source comes from within.

But do not mistake a passing pleasure for the joy that comes from deep reflection and a true understanding of where value is created. You enjoy eating, drinking, and dancing, and your heart is light. Joy is what remains when the things you enjoy are taken from you.

Finding joy in oneself will not happen by accident. It takes preparation, contemplation, and study.

The business of being happy is a serious business.

- Have you trained your mind to be content with nothing or little?

- Have you curbed your passions to the extent that the words of others arouse neither your praise nor your ire?

- Though your body fails you in innumerable ways, adding insult to injury, does your mind rise above to remind you that the body is just a vessel and the container is not the content?

It is true, dear reader, that if you enjoy only superficial pleasures, then you will suffer from superficial worries. But many a person has drowned themselves in a puddle of concerns a mile wide but only an inch deep.

If you can find space for deep thinking, you can create the conditions for uncovering deep joy.

If you do things for the right reasons, uncompelled by anyone and anything external, not needing luxuries or status or wealth for your happiness, then you are on the path of finding a wellspring of joy that will never cease flowing.

I return to Ralph Waldo Emerson to borrow from his fount of wisdom, for I know that his well cannot be run dry:

> To be yourself in a world that is constantly trying to make you something else is the greatest accomplishment.

The temptations of modern life are unavoidable, and so are the voices whispering to you that your happiness lies in their hands. If only you had this car, that handbag, those shoes, and a promotion, then you would be satisfied.

Never mind that in the time you spend longing, you are postponing living. And buying today's must-have items only puts you on the treadmill to be compelled to purchase tomorrow's.

The only thing you truly control is what you think. Thus, the path to happiness is not built upon pavers of enjoyment, but from choices: You must decide what you want and stick with your decisions. If you make well-considered decisions and are happy with your decisions, you will be on the way to lasting joy.

I will add two sayings to balance my accounts and tip the scales in my favor. They come courtesy of India and are proof that we need not look for glitters of gold to find treasure lying in plain view.

Guru Paramhansa Yogananda directs:

> Learn to be calm and you will always be happy.

He speaks of the well-ordered mind that is the pre-condition for joy.

And the Buddha in his wisdom reminds us of what reward awaits us when we focus within:

When desires go, joy comes.

Though I myself do not desire to part from you, I take joy in knowing that you will come to understanding when my letter comes to you.

Be well.

Chapter Four

On Conquering Fear

I will tell you how to banish the demons that bedevil you

You commented that you are finding ways to find joy and not mere enjoyment, but that your mind is still troubled by the troubles that people too active in the world of business face.

- You are fighting frivolous lawsuits filed by unscrupulous lawyers, you must fend off unfounded accusations from claimants who would profit from your pain.

- You are at risk of shareholder lawsuits and regulatory investigations, and sanctions hang over your head like the Sword of Damocles.

It is a wonder to me that you find any tranquility at all when you allow this parade of demons to march through your thoughts unbidden!

The future is uncertain for all of us, dear reader. Why destroy your happiness today because it may come under attack tomorrow?

I will tell you how to banish the demons that bedevil you. Contemplate from the safety of your home the worst that may happen in each of your disaster scenarios, and how much those outcomes would trouble you.

Draw worries out of your mind like you would draw venom from the site of a poisonous snake's bite. Spit them out on paper so you can study them at your leisure where they cannot harm you.

The actual harm awaiting you is often not nearly as bad as the amount of anxiety you create in anticipation. Laugh at the myriad ways in which your mind seeks to burden you with cares.

The ultimate harm that can come to you is either not worth your bother, or it will be so serious that it will also end your life and with it your worries.

You know from what we have discussed earlier that the loss of power, prestige, or possessions should not discomfit you, for these are fair-weather friends and no basis for inner peace.

"But" you say, "what if I fear a lingering and gruesome death from cancer? What if I lose not my possessions, but my self-possession, in losing control of my faculties?"

In the first case, there is no such thing as the unendurable. You either endure or succumb. And anything you bear willingly you reduce the sting of suffering from.

If, however, you prove in the circumstance to be unwilling or unable, your fate is the same as countless others who have gone before you under every circumstance imaginable. In the great sweep of time, your and their suffering ends just the same.

In the second case, you either know your mind and your thoughts, in which case you are still their master, or you do not, in which case you are not there to bemoan their loss.

Your loved ones may suffer to see you thus incapacitated, but you do not suffer directly because another suffers. And keep in mind that if your loved ones would hear and honor your wishes, they would not suffer either in seeing your condition, for no one wishes their loved ones to suffer on their account.

The only proper occasion for suffering comes when, knowing right from wrong and being of clear mind, you choose to go against your better judgment.

Compared to such weighty questions as life and death, are you really going to be weighed down by things like the fear of getting canceled, of losing a friend, or even of your business failing?

Beware of those who offer to sell you an insurance policy against bad luck. Before you reach for your pen to sign up for such a policy, call to mind the words of the Dalai Lama:

> Remember that not getting what you want is sometimes a wonderful stroke of luck.

It may be that the superficially happy person is one whose luck has not yet turned. Better the one whose mettle has been tested and whose peace of mind has not been found wanting than one who has never had cause for complaint.

Fear of loss is just an emotion, and you are not your emotions. Even when your fears arise, in the stillness of your well-ordered mind, you can recognize them, observe them, and ignore them. Your fears will then lose their power over you and fade away.

The Bene Gesserit were the philosophers of Frank Herbert's Dune series. Whenever they felt their emotions rising, they chanted the Litany Against Fear:

> *I must not fear.*
> Fear is the mind-killer.
> Fear is the little-death that brings total obliteration.
> I will face my fear.
> I will permit it to pass over me and through me.
> And when it has gone past I will turn the inner eye to see its path.
> Where the fear has gone there will be nothing.
> Only I will remain.

I do not fear Greeks bearing gifts, at least when they come in this form, and today's gift comes courtesy of Epictetus:

> Men are disturbed, not by things, but by the principles and notions which they form concerning things. When therefore we are hindered, or disturbed, or grieved, let us never attribute it to others, but to ourselves.

We fear the loss of things because our fellow humans pursue them with such vigor. They would be devastated by losing their possessions, true, but that is no reason for you to lose your mind with worry.

Though a thousand tell you that wealth is the true measure of a person, and consequently, that loss of wealth is the worst that can happen, saying it does not make it so.

Fools do not make any more sense just because they are shouting.

Be well.

Chapter Five

On Admitting Mistakes

Now I ask you to ask yourself whether you can say you have never strayed from the path

Regarding the latest string of journalistic malfeasance at our favorite national newspaper, we must apply different treatments if we hope to effect a lasting cure.

The mistakes of the junior reporter are different than those of the senior editor. The first must be corralled gently but firmly back within the guidelines, while the latter requires a stiffer sentence.

We are no friends to our friends if we let misdeeds go unremarked. Leniency is appropriate only when the student appears to have learned their lesson.

"Why on earth" you ask, "do you think your message will penetrate the editor's head? The past several years have shown their slanted reporting is deliberate and no accident. Surely this one will acknowledge no mistake."

I may not be successful in my efforts, dear reader, but the only sure way to fail is not to try.

- Even though our patient seems too far gone for our medicine to bring relief, still we minister attention in the hope of recovery.

- For unlike terminal illnesses of the body, the mind may be regained no matter how far astray it has been led.

The reporter has already suffered from shaming and is open to guidance. The grooves of his mind are not so worn, such that the shock of public scorn will not move him.

So, because he is malleable, we shall shape his thinking in the direction of long-term value, not immediate gain. A shortcut to meet a deadline that cuts short your career is a poor bargain indeed.

The reporter has had his lesson reinforced and will walk the straight and narrow for now.

But I fear the temptation is only temporarily gone and not forgotten. The horse that once strays needs a tighter grip on the reins, for it has tasted the grass growing out of reach of those who follow the rules.

We may certainly redeem ourselves, but we bear watching until we prove again, if only to ourselves, that we are able to resist temptation.

Now I ask you to ask yourself whether you can say you have never strayed from the path.

- You are making progress in learning the things that are truly valuable, but you still value tangible things.

- Physical needs are slight, while wants know no limits.

- Wants multiply in your mind and the more you try to satisfy them, the more you burden your retinue with a train of baggage that stretches out behind you.

I will draw upon the account of the Buddha to enrich us with this saying:

> Empty the boat of your life, O man; when empty it will swiftly sail.

Leave behind all that does not lift you up, or you will be weighed down as surely as by any anchor.

When pointing out the flaws in others, it is all too easy to forget that we are not perfect ourselves. Thus, even as we are watching over our friends at the paper, you shall be an equally vigilant guard over your own thoughts.

ON ADMITTING MISTAKES

You will allow me to stay in the Buddha's debt with this advice:

> Think not of the faults of others, of what they have done or not done. Think rather of your own sins, of the things you have done or not done.

Look first within.

Lest you think we profit today only from the Buddha's wisdom, take into your mental ownership this insight from A Father's Book of Wisdom:

> When you judge others, you are revealing your own fears and prejudices.

I have written to you before about the dangers of hypocrisy. I do not mean here just the dangers to your reputation, real enough though they are, but rather to yourself.

When you criticize another for something you do yourself, you are not only a false teacher, but a false student.

When you freely admit to your own mistakes, you render your opponents harmless. The best weapon is one you wield against yourself because this type of attack only makes you stronger.

Be well.

Chapter Six

On Traveling to Change

What does it matter how many miles you put on your shoes if you do not first orient yourself in the desired direction?

You are not the first person to be fooled by thinking that a change of place will lead to a change of heart.

Though you were told "A change is as good as a rest," your heart is heavy that you have not benefitted from changing jobs and changing house.

This is because you are looking for change in all the wrong places. If the lens through which you look at the world remains affixed to your eyes, is it any wonder you see the same things no matter how far you wander?

You may be the most minimalist of packers, needing nothing but a toothbrush and your ID, the Jack Reacher of philosophers. Still you are laden with that most weighty of baggage: yourself.

Pluck a small-minded person from Anywhere, USA, and place them down in a foreign land. Their prejudices will have made the trip without having paid a penny for the fare.

What does it matter how many miles you put on your shoes if you do not first orient yourself in the desired direction? You cannot outrun yourself. As Jon Kabat-Zinn put it in his book of the same name, "Wherever You Go, There You Are."

This is not as trivial as it sounds, so pause a moment and dwell on the thought and what it means to you.

If you do not know yourself at home, abroad you are but a stranger who also doesn't understand the local ways. Rather than easing your burdens, they become heavier with each step you travel, because now you are uncomfortable as well as confused.

When you carry a stranger within yourself, you will be bothered by strange food, strange smells, and strange faces.

When you are buffeted on all sides by a cacophony of voices, how likely is it you will listen to that small voice inside yourself? Some say it is the measure of success to be comfortable in discomfort and at ease when others are weary.

When you are learning to tame your mind, dear reader, you can be measured in the measures you take to test yourself.

A wise man does not subject himself to needless stress. Yes, we can overcome and thrive in any setting, but that does not mean we prefer to suffer. Put yourself at ease so that you may more easily confer with your inner thoughts.

You have time enough for displays of virtuosity when you have become master of yourself. I say be like those who have not traveled beyond their front porch but first explored the uncharted territory within.

Before I stop I will pay the toll for my fare today, and I will do so in the coin of Edith Schaeffer:

> People throw away what they could have by insisting on perfection, which they cannot have, and looking for it where they will never find it.

If you focus on your thoughts and motivations and values, you have a chance to earn peace of mind that no destination can afford you. The change that lies within you is one no change of place can deliver.

Be well.

Chapter Seven

On the Value of Work

The true value of work is when it brings you not possessions, but self-possession, and knowledge of what is worth pursuing and what can be safely cast aside

Dear reader, I see you clearly among the crowd. By your actions, you turn your potential into practice.

Keep along in this fashion, and you will be successful in the ways that matter most. You will learn self-knowledge and self-possession, and from these, you will know which things are to be valued and which are to be shunned.

Thus, will you have the elements for a happy life.

Your progress is under constant threat, not least when you are in the presence of other people. They will push you and pull you and exhort you to one course after another because that is the way of society.

The direction of travel does not matter so much as going along with the crowd, wherever it is headed. We can tolerate a foe in our midst more easily than a free thinker. The enemy's purpose and maneuvers we understand, while the independent-minded is unpredictable and subversive.

If you do not wish to be a traitor to your own thoughts, you must remove yourself from the presence of those constantly trying to influence them.

During the 40-day period of Lent, Christians live simply and give up luxuries so as to bring themselves closer to God.

The month of Ramadan for Muslims similarly calls upon the faithful to fast from all food and drink from dawn to sunset. It is not just the body, but also the mind, that is to be sharpened by this rigor: avoiding anger, envy, and other failings.

There is wisdom here, but also folly. If we are put on the path to virtue by relinquishing vices and reflecting on what is truly important, why would we tread that path for but a fraction of our time? Is a man wise who is sober on Monday and mindless the rest of the week?

No, dear reader, if you want to maintain your happiness more than momentarily, you must be the permanent master of your thoughts. Having painstakingly snared a cage full of sparrows, would you release them all only to start chasing them again the next day?

If you lapse, let it be because of an inadvertent slip rather than relaxing your grasp. Hold steady and hold fast to what you have gained. This is serious work and deserves your sincere attention.

The work of ordering your mind is worthwhile, but do not make the mistake of thinking that all work is equally worthy. Work itself is not its own reward.

We all know the aging executive haunting the office halls who says that without work they have no purpose. Without their title, their perks, and their pay, they would be cast adrift.

I say there is little purpose to such one's work. The ox labors mightily plowing one furrow after the other, but for all its exertions it neither knows nor cares in which direction it is pointed.

"How can I be sure" you ask, "if the work that I am doing is worthwhile?"

Only if you purposefully approach your work will your work have a purpose. The aim cannot be only money, or prestige, or power, although these may be by-products of your efforts. If such fruits of your labor come your way, by all means, enjoy them.

But you must guard yourself to ensure that to go without is no Lenten abstinence or Ramadan fast. Do not value a thing if possessing more of it brings you farther from contentment and peace.

Fortune gives and Fortune takes away, and it is not up to us to determine the portions we will receive.

You are not made better by your possessions, nor are you made less by lacking them. So why make yourself unhappy by wishing for what you do not have?

The true value of work is when it brings you not possessions, but self-possession, and knowledge of what is worth pursuing and what can be safely cast aside.

The wise farmer protects the freshly planted crops from predators and plows under the weeds. Each invasive plant you allow to take root will later steal water and light from your crop, reducing your yield. And even if one or two weeds will not overtake your field, remember that weeds grow unaided and multiply unseen.

Be well.

Chapter Eight

On Keeping Your Promise

It should give you pause to consider that the great many who think themselves in possession of their faculties are in fact being mindlessly swept along

You have committed to living a good life. Having made the decision knowingly, you are now in a more precarious position than you were before.

You walk in full knowledge of the pitfalls that lay about you on all sides, and you cannot make those dangers disappear by closing your eyes to them.

Many will cast slings and arrows your way, saying things like "Go ahead, give up wants. Then you won't want to do anything but sit around all day like a lump!"

No, when you are about your business seriously, you can expect to be doubted and misunderstood and questioned without end.

Because you travel in your own measured way and do not keep pace with the many, those who notice you will try to bring you back to their rhythm, like a biker who has strayed from the peloton.

And when you say "Thank you, but no thanks," in reply "I have all I need," they will leave you for a fool.

"By all means," they'll cry, "rush to your death you seem to be so eager to prepare for."

It should give you pause to consider that the great many who think themselves in possession of their faculties are in fact being mindlessly swept along.

They are driven by the whip of desires and wants and emotions as surely as the drover plies his oxen. Onward they pull, carrying every burden behind them, because the only way they know is forward. But we know the only way to escape the yoke is to first realize that it lies upon our shoulders at all times, heavy and unyielding.

The key to unlocking ourselves from our burdens is for us to stop and think, though we are whipped in the resulting stillness by all we think we should be doing.

To go forward in the direction we were progressing is to make no progress. But take a turn ninety degrees in our minds and we can walk away from our shackles as if they had fallen to dust on our shoulders.

Once you know that at least some of your prisons are comprised entirely of your own mind and that you are your own jailor, you will be free to step outside the confines of your cell.

Thus, I say live up to your promise: You have your wits about you, and there is nothing more beneficial than living according to reason. You, having nothing, know that you have everything within yourself, and are content.

The witless are hopeless because they hope for what they have not.

Be well.

Chapter Nine

On Composure

Just as the glib speaker fools the lazy listener, so we mistake fervor in argument for conviction, and conviction for correctness

It is a pleasure to receive your letters, though I repeat myself in saying it. I know that when you address me in this way, you are giving me your attention and more: You are giving me an insight into your mind, so that I may mark your progress.

A letter reveals much, and what has been written can no longer be hidden, from yourself or from your reader. And if I recognize in your words the unveiling of a fellow mind, it is because your letters bring to mind our conversations so well.

Don't fall in love with the sound of your own voice, dear reader. People who are facile with words risk remaining only superficial thinkers.

This is because they can talk their way around any obstacle, without regard to whether they have addressed the substance of their opponent's argument. They can dazzle and confuse with their eloquence, and because they are quick on their feet, the listener assumes they are correct in their conclusions.

But why should something done quickly be considered done well? Yes, efficiency and productivity deserve our praise, but not in all things.

And just as you can take an obsession over detail too far, so can you exaggerate in moving quickly. In what area of human endeavor do we praise the slapdash effort as the best one?

- Would you rather your painter spilled out color at great volume regardless of who or what gets splattered in the process?

- Or do you prefer the professional who carefully tapes off what they are working on and painstakingly addresses every detail?

Keep your wits about you, and let the wags rattle on. Just as the glib speaker fools the lazy listener, so we mistake fervor in argument for conviction, and conviction for correctness.

Shall we not be a little wary of the one who rages and foams at the mouth? Is their point made stronger by being delivered strongly? If we shower our audience in spittle, do we expect them to lean in for more, or to lean away?

Logorrhea of speaking or writing, with its diarrhea of words and repetition, is unpleasant to hear or read.

And it is not just unconvincing for all its volume. The more words you spill out, the more you will open yourself to criticism.

A carefully tended chain of thought has fewer but stronger links. An argument that stretches on for miles will be easily broken at many points, and so the whole of the journey may be called into question.

My core message is this: think long and speak short. Spend so much time in the company of your thoughts that you can deliver them briefly.

Be well.

Chapter Ten

On Rumor and Fact

When we look at others, our views of reality are shaded by the tint of our own minds: our prejudices, our fears, and our faults

You are wondering how I have found out what you were planning when you did not tell me yourself.

Nature offers up many seemingly inexhaustible resources: Water raining down to create lakes and oceans, fish to fill them, and sun and wind to keep the weather cycles streaming.

Another resource we will never run short of is rumors.

The tabloids at the checkout counter fill us in on the intimate details of the lives of the rich and famous. What would be trivial about any other, "He was spotted in Starbucks wearing an old sweater," is consumed avidly and questioned rarely.

We don't stop to question our prurient interest or our voyeuristic bent. So let me ask you, dear reader, why do you think we cannot look away?

I suspect one reason is this: People are poor at determining the value of something that stands alone, but we are savants when it comes to comparing two things.

Ask a person, "Do you like fruit?" and you will elicit a lukewarm "I guess, yes." Now ask them whether they prefer apples or bananas and you will hear them answer with confidence.

When it comes to celebrities, the tabloids hold them out to us not in splendid isolation, but as an implicit contrast to our own lives. "Look at their mansion, behold their supercar, bewonder their Caribbean vacation!"

These displays do not drive our admiration, but more often only discontent with our own lives.

We are much more likely to find bitterness, envy, and resentment when we peer over our neighbors' walls. The French have a proverb:

> What makes us discontented with our condition is the absurdly exaggerated idea we have of the happiness of others.

We see the outward signs of others' success, and we forget both the sacrifices that were demanded and the inner struggles that remain.

When we look at others, our views of reality are shaded by the tint of our own minds: Our prejudices, our fears, and our faults.

The rumor we read on the page or concoct in our heads is never reflective of reality. So why do we collect and pass on rumors, like couriers supplying narcotics to their addicted clientele?

It is because we know a scandal or fall from grace is never far. Rumors bite, they bleed. They tell us that our life cannot be so bad, because look how badly that one screwed theirs up.

This is a comparison we gladly make. It is the promise of a boost that comes from another's fall that keeps us coming back to the water cooler. But it is no noble thing to delight in another's misery.

To not feel elevated by another's fall is the first step in understanding that your worth is measured only by your own thoughts and deeds.

Focus on the facts of your own actions and give rumors no run of your thoughts.

Be well.

Chapter Eleven

On Role Models

Those who see much while believing they know little are much rarer and more valuable than those who believe they know much and consequently see little

Like hikers caught in a sudden snowstorm, dear reader, we are easily led off the path we wish to follow.

Despite our strenuous effort and determined gait, we can find ourselves after a lengthy march only to have wandered in a great circle and ending up back where we started.

When it comes to matters of desire versus reason, wishful thinking is no guide at all. What we need is the philosophical equivalent of a satellite high up in space, untouchable yet reaching out to us with a steady signal to remind us at all times not only of our current position but our heading and speed as well.

Where are we to find such GPS guides for the soul?

Consider first whether the truth of a proposition depends on who is propounding it. This is not as easy to see through as it seems, so let's spend some moments here before we move on.

At one extreme we have acknowledged experts, which is to say people who have devoted serious time and attention to a topic. You will identify them by their credentials and degrees.

Surely, we should grant the expert the greatest degree of credibility? I am reminded of what Napoleon supposedly said about the practice of law, namely that it sharpens the mind by making it narrow.

Those who see everything through a single lens miss all that is outside their immediate gaze. It is when you are in the midst of the most credible, dear reader, that you should most hold fast to your credulity.

Experts are among the easiest to fool, not least when they are fooling themselves in pursuit of publishing. Thus forewarned, you will more clearly see the signs of their folly, which are to be found in the fact that they are either speaking or writing.

At the other end of this uneven seesaw, we find the great mass of humanity. I do not doubt that many have the talent and ability to uncover truths if they would but put in the effort.

Alas, the easiest road to travel is the one that leads down the path of least resistance.

So not having the inclination to study a subject deeply themselves, they incline to the best available proxy: What does everyone else think? If we can find it on the front pages of the New York Times or the Washington Post, why should we tax ourselves to travel a step further?

The absolute truth of a matter is irrelevant if everyone in your neighborhood believes the opposite.

This is how we find supposedly serious people debating which way the weight of consensus opinion tips. As if such light things as opinions could be tallied up to create something of substance!

A googol of zeros does not add up to more than one hundred ones multiplied by one another. And yet a single dissenting voice can reveal a previously unseen flaw that renders entire foundations of science unstable.

Who are these few who can, with a word, end the debate? Or if they do not bring it to its terminus, who can shift the train of discussion in an entirely new direction?

The truly wise do not come in common guise, dear reader, although we can call forth some common properties among them. One who sees much and says little is more likely to scatter treasures after them than trifles.

The Buddha identifies their opposite number when he reminds us:

> One is not wise because one speaks much.

Those who see much while believing they know little are much rarer and more valuable than those who believe they know much and consequently see little.

In "*The Art of War*," Sun Tzu describes the clever fighter as

> one who not only wins, but excels in winning with ease. Hence his victories bring him neither reputation for wisdom nor credit for his courage.

If you have clawed back from the brink through mighty effort, but it was your own actions that placed you first in peril, why should we celebrate your heroics?

If you agonize over every choice and second-guess yourself the moment you decide, are you a better arbiter than the one who silently chooses the correct path and simply implements it?

The most virtuous role models are not calling out to lead. They do not call out at all, because they do not believe their right to speak outweighs any other's.

You will see their handiwork in their actions, not their proclamations. They know that they are no farther than a single step from a fall, so do not claim to be perfect. This, even though you never see them place a false step.

"But you still have not told me" you cry, "where and how to find these gurus. If they are not among the ranks of experts, nor to be found among the bestsellers list, where should I turn to for guidance?"

I have two suggestions, dear reader, and you will not be surprised at the first, which is to look within.

All that is good (and not coincidentally all that is bad), is discerned by your reason. You are your own most trusted guru, for none knows you better.

If you slow down enough to query the truth of your honest heart and your well-ordered mind, you will know the wisdom of your actions before you lift a finger.

But we rush to action without thought when we should be rushing to pass judgment on our actions.

If you must look without, then look to that which has passed the test of time. I don't mean what passes for consensus opinion, but rather that which bears up under the weight of the ages.

Human nature bedeviled our ancient forebears as much as it bedevils us now. And because they had both great tribulations and few distractions, our ancestors busied themselves with the enduring questions of what it means to live a good life in accordance with one's nature and reason.

And if we find ourselves still returning to their answers more than 2,000 years later, the chances are good they gave good answers.

Again, I caution you not to be misled by a name.

- As much as Seneca illuminates, he sometimes sheds light where it does not help us.

- As poignant as Marcus Aurelius' meditations are, he was reminding himself of some things that we do not need repeated.

- And even the sayings of Confucius and the Buddha are but map and guidepost, not the territory itself.

Study the greats carefully so that you can imagine them standing before you when you are contemplating your own actions. Look to them as role models, not for what they say, but for how they would act.

Be well.

Chapter Twelve

On Calm Amidst Bedlam

To retire from work life does not mean you have retired from your worries. To take the one step without taking the other is to change places but not position

The well-ordered mind in relaxation provides deep tranquility. Can it be achieved in conditions of disturbance?

I wrote you that I traveled to New York, and I fear I exaggerated the petty insults of the journey to make my point.

My tests were not passed upon my arrival, dear reader. For my hotel was directly on Times Square, and I will not say who recommended this as a good idea. Perhaps they thought I wanted to be close to all that New York has to offer and, if so, they know me not.

The only proximity I sought was to my own thoughts, though this is what was in fact near to me in my cell above Broadway and 43rd Street:

- a constant background din that must be experienced to be believed, consisting of a byzantine blend of taxis honking their horns;

- delivery trucks' rumbling diesel engines, slamming doors, and metal grating of ramps being slid across rear cargo beds;

- the piercing "BEEP! BEEP! BEEP!" of reversing construction equipment;

- garbagemen banging trash tubs into their trucks' crushing metal embrace;

- police whistles seeking attention and directing traffic;
- storeowners heaving skyward the heavy mesh gates protecting their precious wares; and
- the hucksters and tourists in their simultaneously hopeful and skeptical commerce.

The noise presses in from all sides:

- the thump of suspiciously heavy things dropped on the floor above me, the proverbial penny and other shoe making repeat appearances;
- the inanities of CNN blaring through the walls on one side of me, and the conspiracies of FOX on the other;
- drunken voices now shouting, laughing, and stumbling their way down the hallway;
- hotel doors slamming shut with the solidity of stone tomb lids; and
- helicopters whirling overhead to ferry the prominent to their Hamptons estates.

You observe blackout curtains upon entering your room, and you wonder if this is some paranoid preparation for keeping night lights hidden in wartime.

A glance out the window reveals the reason, for you are as well-served here wearing sunglasses at midnight as at noon.

I wouldn't wonder to learn that neon is no longer naturally occurring, for it seems to have been transported *en masse* into tubes lining every surface of every building around Times Square. If aliens in space nearing our planet need a beacon to guide them on, New Yorkers need but continue to pay their electricity bills.

The only relief from the brilliant flickering glare comes when great gouts of steam rise from vents and tubes piercing the cracked streets like Hell's own ventilation system.

Lest I overdo my dramatization once again, let me tell you, dear reader, that none of this bedlam affected me in the slightest.

When I am deep in my reading or writing, I retreat into a world inside my mind and the outside fades from my senses. Those blaring notes which would deafen another I scarcely note.

In this state, my well-ordered mind keeps me focused within, and external distractions have no power over me.

In contrast, without the practice of calming the mind, you could sink a person in a deep-sea submersible to the bottom of the Mariana Trench where no light or sound or sensation intrude, and yet they would be bothered.

We carry our troubles with us and can raise ourselves to states of excitement wholly out of proportion to any external instigation.

Though the decibel meter shows absolute silence, still the troubled hear the voices of arguments raging inside them, the pitiful cries of regret, and the insatiable calling out for more.

I have urged you to hold fast to your plans to retire from your post, dear reader, and to join me in retreat from professional pursuits.

To retire from work life does not mean you have retired from your worries. To take the one step without taking the other is to change places but not position.

If you are successful in letting reason order your mind you have no reason to be discomfited by all the noise and bustle that accosts you, whether it be from opinions of the ignorant, from praise or blame from any source, or from being in the busiest of cities.

Whisk a wise person into the center of Shanghai, Mumbai, or Mexico City, or into the center of a maelstrom of argument whipped by heated emotions, and they will be as at peace as in a mountainous meditation retreat.

Though we test ourselves periodically to ensure we are up to the task, we should not live permanently in the madhouse to prove we are sane.

I am just as happy to walk easily as I am to make my way uphill, and I do not seek out the treacherous path if I can easily detour past it.

Thus, I will soon depart from this bedlam and would that more people understand that the door is unlocked, and they too are free to walk away from their personal prisons!

Be well.

Chapter Thirteen

On Outrunning Yourself

Rather than looking to travel in more luxury and greater style, we should sit still with ourselves and consider whether we are running to something or running away from it

Departure day and I am on the road again!

I aim always to be a sincere student, dear reader, and this means learning the lessons from my trials. Hence it was that I made my way by foot from the doors of my Times Square hotel and down the broad sidewalks flanking Broadway.

No taxi to lure me in like a Venus flytrap only to hold me immobile and despairing of escape. I walk on past the stairways leading into the steamy depths of the subway, for there is nowhere they can transport me I want to go.

And none of JKF, LaGuardia, or Newark will tempt me today only to leave me sitting. For there are only waiting gates and delayed gates, but no departure gates.

"How then" you ask, "did you plan to make your escape from the city, if you were avoiding all these means of transport?"

Ah, my clever plan was this: Take to my own two feet, which have never failed me. I journeyed south down Seventh, west on 42nd, and there avoided the first shoals of my journey.

The Port Authority Bus Terminal was not my plan, for I was seeking to make my escape from madness, and not to become mired in the quicksand of lost souls.

Safely past to the corner of Eighth, and I strode on down to Penn Station. The iron rails were my last refuge, dear reader, a hitherto reliable link to the state capitol, where Albany's little airport beckoned.

Though I am unwillingly online, I knew enough from prior journeys to both order my ticket in advance on Amtrack.com and to reserve a seat on the grandly named Empire Service.

Past the lingering lines of the lost snaking their way to ticket windows, the self-service kiosk cheerfully spits out my ticket with no more than a passing greeting from my credit card.

Oh, to see the great hall of Penn Station, where travelers direct their gazes up to the screens overhead, eagerly awaiting announcement of their track.

- Don't watch the people, play with your cell phone, or let your attention wander.

- Suddenly a group takes off at a sprint, dragging suitcases and clutching loose bags to their side, their number has been called!

- If you have positioned yourself at the wrong end of the station, if you hesitate, you are left behind.

Past trips have left the bitter taste of experience in my mouth, for I know that though the Empire Service may originate on a different track each time, the line for boarding always forms in the same place.

On the side of the great hall, in sniffing distance of the Dunkin Donuts if not quite close enough to touch, you must wait. Line up an hour before your train is to depart, and you will not be too early.

Book in hand, your hour flies by, and you are on the train moments after the boarding has begun. Locate your seat, tend to your bags.

Then begins my favorite part of the journey: The first half hour as the train haltingly navigates the secret underground corridors of New York and emerges into the wide-open Hudson Valley.

The lights on the train flicker on and off as the train shunts from track to track. Is the train supposed to lurch from side to side that much?

Periodically you hear the static of a conductor's announcement, the crackle a hint that something is being said, but I have never deciphered a single word.

In those moments when the train is dark and you are still underground, sometimes a beam of light thrusts in from an improbable angle above, lighting up fantastic and ever-changing manmade landscapes.

Graffiti, of course. I cannot look away. I will not be surprised if the first sign of non-human intelligent life we find is a graffiti tag left behind by a bored alien teenager at the base of a red cliff on Mars.

Then there are the detritus of human existence, some expected, like bottles and cans, filthy blankets, paper scraps blown in from the streets above, a mattress, rats, both living and not, but other things so unexpected that you marvel at what extremity brought them to these places: The shopping cart at least has wheels, I guess someone could have wheeled it there, but the refrigerator, the set of dining chairs?

Though your eyes strain in the dark, and you almost imagine you saw a shadow receding into the corner, I have never seen the citizens who must make their homes here or at least pass some time among the dusty cinders.

How do they access these realms, and how again do they alight? And what do they think when they see the lit windows of the Amtrack car? The faces of all within reflecting the blue glow of their phones and tablets, for am I the only one looking out?

I think the reason people so readily focus on outward appearances, dear reader, is that they are afraid to look within.

When I tell you that the worth of a person is not to be found in the clothes draped on their shoulders, or the car they adorn themselves with, think for a moment how hard we two work to ensure reason holds pride of place in our minds. Think how much toil is required to achieve this ease.

Many all too willingly embrace the external to avoid facing the internal. For how many would find within themselves well-ordered and well-lit rooms instead of scattered debris, cast-off possessions, and wild-haired inhabitants lurking in dark corners?

Though we travel to the ends of the earth, we cannot outrun ourselves.

Rather than looking to travel in more luxury and greater style, we should sit still with ourselves and consider whether we are running to something or running away from it.

If we work to clear away the weeds from a portion of our mind and carefully pick up and discard the broken glass of poor decisions in our past, we may create a place of rest and calm within us that we can retreat to at will.

Be well.

Chapter Fourteen

On Joy and Enjoyment

Joy as we understand it does not depend on what possessions you are currently enjoying, and what pleasurable experiences you may be seeking

I enjoyed reading your latest commentary. I say enjoyment in the usual meaning of the term, dear reader, and not the philosophical mean we aim for.

Enjoyment is what one commonly feels when the way is easy, and distractions are few. I would normally tell you that enjoyment is no sign of virtue, but rather of an uncontrolled mind.

For most, enjoyment is the condition that signals its opposite is not far behind, and is thus not to be confused with joy, which when attained is lasting.

Joy as we understand it does not depend on what possessions you are currently enjoying, and what pleasurable experiences you may be seeking. It is a condition arising from a tranquil mind, undisturbed by external things.

You may take enjoyment in your friend's business success, her new house, and her doting spouse, but when we remember that all of these are potential fault lines from which future disappointment may yawn wide, we will not mistake the feeling for joy, which cannot be undone by any reversal of fortune.

I did take pleasure from your commentary, and I will tell you why I enjoyed it.

You put words into service with purpose and meaning, and your army of words is both varied and wide. The rich vocabulary you call into the field is employed to illuminate and not obfuscate.

I am compelled to pay attention, but I do so eagerly because I am not kept long waiting for a tangible example to illustrate an ephemeral point.

Sometimes I am rewarded with a simile, like when you compared the author's writing to orderly rows of corn in the field, stretching uniformly into the distance.

Sometimes it is a metaphor, for example, calling wealth a weight that pins us down to places and pursuits that hold us captive more than they free us.

If I can draw an analogy, the evidence of your clear thinking can be found in your clear writing, just as a pure source of water will generate a clear stream even though it travels over a muddy bed.

I will not go on in this vein, because I am mindful of what Confucius once said of his student:

> Hui does not help me — he takes such delight in everything I say.

I would help you, and not just praise you, so I will tell you what else Confucius brings to mind on this topic. It is that wisdom bubbles up from many sources, and these springs flow freely for us all.

If you want confirmation that we are but keepers of the waters of wisdom rather than its possessors, consider this: The Roman philosophers we are so fond of reading were performing their mental gymnastics some 2,000 years ago, and they made frequent reference to the "ancients" that were their inspiration, including the Greek thinkers that pre-dated them by half a millennium.

In the East, Confucius lived and died 500 years before Cicero walked the earth, yet Confucius looked to the principles of the Zhou religion that were ancient in his day.

Considering the pace of technological change, the year 2500 is as far from us today as we are from the Roman Stoics.

Should we doubt that those who follow in the centuries long after we are dead and gone will look back upon our "modern times" and consider our practices and our troubles ancient?

But the wisdom we lay claim to is not ours, it is the common property of humankind.

When we look back into the deep recesses of time and compare what our forebears had to bear, many people living today have every reason to be masters of themselves, for they have been given rich advantages:

- a lifespan that is three times as long as what humans enjoyed even two hundred years ago, and one that is marked by remarkable health and curing of disease;
- societies freely organized under principles of individual freedom and inalienable rights;
- the accountability and certainty arising from the rule of law, with life, liberty, and property coming under the protection of the state.

When the ancients talked of freeing themselves from the burdens of fortune, their concerns included

- imprisonment, banishment, war, slavery, torture, and death, to name but a few. Not only their own deaths, but those of their children, siblings, partners, and friends;
- reversals of fortune that would keep Hollywood scriptwriters salivating for years;
- the rise and fall of empires!

In our absolute comfort and ease, with ready access to all the world's wisdom, and with the least to objectively complain of, we are among the unhappiest of all generations.

How to explain the riddle that for all our enjoyment, joy consistently eludes us?

In being surrounded by plenty we have not grown virtuous but have grown accustomed to vice. Our enjoyment of easy pleasures has made us flabby of mind, as undisciplined as a college wrestler gone to fat in middle age, maintaining bulk while losing substance.

Used to having everything at our fingertips, no more than a one-click order and same-day delivery away, we no longer appreciate what we have.

When your freedom and your very life are forfeit to the whims of chance, you cannot help but think about what things are of real value. When you not only cannot control your own suffering, but you see it meted out with a generous hand all around you, you appreciate fully when you are not suffering.

The ancients faced mighty troubles and found ways to nonetheless not be troubled.

The purpose of holding troubles in your mind, dear reader, is not to be consequently plagued by worry about what might happen or not happen. You become the thief of your own peace of mind when you worry about others taking it from you.

Think on troubles to remind yourself that these are troubles only in your thoughts and hold no power over your mind. You will achieve lasting joy by remembering that while it may be found in enjoyment, enjoyment is not its exclusive domain.

When you are free from doubt, worry, and jealousy; when your course is the same whether you are pushing into the headwind or blown along by a tailwind; when you delight in stillness as much as you do in motion; when you do not rely on external things, joy is your reward.

Be well.

Chapter Fifteen

On Endurance

Virtue lies not in hard circumstances themselves, but in being able to endure hardships without upset or complaint

I am just returned from a run through the forest paths and farmer's fields near my home.

In springtime I run the risk of encountering every condition when I step out my door: Though the sun is peeking out behind clouds when I set out, I may be confronted with a sudden squall of rain, by hail if I am unlucky, and wind that whips the treetops, not to mention my bare legs.

This time I was blessed with all that nature has to offer, with the result that I got first overheated, then soaked, then chilled.

I now warm myself with the prospect of a pleasant conversation with you, dear reader. Not a heated one, but one in which I can bask in the reflected glow of a point well-made, and a connection made between minds.

Judging from your questions about my recent letter, I cannot take my rest yet, but will put my efforts to explaining one particular topic that seems to be bothering you.

For you ask, "If the first-order and second-order pursuits are equally valuable, that means they are equally desirable. And if they are desirable, that means I should seek them out. But how does it make sense for me to welcome the ill-winds of conflict, to court obstacles, or to look for ill-health?"

I have learned physical endurance from my running training, and you have learned endurance of another kind reading my letters: Patience with me getting to my point. So let me get straight to the substance here.

Just like the courts draw a distinction between murder and manslaughter, though the victim is just as dead in both cases, so must you draw a distinction between these different circumstances, dear reader.

The state of mind is the key, your intentions are everything. Virtue lies not in hard circumstances themselves, but in being able to endure hardships without upset or complaint.

When you let reason rule your mind you will not prefer a fight, but you will address it head-on when it cannot be avoided.

- You will not knowingly or unnecessarily make your path more difficult, nor will you complain about the obstacles you inevitably encounter.

- You do not welcome the fever you feel accompanying a cough, but you also do not recoil in terror at the thought of what you may have caught.

Imagine what a world it would be if we could only find value in things that were pleasant and easy! How many would suffer without end, because it is the fate of many to be without pleasant and easy times.

There is virtue in rising to your circumstances, whatever they may be. The things you work the hardest for are consequently easiest to see the value in.

Meet your challenges openly, calmly, with reason ruling your passions, and you will be rewarded with a well-ordered mind that brings peace, no matter the chaos you find yourself in.

I reward your attention today by stopping, lest I run on in this letter like I have done before.

Be well.

Chapter Sixteen

On Adversity

The only misfortune you need to focus on is the fact that you feel the need to resist and complain

After all we have discussed, I see you are resisting and complaining about the misfortunes that have befallen you.

Have you not learned the lesson, or have you forgotten, that the only misfortune you need to focus on is the fact that you *feel the need* to resist and complain? There is no sadness for people in existence unless they find something in the world they think is sad.

- I am weary from work and my body is becoming frail; that is my fate and the fate of all people.

- None of the cryptocurrencies I buy are promoted by Elon Musk, my blog had just three visitors last month, and I have forgotten more passwords than I can remember.

- On all sides, I am beset by selfish neighbors, ungrateful employees, and greedy customers.

None of this daunts me. The default state of existence is hardship, not ease. I tell myself this not only to learn to *accept* the nature of life but to *expect* it.

I will not be surprised by the adversity that comes my way. On the contrary, I welcome having revealed to me each day what difficulty I must now overcome. I greet my obstacles with relish and a ready smile.

I understand your dismay, dear reader.

Between the lines of your anxious letters, I read your worry about your sudden insomnia and hair loss. Here now, I will say what you could not. You dread that you have some form of cancer, as if by not saying the word you can keep it from finding its way to your door.

The longer one lives, having survived all the outrages and accidents that carry off the young, the more likely one is to fall prey to an ailment from within. Replication errors within your DNA multiply exponentially as you multiply your years and expose your cells to ever more free radicals.

Are you not supremely greedy to wish that you alone can be made exempt from the laws of nature?

It is human nature to suffer and to struggle. I say open your eyes fully and accept the reality that surrounds us.

Embrace the battle and become master of your fate, not subject to it. Face adversity head on and you will be the hero of your own life, and there is no better way to live your life.

Thus you will understand me when I wish you all the best by wishing you a life not free from adversity, but full of clarity.

Be well.

Chapter Seventeen

On Self-Care

There is no distance we should not travel to find a cure for what ails us. But I would have you reflect that no amount of travel will help us if we are treating the wrong illness

Over the centuries, we have tried many ways to cure the ailments that afflict humankind.

Before we understood antibiotics, the sanatorium was the preferred course of treatment for tuberculosis. Patients were sent off to new facilities in the hopes that fresh air and good nutrition would cure them.

There was money to be made from the treatment, never mind the cure, and so people experimented with many different methods.

- Altitude and cold mountain air became the approach for Switzerland; in Finland, it was remote forests that offered the best environment.
- In the western United States, we tried a mix of scenery and a lack of stress in North Carolina and later deemed the dry desert air of Arizona best at effecting a cure.
- Long after the lake air of the East Coast was tried, the ocean breezes of the West Coast emerged as front runners for convalescents.

For much longer than we shipped off the ailing on their healing journeys, the healthy made pilgrimages in the name of wellness.

- We have tried hot springs and spas, with volcanically heated pools and minerally infused waters.

- We heated saunas to steam us like so much slow-roasted pork.

- Then there are those who take the opposite plunge, submersing themselves in glacial waters so cold it snatches your breath away.

- Or consider mud wraps, salt scrubs, and seaweed masks. All the things we would normally wash away with alacrity if we fell into them by accident, we now pay great sums to have slathered on our bodies.

- Pedicure, manicure, massage; massage in every variation: Hot stone, deep tissue, full body, Swedish, sports, Shiatsu. Who knew there were so many ways to bring a recalcitrant muscle back in line?

Lest you take my list for a complaint, dear reader, let me make clear I do not object to self-care. Self-care is critical for well-being.

There is no distance we should not travel to find a cure for what ails us. But I would have you reflect that no amount of travel will help us if we are treating the wrong illness.

Some of us have serious physical ailments, it is true, but we all have mental afflictions. And these are not cured by our spa pilgrimage, no matter how expensive it may be. To effect a cure of our mental ills we must first journey within our minds to identify the sickness.

The most common cause of mental stress is to place the wrong value on external things.

The many who think wealth is a worthy pursuit are plagued by not having attained it. No matter how much they amass, they are goaded on by the fear of it never being enough and by envy of those who have still more than they do.

We all know a person who makes themselves ill with stress and a hypochondriac who in worrying about becoming ill actually accomplishes the feat that nature did not.

Before you take in the water, the air, or the scenery of a new destination, take a moment to consider the value you place on things. Take instruction from the great philosophers before you take the physician's cure.

Rather than having your muscles pulled this way and that, pull yourself out of your comfortable, unquestioning existence. You do not need to travel to resorts or spend money in spas to realize that your satisfaction does not come from the outside.

You are most pleased with yourself not when everything goes easily but when you have encountered and overcome obstacles and met your challenges head-on.

The hard way is hard, but along that path lies satisfaction and peace. And in any event, you cannot avoid the hard path in life, so are well-advised to embrace it when it comes even if you do not seek it out.

The easy path only seems easy, because going down this road leaves us flabby and unfulfilled, unprepared for the slightest setback. If we can only be happy when everything continues to be perfect, we are living a precarious existence indeed.

Knowing that hardship is part of what it means to be human, we take better care of ourselves when we are prepared for adversity. We prepare by contemplating the lessons of philosophy.

Though this commitment is also a cost we must pay, unlike the bill at the spa the investment in philosophy pays dividends our whole lives long.

Be well.

Chapter Eighteen

On Accepting the Inevitable

Think about the possibility of a hundred hardships. Better yet, expect them to afflict you at any moment

I can scarcely believe my ears to hear you carrying on so, dear reader. Have you forgotten everything we have been discussing? Does it take no more than an inconvenience to throw you off course and set you back to the beginning of your studies?

Three of your employees have given notice that they are leaving for greener pastures. That is their perfect right, or have you in your delusional state also forgotten that you work with paid employees and not Roman slaves?

If you paused in your lamentations to examine your thoughts, you would realize the true cause of your anguish.

- You are put to some inconvenience because you must now conduct a replacement search, and not just one but three! This takes time and is certainly a distraction from the daily business.

- Worse, you are worried about what your colleagues may think of you. Will they consider these defections a reflection of your leadership?

- But I think most of all, you are secretly worried that your former employees are giving not just two weeks' notice to the company, but giving *you* notice of some defect in you yourself.

I can almost hear you wondering whether the old saying is true "Employees don't leave companies, they leave bosses."

Recognize these thoughts for the signs of weakness that they are, dear reader, and give them no leave to plague your mind. You will no doubt spend some time finding your new teammates but think about what opportunities this gives you to upgrade your team.

I have taught myself to find the positive in every situation, for this is a habit you can practice like any other. If you have yet to find the upside, assume it is because you are not looking in the right place and keep looking.

Your colleagues may think ill of you. What of it? You know as well as I do that people project onto others their own fears and desires. If they are prone to assume that your employee turnover signals trouble, then you may entertain the thought that they have their own troubles to deal with.

And as to your self-doubt, this is one condition that you can bring about and multiply merely by thinking of it.

Remember instead that all feedback is useful to you, either revealing something of the giver or something about you. In either case, make it your own and use it to better yourself. If the feedback is from a trusted source and true, you now have a profitable topic to pursue. And otherwise, the input should be easy to dismiss.

Epictetus provides a helpful summary of the point I would have you take from this discussion. Perhaps his words will resonate with you if mine have not:

> Some things are in our control and others not. Things in our control are opinion, pursuit, desire, aversion, and, in a word, whatever are our own actions. Things not in our control are body, property, reputation, command, and, in one word, whatever are not our own actions.

The broader point I would make is this: Ask yourself in all situations, do you improve your position by complaining? This typically only serves to magnify minor complaints into larger ones.

And even if your misfortune is truly major — the death of a close friend, failure of your business, or a diagnosis of serious illness — will you make it worse by losing your well-ordered mind and railing against fate? What is the benefit of making yourself unhappy and irrational because the things that are destined to happen to humankind in fact happen?

"But they are not destined to happen to me!" goes the reply. "*Others* will get ill and die and suffer bad luck. I expected *my life* to be charmed at all turns."

This is no more than a pleasant fantasy, a daydream for children. Do you complain that the world is unfair? That you have not been allotted the same portion of good luck as some other, imaginary person? You would be as justified to complain that the sun rises each morning to disturb your sleep, that ants invade your picnic, or that your lottery numbers never get called.

Though fairness in life is unevenly distributed, there is one thing that we all share alike: Our mortality. We are each destined to die.

If you wish to feel better about the unfairness of it all, consider that the luckiest, wealthiest, and most beautiful people are all going to die. They are going to leave their charmed lives behind all the more grudgingly compared with those who have endured hardship and defeat. Tell me, will their deaths be any less final than your own?

You should not become spiteful in considering the fate that awaits all humankind. Nor should you become fearful at the thought of the misfortunes that may befall you.

By thinking about all the things that can happen to you, you prepare yourself to deal with them appropriately. The fact that bad news comes as a surprise is often all that is necessary to throw your reason temporarily out of balance. It can come as no surprise to one who has contemplated misfortune in advance.

Think about the possibility of a hundred hardships. Better yet, expect them to afflict you at any moment. Not only will you be ready for whatever comes your way, you will say "Is this all? I expected much worse."

The same situation, happening to the same person, but the reaction makes all the difference. If contemplating misfortune is part of the cure from misery when ill winds blow, are you better off dreaming only of pleasant things?

I leave you with the words of American theologian Reinhold Niebuhr, who also manages to summarize my point in far fewer words with his aptly named serenity prayer:

> God, grant me the serenity to accept the things I cannot change,
> courage to change the things I can,
> and wisdom to know the difference.

Be well.

Pragmatic Wisdom
Vol. 7

Stoic Lessons on Money and Things

James Bellerjeau

A Fine Idea

Contents

1. On Wealth — 381
2. On Deprivation — 385
3. On Things of Lasting Value — 389
4. On the Meaning of Life — 393
5. On Class and Philosophy — 397
6. On Cohen's Condos — 401
7. On a Holiday Rental — 405
8. On Living Simply — 409
9. On Our Rotten Times — 413
10. On the Value of Wealth — 417
11. On Slippery Slopes — 421
12. On Stepping Off the Treadmill — 425
13. A Little Philosophy Goes a Long Way — 429

Chapter One

On Wealth

Once one's feet are stuck on the path to wealth, the scantest few manage to pry themselves from it

The ties that bind us to bad habits are no less restrictive for being attractive at first glance. The one whose arms are bound by golden chains is no freer than the one in iron shackles.

I am talking about the seductive charms of money, and they have led more from the path of wisdom than any siren song did sailors to their deaths.

"Surely" you say, "I am entitled to take care of myself and to ensure that I have enough to live on." If ever a paving stone belonged on the path to hell, dear reader, it would be this intention.

I grant you that it is suitable and even beneficial that you provide for yourself, and do not need to rely upon the charity of strangers. When you are paid for your toil, you learn the value of work and equally the value of leisure.

Both work and leisure are gifts, and both deserve our deepest contemplation.

But once one's feet are stuck on the path to wealth, the scantest few manage to pry themselves from it. For if a little money is good, more money must be better. But you already know from my earlier letter, that a desire that can never be satisfied is not a true desire.

Plug your ears, then, to the siren song of wealth, but leave open your mind to the alms of philosophy. A true understanding of what it means to live a good life will help you avoid this false temptation.

I was pleased to discover that we have more modern-day Stoics among us than many realize, and it seems that some lessons have made their way safely down the ages.

Though they do not call themselves Stoics, the FIRE movement contains kindred spirits. I refer to "Financial Independence Retire Early," of which we have several different schools of thought. They differ in the sense of how much money the practitioner saves, how much they spend, and what they do with their time.

For our purposes, the operative word for all students is this: Independence. Each works towards passing the test of being in control of their time, and of not relying on others for their contentment or fortune.

However financial independence is defined by each, the FIRE adherent knows that attachment to things impedes progress. You need few possessions to acquire that most valuable thing: Self-possession. Do not spend your time earning money but spend your money to earn yourself time.

Also, who is to say that you would not learn more from dealing with adversity, i.e. by being poor, than you would by never having to deal with want?

To give your mind leisure, do not accumulate things, whether because you cannot afford them, or you have trained yourself not to acquire them. The less you have, the less you worry about. No one will try to take your possessions if you do not have any. Nor will you spend any time worrying about maintaining them.

When your possessions number more than you can hold in your hand, you must worry about how you will carry them about or keep them safe. Here is our old friend Thoreau saying it as he does best:

> Simplicity, simplicity, simplicity! I say, let your affairs be as two or three, and not a hundred or a thousand; instead of a million count half a dozen, and keep your accounts on your thumb-nail.

Now, dear reader, let me caution you as you make your own calculation of how much your independence is worth.

Whatever number you have set for yourself as being enough to allow you to start to live purposefully, it is very likely too high. People today live lives of luxury unimaginable to those of just a few generations back, never mind those stretching back thousands of years.

Lest you think I exaggerate to make my point, let me describe for you a result the Swiss bank UBS found when they surveyed the most successful savers. Across every wealth group, from the mere millionaires to the mega-rich, UBS discovered what we already know: that standard of living expectations increase in line with wealth.

- Those with $1 million felt they would be satisfied with $5 million.

- Those with $5 million thought they could make do with $10 million.

- And those few to have amassed $10 million felt that their way of life would be secure with $25 million.

Like the rabbit leading on the greyhounds, the benchmark moves without the chaser noticing. For it is never the amount as such that makes you feel secure, but the feeling of accumulating more.

Just as a dinner guest shows their appreciation in advance by bringing their host a small gift, I have an offering for you:

> To be content with little is difficult; to be content with much, impossible.

This wisdom comes to us from the pen of Austrian author, Countess Marie von Ebner-Eschenbach. She was born of a Baron, lived in a castle, and was surrounded by libraries of books.

The Countess knew of riches both material and immaterial. It is to our benefit that she placed greater weight on the latter.

Be well.

Chapter Two

On Deprivation

You do not need what you think you need to be happy, because all you need is within you

Another New Year's Day, which means another spate of New Year's resolutions. We promise ourselves that we will change in the new year. The tight waistband of our favorite jeans, the low step count on our Fitbit, the exercise equipment collecting dust in the corner, all that will be different now.

If you were here, dear reader, I would happily listen to your recommendation. Should we be resolute in our retiring ways, or join the crowd in making resolutions? When everyone around us declares their good intentions, what misers are we to withhold our contribution to a more hopeful future?

If all eyes around us turn towards the sky, only a few can keep their gaze on the ground. We are social animals, and to go against the herd is to go against our very humanity.

I know that you are up to the test I will put to you now. Do not be about the setting of annual resolutions, if these be expressed in the form of a goal you wish to achieve. Goals are but wishful thinking.

Better orient yourself along the right path, and follow a system designed to move you in the direction of your choosing. You will arrive in places beyond what you could have imagined using mere goals.

If you have a resolution, let it be this: You will learn to develop new habits, by taking a small thing and practicing it daily for two weeks. In that time, you will either adopt your new habit with relative ease or determine that it is not the one for you.

No need for self-doubt. There are many paths leading to good outcomes, and you will simply choose another. Not the goal, mind you, but merely the path along which you will walk.

What you will learn from learning to adopt habits is that habits are everything. And how wonderful that, despite being so foundational, habits are disarmingly easy to form.

Do you wish to be content with what you have? Practice going without and do so as often as you feel your resolve weakening.

For all those who think "But I need to travel in Business Class, or I will suffer most grievously on the flight" I say this:

- Put yourself happily in the back of the plane, one row from the restrooms.

- What are eight hours when you have a good book to distract you?

- Should I have lost a moment's peace worrying about being a few meters further back in the same plane?

- Am I not especially ridiculous when I imagine the anguish of those who sit one cabin ahead of mine when *they* contemplate the luxuries being lavished on the lucky few in First Class?

- And even those elite are secretly irked by the thought that flying private is so much more civilized.

Better yet, make your vacation one in which you do not set foot in an airport. Let your feet do the work and take a walk to a nearby scenic viewpoint.

For nothing more than the trouble of walking out your door, you can attain peace of mind for no price. A walk in a forest salted with birds is better than any time spent in a concrete jungle, with only the outraged honks of taxis to serenade you.

The lesson you are reinforcing as a diligent student is that you do not need what you think you need to be happy because all you need is within you. When you deprive yourself of things, particularly of comforts, you weaken their power over you. And such is the power of comforts that it leads many to lives of discomfort for fear of losing them.

Not you. By going without, you learn not to fear privation. Besides learning the nature of which things are worth fearing and which are not, you learn not to take for granted that which you have.

After you have been cold and thinly dressed, wet and without an umbrella, hungry and without food, then truly do you become a connoisseur of a warm, dry room and simple food.

When you have trained yourself to be happy with the most basic of nature's offerings, then you have learned to live true to yourself. Happiness never lies in external things, and if it takes our depriving ourselves of things to relearn this lesson, then better for us to cast off all possessions than be weighed down by the slightest of them.

My finger hovers over the send button. "Not without another installment payment on your account," you say. I call on the fortune of the Buddha to help pay this week's debt:

> Holding on to anger is like grasping a hot coal with the intent of throwing it at someone else; you are the one who gets burned.

The wisdom here is apparent to everyone who has felt anger and been fortunate enough to have it fade away. Some spring repeatedly to anger at the slightest provocation. Anger is satisfying to give vent to because it drives out reason. You are no longer responsible for thought, you are spurred to violent action, be it words or deeds.

You do not wish to be someone who gives up their reason so readily, for this too is habit-forming.

Self-possession means more than not needing things. Self-possession means keeping a tight grip on your reason and not letting anyone or anything external hijack it from you.

Though you may safely cast all else aside, your mind is the one possession you do not make better by depriving yourself of it.

Be well.

Chapter Three

On Things of Lasting Value

Not all appreciate that hard work and sacrifice are not just the price for rewards, but a necessary precondition for valuing them

"Not another sermon" you say. "I have heard you preach to others, but do you practice your own lessons? Are you so advanced that you have endless time to pass on your wisdom to those less learned?"

I do not pretend to point out the mote in my brother's eye while ignoring the beam in my own. Consider that I am trying to describe a landscape that I see but dimly, and that by comparing notes with my fellow observers, we each gain a sharper view of its contours.

You are thus my sounding board for good sense. Though I may be just talking to myself, putting my thoughts into words still helps me understand the message.

I tell you one lesson that I must practice and practice, and hence I preach it to myself as often as to others: I shall seek an end to my wants before I come to my own end. As often as I banish wants, still they sprout anew like perennials each spring.

"What harm," I muse, "in this small indulgence? I can afford it, and truly there may be no consequence for my weakness of the moment."

But what a tiny bounty this small pleasure buys, when compared to the erosion of my foundation of self-possession and well-ordered thought! What an unfair trade to grab onto a momentary enjoyment and let go of long-term contentment.

For though the pleasure is fleeting, the memory of it remains. And the memory is not of the enjoyment but of my lapse, or as the saying goes: Act in haste, repent at leisure. With each slip, my footing grows less stable, until I am scarcely able to stand without support.

Contrast this with the memory of virtuous decisions resulting from clear thinking. Rather than death by a thousand cuts, each of these decisions can be safely savored in leisure. They represent a fortification of the soul and not an assault.

Standing firm is the only way to continue to stand firmly, and thus the only path to lasting value is to be true to your values.

There are more obstacles in our path than aids, dear reader, even though it appears that the opposite is true. Consider:

- We live in an age when virtually all knowledge is available at our fingertips, courtesy of Google. The instant a thought or question arises in your mind, you can slake your thirst with a search.

- How many drink deeply enough to fully quench desire, instead of sipping at the sources of wisdom? Though they have been handed the keys to all the libraries of the world, they cannot unlock wisdom.

There have never been more well-informed idiots who know all of the facts and none of their implications.

I put it down to instant gratification. Not only do we feel entitled to satisfy our every want, but what we think we deserve we want right now.

The worst thing you can do with a child is to satisfy their every want, for then they never learn the difference between wants and needs. Are we to be spoiled children into advanced age?

Not all appreciate that hard work and sacrifice are not just the price for rewards, but a necessary precondition for valuing them.

- If I give you something for free, and you have invested no effort in obtaining it, you will value it as highly as any other common thing you can pick up off the ground.

- Because free and easy are today within short reach, few grasp past them to the costly and the challenging.

But if we wish to ensure our safe passage, the hard way is where our path lies. The longer we toil upwards, the greater will be our reward.

The joy that comes from mastering your thoughts is not only the greatest possession, it is the one that cannot be taken from you by another.

I pay now my debt and take my leave:

> The greatest wealth is to live content with little, for there is never want where the mind is satisfied.

This comes courtesy of Lucretius, and you marvel at the many routes by which I return to this point.

That is because it is a road you must travel down before you are safe to venture further on. It is also the road to which all others eventually return.

I would have you hear this lesson until it becomes second nature, and you are a safe navigator for yourself and others.

Be well.

Chapter Four

On the Meaning of Life

How do we find meaning? By learning to identify all those things that are meaningless, and serve only to weigh us down

So, I understand your friend is trying to convince you he has figured out the meaning of life.

I recommend a healthy skepticism towards anyone who says they have it all figured out. Exercise particular care with the ones who are selling you a simple solution.

Do you know how rare it is that a person becomes truly enlightened, in the sense of the Buddha or the Dalai Lama? A person who puts their worldly cares behind them and lives a life of joy and compassion?

Perhaps we see signs of it in children. This transcendence is so seldom achieved in adulthood, and so striking when we do find ourselves in its midst, that you will have no trouble mistaking the practitioner for the master.

"My friend is calm and composed" you say, "when others are incensed by small things."

You can observe a cobra from a distance every day and never see it bare its fangs. Until you do. Perhaps it is simply that your friend has not been sufficiently provoked.

Do not be impressed by a person who remains calm when there has been no disturbance. The fact that others are disturbed by small things tells us nothing.

"He condemns politicians who abuse their power, who tend to themselves rather than their constituents."

This says nothing of his true nature, dear reader. For among all those who shrink from the whip, there are but few who would not themselves wield it willingly if the whip should fall into their hands.

The only thing preventing the average person from becoming tyrants themselves is they lack the means to implement their whims. Situations make most people who they are, and it is exceedingly uncommon for a person to make themselves in spite of their limitations.

Though your friend is unlikely to be a guru, if for no other reason than he professes himself as such, there is no shame in being a practitioner.

We are all pilgrims walking the same path and the value for most of us is in the progress we make. Point yourself in the right direction and take a single step, and you have advanced farther than those who run a thousand miles aimlessly.

How do we find meaning? By learning to identify all those things that are meaningless, and serve only to weigh us down:

- public opinion and trends;
- fashion, fame, and fortune;
- anger, envy, and longing.

Note how fickle these things are, and how insubstantial. Though you cannot see them or hold them in your hand, still they are the heaviest of burdens.

With each of these chains we shrug from our shoulders, our load becomes lighter, and our steps more carefree. Satisfaction and joy lie along this path, and the cost to us is giving up things that require us to pay a price, whether in money, time, or attention.

For everything we plan to seek in life, let us first understand the cost to obtain it. Naval Ravikant shows wisdom when he says:

> Desire is a contract you make with yourself to be unhappy until you get what you want.

What is keeping you unhappy? What you want. What do you want? ... Happiness

We do not want things. We want what we think those things will bring us. No matter how eagerly we sought a possession or a promotion, notice how quickly they start to lose their luster the moment we attain them.

- The new car becomes a used car the instant you drive it off the lot.

- The new phone is soon outshone by a rival as sure as the sun will rise tomorrow.

- The big new office that comes with the big new job is quickly filled with the big new problems that you now feel weighing you down.

To make yourself unhappy by wanting things that will not make you happy is not a recipe for success. Let me end again with Lucretius because it bears repeating:

> The greatest wealth is to live content with little, for there is never want where the mind is satisfied.

Our most important possession is our self-possession, and once having taken ownership of this, you have all that you need for a meaningful life.

Be well.

Chapter Five

On Class and Philosophy

Philosophy holds out to us the exact same opportunity, regardless of birth, gender, class, or wealth. Truly the way is open to all

You say that you come from humble origins, that your family was lower middle class at best, as if this had anything to do with your ability to mine your reason and become truly rich in happiness!

Philosophy cares not a bit for your social class.

Though your family may be rich or impoverished in money and circumstance, we are each born with the same inalienable rights: Life, liberty, and the pursuit of happiness.

Think how much better your situation is today than humankind throughout most of history, a third or more of whom toiled in slavery. To become wealthy and powerful was the province of kings and generals, and even these could never rest easy because they could lose everything in a moment's weakness.

Today we are born free, and we are free agents, able to direct our attention where we would like and reap the consequences of our actions. That which we create with our own hands and by our own effort belongs to us, which none can take without due process of law.

If you wish to climb the ladder of social mobility, dear reader, there is no better time to be clutching the rungs of progress than today.

Your own career bears out the proof of what I say. Though you were born into poverty and obscurity, you have risen to your current position of prominence through your own hard work.

It is your own efforts you should applaud, for which of your ancestors labored alongside you in getting you to where you are today?

Go back down the family tree of mankind, and you see that we all share a common ancestor. Do you want noble blood in your family? Look but a bit further and you will find your kingly kinship.

But take little comfort from your royalty, because you will also find all manner of rogues and scoundrels among these relatives, who wreaked havoc and destruction on humanity.

If you wish to bask in the reflected glory of others' deeds, you must also accept to be doused in shame and remorse from their misdeeds.

No, it is our great luck and our greatest burden that philosophy holds out to us the exact same opportunity, regardless of birth, gender, class, or wealth. Truly the way is open to all, though few tread these paths and fewer march confidently in a consistent direction.

"The good fortune I understand" you say, "because I see that we all have potential. But why do you say our opportunity is also a burden?"

Responsibility is both wonderful and terrible, depending on *whether you take it*. Taking responsibility for yourself and your progress gives your life meaning. Nothing makes an achievement sweeter than knowing it was hard-earned.

But look how many shirk from responsibility, from the consequences of their thoughts and actions. Because we live in an age of peace and prosperity, a person can choose to be idle, to be uninspired.

But to be average in your ambitions when others excel, where no one has forced your hand, is to know that you could have done more. Thus, people either willfully ignore their promise, or are weighed down by their potential.

This can be more damning to their spirits than if freedom was taken from them against their will. In the latter case, at least their lot is not their fault, and they are freed of the burden of responsibility.

Let me give you a final reason why you should be happy for your modest social origins.

Those born to privilege are surrounded by fine things in their cradle, and their tastes quickly grow accustomed to rich fare. Great is the risk they will set out on a path to maintaining their status and wealth.

How many will have cause to question whether wealth consists of things? And if they never question the wisdom of their choices, but blindly pursue prosperity, why should philosophy hold any appeal to them?

Though they amass wealth and power, they remain unsatisfied the whole while, and worst of all, do not know why.

I say the fortunate at birth are those who have few luxuries. For though they may start by fervently wishing for all they do not have, they have a better chance of realizing that happiness can be found in more places than their bank account, such as a walk on the beach, a vibrant sunset, or a meal with friends.

Because their progress is not assured, they take responsibility for their actions, and in this way find meaning.

The lessons of philosophy take root more readily in such a one because admission to this club requires only a well-ordered mind.

Be well.

Chapter Six

On Cohen's Condos

We assume the prominent are thrilled with their privileges and made content thereby. But what do we know of their inner thoughts, their joys, and their worries?

I flew into JFK airport not long ago and marveled once again at the miracle of modern travel: Boarding a plane in the morning, crossing an ocean, and arriving at a new continent in the afternoon of the same day.

The speed with which we can conquer by air the distances of the globe is outdone, though, by the time dilation that occurs on reaching the ground, at least in New York.

It starts with the rush from the plane's door down endless, empty corridors to the customs hall.

The legs fairly leap after being caged for eight hours, and you are happy to stride energetically past the moving walkways. Why stand like a statue after you've been sitting immobile like a mummy in its sarcophagus?

The sunlight streams through the glass windows along the hallway, and your heart briefly soars with optimism that this time will be different.

Your face soon falls in line with your dashed hopes as you turn the final corner to see the Brownian motion of thousands of fellow travelers inching imperceptibly toward the next hurdle.

Quickly, which line is for you? Citizen, non-citizen, crew, green card holder, Global Entry ... choose wrongly and you will be forced to backtrack, letting who knows how many ahead of you in line and adding perhaps hours to your wait.

So, you run to then stand and shuffle while wondering for the 50th time whether those signs saying "Cell phone use prohibited" are really enforced.

There's a fellow traveler from your flight, and how on earth did they get so much farther ahead of you? They were sitting in the same row as you. Oh, there's another, and you stifle a secret laugh that you are far ahead of them.

Eventually, I clear customs, relieved to be spared the indignity of being fingerprinted and photographed like the potentially criminal non-citizens.

The baggage hall is one circle of hell I may circumvent, for at least today I am traveling light. With a pitying glance at those in the purgatory of lost baggage, I make my escape through the doors to freedom or, as it turns out, merely the arrivals hall.

I feel like a marathoner approaching the finishing line, for the way is lined with spectators holding up signs, each eagerly looking to catch sight of their runner: "Mr. Pletros, Marriott," "Electrolux," "Al Walheer, The Essex House."

If you were willing to assume a new identity for the afternoon you could be whisked any place you wish in leather and air conditioning.

In my case, I put my person into the care of that most venerable institution, The Yellow Cab Company.

Though I made my way from the plane's door with the alacrity of a seasoned competitor, first to the line, fastest out the gate, leaving less experienced runners far behind, the halls of JFK strain from the disgorge of disgruntled passengers.

Fast as I have been, before me waits another Amazonian line winding distantly to the taxis.

To truly understand motion that yields no progress, dear reader, get into a New York City cab at the very epitome of the oxymoron that is "rush hour."

- For hours you will sit, wondering whether your destination is nearing faster than the figure on the meter is rising.

- Many times, you will be tempted to fly your yellow cage and take to the streets by foot.

- Would that you had descended into the bowels of Jamaica Station and taken the E-train! The subway, with all its chance encounters and strange smells, at least gives you the sensation of movement.

It was while this run of thoughts ran riot through my tired brain that I looked out the window at 58th Street and spied a former home of hedge fund billionaire Steven Cohen.

Twenty-four-foot ceilings, spread over two floors, and in the news as much for its storied owner as for its views over Central Park.

Forced by an insider trading scandal to close SAC Capital Advisors, his eponymously initialed hedge fund, the firm paid the largest insider trading fine of all time at $1.8 billion.

Mr. Cohen was reduced to managing his own money, perhaps a mere $10 billion at that point. He had also reduced the $115 million selling price of his condo multiple times since putting it on the market in 2013.

The headlines reported it attracted a buyer after eight years and a 74% price cut. "Hah!" we laugh, "The brilliant trader has lost his golden touch." But read a bit further and you see the bargain price of $29.5 million is still $5.5 million above what he paid for it.

I am not writing to begrudge anyone their wealth, their acumen, or their pursuits, dear reader.

I would have you see that the breathless reporting of billionaires' mega apartments, art collections, and philanthropic contributions is a symptom of something else and a distraction from what is truly valuable.

The amount of ink spilled over the prominent hides as much as it reveals.

We assume the prominent are thrilled with their privileges and made content thereby. But what do we know of their inner thoughts, their joys and their worries?

Do you think the shuttering of SAC Capital's doors made Mr. Cohen any happier to open the doors of his Hamptons home?

It is not the painted walls of a grand villa that make one bright and happy. The riches that philosophy offers are available to all, regardless of what's in their wallet.

If you can but purchase peace of mind, you will see that you do not lack the means for any further purchase.

And moreover, you will see that you pay the cost of your things well after you've paid the price. The maintenance fee on a million-dollar condo is much more than what flows from your bank account each month!

When you think you are building a bulwark against uncertainty by piling up stacks of cash, be careful you are not building the walls of your own prison of discontent.

The condo I would have you inhabit is one entirely of your own making, and though it be free of adornment, you will spend more carefree days there than in any luxury building.

Be well.

Chapter Seven

On a Holiday Rental

Sometimes progressing on the journey of life means leaving the comfort of what made us successful in the past

I have rented a beach property on a barrier island off the southern coastline. I hope to wile away there some sultry summer hours in rest and contemplation with my family. We will take a collective deep breath to catch up from this manic past year. I think also as much to gather our strength for what lies ahead.

Changes are afoot at summer's end, dear reader, not just in my own work life, but for all of us.

- My daughter switches universities and Cantons, leaving home to stay on course with the next phase of her studies.

- My son ends his apprenticeship and graduates with his certificate, also to begin new studies towards a degree.

- And my wife and I are moving house and moving countries, leaving our adopted home of more than two decades to return to the land of our birth.

My wife and I are to become refugees in all but name, for I fear we have become strangers to the land that was once all we knew.

Every significant life change makes us into temporary strangers. We become strangers to our old habits and our old ways, even as we are not yet familiar with our new surroundings.

We will be fools for a while, not knowing how to get simple things done, embarrassed and uncomfortable in our ignorance.

Why do it then, one might reasonably ask? Why not just stay in our known environs? To grow and develop we must confront the new. It is an illusion that we maintain our position when we stand still because we run the risk of lapsing into complacency. Still water more easily stagnates.

Sometimes progressing on the journey of life means leaving the comfort of what made us successful in the past.

To stay successful in the future, we must take with us all that we have learned along life's journey. The cargo of life's lessons is not heavy if we pack it carefully about our persons.

One of the great opportunities a change offers us is to leave behind all that we no longer need. Jettison the dead weight of bad memories and bad experiences, of second-guessing and regret. Assimilate to yourself the best of all you have experienced and all you have learned, and not only will your steps be light, but you will be well prepared for your next step.

Remember that you have surmounted countless obstacles to get where you are today. Let the confidence of your past victories, your triumphs over so many struggles and worries and cares, carry you into the unknown with your head held high.

Will everything go according to plan? This I can tell you is hardly to be expected. Will you encounter new challenges and unexpected setbacks? Almost certainly. Will you overcome them? I have not the slightest doubt.

Can I tell you how you will overcome what comes your way? No, I cannot. But I am nonetheless supremely confident that you will prevail because you have all the lessons and skills that brought you to your current position.

Now in my case, we are not traveling so far for our summer rest that I have outrun my sense of the absurd. For starters, I cannot seem to outdistance my own folly, for I have fallen into the trap of reading the marketing material about the vacation properties on offer. As if this could tell me anything about what sort of environment will foster relaxation and restoration!

ON A HOLIDAY RENTAL

The greatest threat to our peace of mind lies within our own minds, and these we carry with us no matter how distantly we travel.

But there I was, dear reader, reading about houses arranged in military order by the number of bedrooms, bathrooms, and rows distant from the beach. Shocked at the geometric progression in price as properties inch closer to the shore and the surprising jumps as each bedroom gets tacked on.

After some time perusing the offerings, you could be forgiven for thinking that a home without a television in every room is akin to a prison sentence, each silent room promising the torture of temporary boredom.

"Can you believe they only have TVs in the bedrooms, dining room, and living room, and not the kitchen or bathrooms? How can I possibly evacuate my bowels if I am not accompanied by a screen before my face?"

"It is a hardship, dear, but I suppose you could take your iPad with you when the need comes upon you."

If I sound unkind, and I do to myself as well, it is because I am so disappointed to be reminded yet again that this is apparently what we want.

And it must be what we want because this is what the market offers at every turn: Private pools, spas, and furnished patios with gas grills; flat-screen TVs in every room and Wi-Fi throughout; a laundry room, a garage, and a walkway to the beach.

Tell me, dear reader, is it the warm embrace of your heated pool, the closed walls of your private gardens, and the flat screens facing your king-size beds that bring us to the seaside?

Or is it that moment when you slip off your shoes and socks near the end of the wooden slat walkway and feel the sand between your toes? When you first note the stiff breeze of the Atlantic wind across your face and the unmistakable smell of salt in the air?

Could it be upon hearing the reeds in the dunes rustling in the wind as you round the final curve and lay eyes on the ocean? Surely by the time you are out of the soft, dry sand and onto wetter and firmer ground, you will once again be on the way to grounding yourself in what's important.

To walk along the shore just above the sandpipers, who are themselves rushing to stay just ahead of each advancing wave, is to walk away from worldly cares.

With pelicans silhouetted by the setting sun, and dolphins' beaks occasionally breaking the surface, at that moment who cares whether you walked from the third row or the seventh? Whether you will return to a private pool, a community pool, or no pool at all? Yes, you may have a TV on every surface but still find that you are happiest leaving all screens dark.

It is outside in the wind and salt and sand that we will find ourselves closest to nature, and perhaps our own true natures.

And it is inside in the close confines of a family conversation that we will find satisfaction, and perhaps peace.

Be well.

Chapter Eight

On Living Simply

When traveling light you think carefully about what you really need and leave aside all those things that you might need. I think that is the reason I so love the practice

There is nothing that gives me greater pleasure than embarking on a journey with nothing more than what I can carry about my person and in a backpack!

There are now numerous websites devoted to traveling light, filled with one-bag travel adherents who have learned to love minimalism on the go. I can now travel for two weeks for business or pleasure, dear reader, with no more than the clothes on my back and an easy armful of items I can keep with me no matter how cramped my quarters.

I make my way in every environment, be it hot or cold, wet or dry, formal dress or beach casual. No hobo with their possessions tied in a sack flung over one shoulder ever felt so free of burdens as they pointed their shoes down the next highway.

When traveling light you think carefully about what you really need and leave aside all those things that you *might* need. I think that is the reason I so love the practice. It is good practice for the greater concern we continually face: Making distinctions about what is necessary to live a good life.

If only this small practice while traveling left more permanent lessons once home again. But in my familiar places, I find myself needing to remind myself over and over about what is important, lest I twist about in pursuit of possessions.

People will twist themselves into knots to avoid confronting a hard truth or to give themselves permission to believe something they desperately want to be true. Nowhere do we see this more than in the perennial question of possessions and wealth.

It is not just philosophers who have grappled with this question. The Bible addresses it frequently and generations of religious scholars have interpreted and re-interpreted its teachings ever since.

In a document as rich and complex as the Bible, no doubt you will find support for many propositions. Just like philosophers tied themselves in syllogistic knots by defining propositions and then letting logic twist all meaning away, so too have theologians found the Bible to contain a multitude of paradoxes to say nothing of support for competing propositions.

Here I would give you a general caution, dear reader, to never trust a researcher who starts with their conclusion and then scours their data for any means to support it.

We struggle to put this advice into practice because researchers often take pains to be crystal clear about their results while remaining opaque about their motives. And this assumes they have a clear idea of their motives, which you must also not take as a given.

Though you will find them less frequently, look for those researchers who first publish their hypotheses and make testable predictions. Then you may share their eagerness to experiment and check whether reality agrees.

But let me return to the Bible. Even though today we are far removed from being able to check any of the authors' motivations, some I will take on good faith. Thus, it is in the gospel of Matthew that we are told that Jesus said

> it is easier for a camel to go through the eye of a needle than for a rich man to enter the kingdom of God.

This was in the context of Jesus answering a young rich man's question about how he could achieve eternal life. Jesus's advice was for him to sell his possessions to give to the poor, and then to follow Jesus's teachings.

This prescription proved to be bitter medicine, as it has for striving people throughout the ages.

Amidst much truth-telling and honest acknowledgment among the faithful, there also followed a millennium of pretzel logic. Would there be a way to turn this simple advice entirely on its head? To say that riches and possessions here on earth were a sign of God's favor, confirmation that one was living a virtuous life?

Indeed, there arose a host of pastors preaching so-called prosperity theology, which teaches exactly this. If spiritual and physical realities are interconnected, the thinking goes, and we are entitled to well-being, then material wealth can be seen as a blessing from God.

The desire to believe this is so strong that adherents have managed to overlook a mountain of contradictory indications in the Bible and elsewhere.

The followers of conjoined spiritual and material wealth also seem unconcerned with the inherent contradiction that making regular donations to one's church is apparently a primary vehicle meant to bring about God's blessing.

This will no doubt bring material wealth to some, but I fear it is only to the lucky church receiving the faithful's donations. At this point, I am reminded of American Pastor Creflo Dollar's rather direct request to his congregants for $65 million so he could purchase a Gulfstream jet.

We do not need a Gulfstream jet to bring us great distances, dear reader. Of course, I am not speaking only of travel, although the lesson applies equally there.

I believe there is nothing inherently wrong with possessions, or in having possessions. The harm comes from the harm we do to ourselves and others in *pursuit* of possessions.

Having proven ourselves to be untrustworthy stewards of our most valuable possession, that of our well-ordered mind following reason, let us leave aside most external things so that we can learn to appreciate simple things.

If it takes a trip away from the comforts of home to remind us that we are not our things and that we can be happy with but few things, I say dust off your passport, load up your backpack, and head out your door!

Be well.

Chapter Nine

On Our Rotten Times

Just as advances and accomplishments belong to an age in history, so too do the embarrassments that the next generation takes but a few decades to clearly perceive

Have you noticed that each generation inevitably becomes convinced of two things, dear reader?

- First, they have reached the pinnacle of wisdom with current science and civilization; that their way of life and pursuits are correct and good and the one true path.

- And second, they simultaneously laugh at how their ancestors were so gullible and dangerously ignorant in so many things; while they lament that their children are both gullible and dangerously ignorant in so many things.

"Contemptible idiots behind us, and superficial fools ahead of us! Howsoever will the world survive when we are gone?"

It is not the times that give rise to such convictions. The folly is peculiar to humankind itself and so passes unbidden and unseen from generation to generation.

It is true that each generation finds a way to express its failings uniquely. Just as advances and accomplishments belong to an age in history, so too do the embarrassments that the next generation takes but a few decades to clearly perceive.

Humans are powerful in so many things but applying perspective to our *own* imperfections is not one of our inherent talents, nor do we seem to have any desire to develop it.

Is our own generation really the first to be free from error? Have we become enlightened as a whole, such that our every utterance deserves to be inscribed in the skies for all to wonder at?

Let us seek to be impartial judges and consider the evidence.

- We live in times where serious people seriously expound the idea that you can tell something important about the inside of a person by looking only at the outside of that person.

- That all of society can be explained by power, and that there is no objective reality behind power structures, only self-serving and self-perpetuating identity groups.

Consider the supposed attributes of "whiteness," which we are told have been invented and used to oppress non-white people.

- These include that whites value self-reliance, rational linear thinking, and the idea that hard work is the key to success.

- That it makes sense to plan for the future, delay gratification, and make progress.

- That we should have an action orientation and seek to master our circumstances.

Before you find yourself nodding along in agreement with the items on the list, recall that they are held out as symbols of oppression, not freedom.

Social justice movements hold out as heroes the victims of police brutality, as if somehow resisting arrest is the better example of virtuous conduct. Among the most exalted are the ones who have been martyred, and it does not seem to matter what their prior record may have been.

Mobs vandalize and burn city streets, and we call it justice. Crowds loot stores and we call it redistribution of wealth. City councils tell you they expect to see *less* crime when they defund the police and stop prosecuting offenders.

For our own parts, we fill our bellies with junk food, and we fill our heads with junk science. We buy junk products on credit and amuse ourselves with junk entertainment to tickle our ever-shortening attention spans.

We go into debt to pay for educations that fill our children's heads with dangerous nonsense. We borrow money to buy cars and houses that we don't need and can't afford.

All this brings us more sadness than satisfaction in both the pursuit and the possession.

On the national level, our politicians have elevated empty talk to a new art form. With one side of their mouths, they stoke our most base emotions and outrage.

So aroused, with our eyes burning red and our ears ringing, we do not notice when they utter out of the other side things like, "There are no limits on what we can spend and there is no consequence to running our deficit higher and higher."

As if! This is one time when future generations will look back not in amusement but in horror at the delusions we felt comfortable with, for we are burdening them with both our sins of omission as well as those we commit.

No, we would know on a moment's quiet reflection that ours is not the golden age, dear reader. At least, no more than any other age.

Despite our advancements in science, technology, health care, productivity, and more, we have spent little time in the laboratory of the human soul. For all our progress in external things, we have forgotten that the natural course of our minds inclines downward.

Stability in human societies is only ever temporary. We fail and we have never not failed.

The reason is that we have never removed our weaknesses and our vices from the equation. We have too few examples of virtuous behavior, and pay too little attention to the examples we have, for them to tip the scales in our favor.

In their hearts, people are not so easy to fool. We know when we are consuming garbage, though none admits it aloud.

We suffer in our hearts and our thoughts when we proclaim satisfaction with superficial things. These internal maladies do not remain suppressed but are expressed through ill health, depression, and turmoil in society.

Thus, we have sown the conditions for our downfall: Those who are told they are well-off are nonetheless unfulfilled and so restless and eager for change; while those who are told they are suffering are angry and mobilized to tear down the systems that have failed them.

Who will fight to preserve the good that humankind has achieved in its centuries of struggle? Who will ensure that the good humankind is capable of is not extinguished in the fire along with everything else?

In our rotten times, you cannot stand on the sidelines. You are either pouring water on the flames or you are fanning them. By your silence you let the rot spread.

By your words, do you seek to build and fortify or only tear down?

The early few may sacrifice themselves in standing up against madness, true. But if none stand, all will fall. And perhaps we will find that there are others who will stand with us to slow the fall.

Be well.

Chapter Ten

On the Value of Wealth

True wealth comes from not needing to display wealth to be happy, rather than having wealth to display

What good is excess wealth to a parent or their family? I have come to believe that parents who give everything to their children growing up are themselves selfish.

You are wondering if I am being contrary to make a point. You are right to wonder this, but I assure you I am sincere.

"But isn't the very definition of a good parent," you ask, "the one who is responsible and provides for their family to ensure they suffer no material want?"

I say this definition is incomplete and, moreover, insufficient, unless you are raising children to be permanent children, cut off from the cares of the outside world.

The true responsibility of parents is to raise their children to be capable of safely making their own way in the world, and not to remove every obstacle from their paths. This means learning to handle adversity.

Is life trouble-free for any person, regardless of their wealth?

Say a person has amassed a fortune as great as that of the robber barons of the Gilded Age. Does that mean they can now buy their way free from the envy, spite, and double-dealing of their fellow humans? Are their relationships protected against failing, their bodies immune from ailing, and their thoughts free of doubt?

Consider this: How can a child learn to handle adversity if they are never confronted with it?

"What," you say, "shall parents now let their children stumble unawares into the street to teach them the value of pain?"

Life will bring its own troubles soon enough, dear reader. We do not need to invite them in. The point is more that we should not seek to bar the door to every trouble.

Rather teach your children first by your own example that hardship can not only be endured but mastered. When you encounter your own inevitable setbacks show your children how you rise to the challenge, not only well, but willingly.

"I can see your point about the need to confront adversity" you say, "but why do you call parents who seek to provide a comfortable environment for their children selfish? How can wanting to give the best things to someone else make *you* selfish?"

Think about it and you will come to your answer. Will the child live only in the parent's household, or will they one day wish to live an independent life? What then? Will the parent tend to every need until the child has died of natural causes while the parent clings to life? No and no, and no to every circumstance where the outside world will intrude.

The principal thing a parent accomplishes by eliminating any real-world struggles is avoiding seeing their child suffer. Who benefits the most from such a sheltered environment?

Hence, I say this is the ultimate selfishness on the part of the parent, because in saving themselves pain they leave their children unprepared for life. I know that most parents would vehemently disagree, but that is to be expected. I have just called them selfish and bad parents in the same breath.

All right, let us respond to the incensed parent by asking them some questions:

"Reflect back upon your own life. Did everything go easily for you? Was everything you have now simply handed to you? What made you the person you are today? Tell me about a time that you overcame a hardship or a challenge and came out stronger for it."

Some of the most driven people became that way precisely because they were sorely challenged and survived the tests. Not only survived but emerged from their suffering stronger. You learn to confront adversity by being confronted with adversity.

This thought experiment is usually enough to quell the anger of all the thoughtful parents, which I believe is most of them. It quiets their voices because they are now reconsidering not only their approach to parenting but all they have done so far.

But you will encounter some number of others who say something like, "I earned my money through my own hard work. I am paid a lot because I deliver a lot of value, and I am worth every penny. How dare you say I should not give every advantage to my children now and allow them to reap the benefits of my labor?"

Everything in modern society supports the wealthy parent's view, dear reader, and your opponent has the weight of numbers and opinion on their side. Further, they have built their entire lives following a formula that was not of their making, but which they learned to master.

These roots run deep. By digging around the foundations like this you are questioning their values and by extension their very worth as a person. Do not expect your discussion to be easy and do not expect to be thanked for your service.

Be aware that many people are only too happy to be misled if it means they never have to confront painful truths.

Though they cannot permanently lay to rest a nagging dissatisfaction, they can temporarily silence this voice with a new car, a buying binge, or a trip to Vegas. The most you can hope for is to add weight to that persistent doubt so that in a quiet moment it gives them pause to think.

You might get this person to observe that on their travels through, say, Southeast Asia, they encountered many happy people who otherwise lived in poverty. That in fact having money is not the only path to happiness.

And if you arrive at this mutual realization, consider yourself a success and do not seek to go further. Because to a person who has money, the idea that money does not bring happiness is madness. Not only or even primarily for what it buys them, but for what having money tells them about themselves and what it tells others.

Money tells them that they have done the right things and are being rewarded. It tells them they are a good person! And by making lavish displays of wealth, money signals to others that a person is successful. We want nothing more than to be considered successful.

But happiness is intrinsic. I cannot show it on my arm like I can a Boss shirt under a Gucci suit jacket with a Rolex watch peeking out at the wrist. No, for bragging without talking, money beats happiness every time, at least in this person's mind.

Never mind if the parent has learned anything from you. If you have learned anything from me, dear reader, it is to identify the true value of things.

Do you seek to arouse envy in your fellow person or admiration? Does a person admire you for what you have or how you behave?

And will you set your value by the estimation of others, who do not know what is valuable and what is not? Or will you set your value by your own estimation of how well you lived according to your values?

True wealth comes from not needing to display wealth to be happy, rather than having wealth to display.

Be well.

Chapter Eleven

On Slippery Slopes

Can you tell me now which of your indulgences let grown into vices will be your undoing, or will you tell me that you are safe from all temptation?

Some people assert that the slippery slope argument is silly because no trend exists in isolation. For all the forces presently gathered and pushing in one direction, other forces will come into play and provide natural causes for things to slow, shift course, or even cease.

Now, I am the first one to applaud when I hear people say, "Do not look at this issue by itself but consider the larger context."

The biggest hurdle to effective problem-solving lies in focusing too narrowly on the problem we want to solve. By omitting the context, we forget that actions create reactions and that intended consequences are far more difficult to achieve than unintended consequences are to arise.

Most of all we forget that good intentions are all but irrelevant to actual outcomes. You may have had a noble goal in mind, but if you have designed a system that creates incentives that drive different outcomes you are making things worse, not better.

Those who say we should not fear the slippery slope are usually trying to do one of two things: Undermine opposition to a position they would like to see promoted; or convince themselves that their own little indulgences are acceptable.

I'll leave for another day the discussion of this topic as applied to politics and law, interesting though it is. Right now, dear reader, I want to address your question of whether we must be so strict in denying ourselves pleasures and so rigorous in casting out negative emotions.

In other words, are we as people standing on slippery slopes, or do we have ourselves under control?

The highest state of mind, well-ordered and applying reason to each situation, will place the proper value on emotions and guide our judgment and actions.

There is no reason at all not to take pleasure in the things that are necessary for life. One of the goals of our practice is to learn to live a good life, and surely enjoying life is part of that practice.

Similarly, there is no doubt that emotions are part of what it means to be human. To suggest otherwise is to place unreasonable expectations on any person; we are not robots!

No indeed, but just as we are no mere machines, so have few of us achieved that state of having perfect wisdom in all things. We are tempted and we are easily led astray. What begins as a simple indulgence can grow into the greatest of monsters, devouring far in excess of reasoned appetite.

"Yes, that happens" you say, "but must it happen every time with every person? Can't I be trusted to safely manage the smallest of my daily affairs?"

Do you think I exaggerate the dangers once again, dear reader? Consider for a moment how many ways humans can become addicted. It is easy enough to see that most vices start as harmless pleasures no one could argue against in isolation.

- For one group, it is an occasional drink, a cigarette, or watching a few YouTube videos.

- Another group might be tempted by a spot of online shopping, giving in to a twinge of jealousy, or giving vent to a bout of anger.

- Yet another puts a few dollars on fantasy football, takes a flutter at the track, or wants to bet whether the ball will land on red this time.

For each of them, you can say "No harm done, and anyway, those are not my vices. I like a piece of chocolate, placing my bets not in Vegas but on stocks, and leasing a new car every so often. I can afford it and have handled myself without a problem so far. So really, what is the harm?"

Here is how that sounds to me, dear reader. No different than the person who says "I enjoy a glass of wine or a beer in the evening every now and then. What harm of it?"

And they would be right, in most cases, just as you are right. But even when this person's periodic drink becomes a daily drink, you will find them saying "I am in control. I can stop anytime I want. I drink because I want to, not because I have to." We all know where such self-talk has led too many people.

Can you tell me now which of your indulgences let grown into vices will be your undoing, or will you tell me that you are safe from all temptation?

If so, you must also explain to me how it is that the rolls of the Anonymous organizations number so many millions. I am speaking of Alcoholics Anonymous, Gambling Anonymous, Narcotics Anonymous, and the like.

A staggering number of both substances and behaviors generate addictive behavior. From alcohol, opioids, and nicotine, to gambling, gaming, and shopping. You will be thinking but perhaps hesitant to point out that working and exercise addiction afflicts some as well, and you would be right.

And this just scratches the surface.

You know I like to look beneath the surface, so let's do so together. Humans by their nature are designed to seek out pleasurable experiences — food, sex, relaxation — because these things help ensure we survive and procreate.

We can indulge pleasures more safely in times of scarcity because there is little danger then of their becoming vices. But when we can get what we want whenever we want, the danger of overindulgence becomes great.

Things that are good in moderation do not remain so in excess. But there is no reliable guide to tell us when enough becomes too much.

When it is within our power to self-dose, we should be most mistrustful of our ability to find the limit, because it is blurred by the pleasure of the moment. And once in the grip of an indulgence turned to vice, it is far harder to extricate ourselves from its clutches.

The safest course is to never start down the road of idle pleasures.

If I cannot convince you it is safer to forego pleasures altogether, at a minimum you must set yourself guidelines in advance.

For each pleasure you give yourself indulgence to pursue, do not leave your judgment to the time when you are under their influence. When you are of sound mind, decide your limit in all things, and decide to listen to your mind.

Try this method first in small things to see if you can trust yourself. In this way, you may build up habits of self-preservation that keep you from falling all the way down the slope.

Be well.

Chapter Twelve

On Stepping Off the Treadmill

Can we be trusted to treat equally the good luck and bad luck that comes our way, because neither perturbs the reasoning of our well-ordered minds?

About ten years after I started working in-house, I was gripped by a yawning uncertainty. It was that a great deal of the time my team and I were spending was wasted on tasks of little importance and no ultimate impact.

Nothing is more damaging to motivation than to think that you are running flat out but making no progress. In the legal team's case, it was churning through hundreds and thousands of contracts, negotiating the same damage limitation clauses over and over, to no real effect.

It is certainly good to be confident in what you are doing because self-doubt is destructive of peace of mind. But it is better to first be self-critical and to reflect on what you are doing.

Although this questioning is initially uncomfortable, careful thinking gives rise to well-founded conclusions about the wisdom of what you are doing. Bolstered by the assurance of the correctness of your actions, you can tackle any task and overcome any hurdle.

The hours we spend working are not just mindless toil, undermined by the worry that it is also meaningless toil. The work is noble, purposeful, and of our own choosing.

This line of thinking is what causes me to react strongly, dear reader, to some of the more superficial questions we are confronted with.

We have set our lives to the important task of learning to live well. Of what use are word games and trifles, pursuits that distract and amuse us but do not give us any useful weapons to take into combat? I want the answers not just to hard questions and paradoxes for the sake of solving a puzzle, but for learning what to do and what not to do, and why.

- We will be put in terrible situations of pain and suffering. Can we learn not to needlessly suffer, and add to our burdens with burdens made of our own thinking?

- We will be tempted with riches and wonders and given the chance to pursue the same shiny things all our fellows seek. Will we have acquired in our studies the wisdom to respond with as much care to the favors of Fortune as we do to the evils that surround us?

- Can we be trusted to treat equally the good luck and bad luck that comes our way, because neither perturbs the reasoning of our well-ordered minds?

I say we are at greater risk than the average person by virtue of our studies.

"Why is this" you ask? "Are we not better armed by virtue of our careful work? How can the study of philosophy be of use if it only puts me in greater danger?"

The risk of harm comes about precisely because we have learned to avoid many pitfalls. In particular, we have learned to apply the power of continuous improvement to many situations. This means we will experience steady progress and success in many areas of our lives.

- If you wish to pursue wealth, you will be more likely than most to attain it. For achieving material wealth is not intrinsically hard if you apply the right systems and mindset.

- Ironically, the person who learns to be happy with little is likely to be blessed with many small surpluses. Set prudently aside these small gains can easily grow into greater wealth.

Our greater danger does not go uncompensated, dear reader. For one, we are given weapons against the many accidents and insults that life will confront us with. Being prepared for adversity is a most worthy addition to our armory.

And for another, the dangers I am describing come from being showered with successes. Few of our fellow humans would view that as much of a problem.

And exactly therein lies the problem. We remain vigilant because we know that the saying "Success begets success" does not apply universally.

Indeed, I would say that for all but those who are disciplined of mind and in firm possession of their reason, the saying should be "Success begets dissatisfaction."

How many powerful people do you know who, having attained a certain position in an organization, say "I am content where I am. I need nothing more."? How many wealthy people eschew accumulating additional wealth?

And to make the case more generally and more damningly, perhaps the saying should be "Success begets disillusionment." How many people who, having attained a goal they sought most assiduously, value it the same upon reaching it as they did while seeking it?

Far more typical is to say, "It's not what I thought," or worse, to not think about it at all because they have their sights set on the next prize.

For all the celebrities, millionaires, and social media stars that the masses look upon in envy, how many do you think repose in complete satisfaction? Not the self-satisfaction of pampered ease, but genuine satisfaction at their lot in life. Not needing anything external, not wanting anything they do not have, not wishing to be relieved of a burden they are carrying.

You need only look to the carrying on when one of them suffers a public setback to know that their supposed happiness is only skin deep.

I tell you, do not seek to trade places with any person no matter how fortunate they seem to you. For all the visible signs of their success you may be gaining, you are also inheriting their fears, their worries, and their unchecked desires. And who knows if they have half your ability to control themselves.

Take uncomplainingly what comes your way, good or bad and, yes, work steadily towards improving your situation.

But do not make the attainment of external possessions your aim, or you are stepping on a treadmill that is constantly running. This treadmill will make a runner out of you to be sure, but the work serves only to exhaust and wear you down, not to make you more fit.

In contrast, the measured steps you take after careful reflection are much more likely to take you in a direction of your choosing and which will therefore be more to your liking.

Be well.

Chapter Thirteen

A Little Philosophy Goes a Long Way

In our journey to finding happiness, thinking for ourselves is the key to unlocking and then banishing all the bad habits that may have crept into our lives

The best reward for sharing Stoic lessons is the sincere hope they will help you and others live good lives.

Two letters in the series provide a summary and a powerful incentive to pursue the lessons Stoicism offers us, so I'll give you a brief recap here.

In *Thinking for Yourself*, we discuss why some types of nonconformism are good.

While we are rightly critical of unthinking rebellion, or fighting the system for the sake of it, that is not what Stoicism expects. Stoicism asks us to challenge blind conformity to the current system, i.e. doing what everyone else does without questioning the underlying values of what everyone is doing.

The Stoic's task is initially the harder one: Taming one's passions and desires is a greater challenge than looking to change others. But the reward in determining the proper value of things is greater. The Stoic finds happiness by putting it firmly under the control of their reason.

Thankfully, we don't need to address all our needs at once. We make the most progress by taking little steps consistently. Here's what *Thinking for Yourself* tells us:

"My advice is to consider every day as a session in the classroom of life. I feel confident in predicting that on most days you will be confronted with inconveniences, annoyances, or irritants. The varieties are endless.

By applying your reason, you will put each stimulus in its proper place, and you will not be put out of sorts against your will. Either there is some validity to the thing that irks you or there is none.

- In the first case, you have been given an opportunity to better yourself.

- In the latter case, you have been given an opportunity to practice placing the true value on things.

- Over time it becomes easier to distinguish false harms and, so identified, they lose their ability to hurt you. Or better said, you stop inflicting harm on yourself.

The same mechanisms that trick us into adopting bad habits allow us to give up those habits. If doing something regularly for a few weeks makes it habit-forming, then not doing it for a few weeks also becomes habit-forming.

This sounds so trivial as to be useless, but I tell you it transformed my life. My iron willpower is nothing more than the accumulation of little habits, including refraining from things that I have targeted for extinction.

I use my reason to determine the deeper value of things and to think for myself. The main thing I am trying to uncover is what makes me unhappy, so I can do it less. At the same time, I hypothesize about what will make me happy, so I can do it more."

Thus, in our journey to finding happiness, thinking for ourselves is the key to unlocking and then banishing all the bad habits that may have crept into our lives.

In *Reason of the Well-Ordered Mind*, we start with a reminder of why we study philosophy at all:

"We are conducting our studies for a purpose. If we have resolved not to be idle, and even in our free time to obtain some good for ourselves, then surely it is for the aim of living good lives.

Not in the future, or at some point when we will have attained a more perfect state. Right now, today and every day. We have but one life and what a shame it is to be living unhappy or, worse, to be living in a form of suspended animation."

And we conclude by describing how one attains the desired state of living a good life:

What can bring about this state? It is the same thing that disturbs it, namely our minds.

We mistakenly place the blame on external things, but this is an illusion that we can penetrate by careful contemplation. Thus, our highest purpose is to order our minds so that we can follow reason in all things."

I will end with one of my favorite gems of advice from Seneca himself. It is a lesson that bears repeating because so much of modern life pulls us in other directions and causes us to forget:

> Set yourself free for your own sake; gather and save your own time.
> While we are postponing, life speeds by.

Be well.

Pragmatic Wisdom Vol. 8

Stoic Lessons on Understanding the World

James Bellerjeau

A Fine Idea

Contents

1.	On Existence	435
2.	On Fundamental Rules	441
3.	On Studying Beneath the Surface	447
4.	On Studies of Substance	451
5.	On Relative Values	457
6.	On Philosophy's Dividends	461
7.	On Our Rotten Times	467
8.	On What Survives Us	471
9.	On the Independence of Reason	475
10.	On False Fronts	481
11.	On the AI Philosopher	485
12.	On Nature as a Guide	489
13.	On Instincts and Archetypes	493
	A Little Philosophy Goes a Long Way	497

Chapter One

On Existence

If wishes could create reality, would we live in paradise or hell? I fear we are on the path to finding out

How rich our language is, and how wonderful that it is constantly evolving! We inherit everything bequeathed to us by our ancestors and can dissipate none of the fortune.

Rather, each generation can only add to the riches of the English language. The Oxford English Dictionary defines over 630,000 lexical items as of the year 2020, with more than 860,000 separate senses, or meanings of words.

Words are added to the OED quarterly, at a rate of several thousand per year.

In recent years, the OED has been expanded to include new fears such as *astraphobia* (from ancient Greek, a fear of lightning or thunderstorms accompanied by lightning), *transphobe* (a person prejudiced against transgender people), and *fat-shaming* (the mocking, humiliating, or stigmatizing a person deemed to be fat or overweight).

Though from what the pandemic has already taught us, we have more to fear from COVID-19 than from being told the truth about our weight.

But because the last thing most people want to hear is the truth, we have invented new responses for our new fears including:

- *cancel culture* (publicly boycotting a person thought to be promoting culturally unacceptable ideas) and

- *virtue signaling* (acting in a way motivated primarily by a wish to garner recognition and approval).

- The *keyboard warrior* (one who posts abusive messages on the Internet, typically with a username that conceals his or her identity) is today alone mightier than armies,

- no mere *griefer* (a person who derives enjoyment from spoiling the game for others by playing in a way that is intentionally disruptive and aggravating) but able to breach the stoutest defenses,

- for all we are tempted to dismiss them as a *crybully* (a person who harasses or abuses others yet, following resistance or disagreement, claims to be a victim of ill-treatment).

All around us, some see signs of *structural racism* (discrimination or unequal treatment arising from systems, structures, or expectations that have become established within society), so please *take a knee* (to go down on one knee as a peaceful means of protesting against institutional racism) to start redressing your *unconscious bias* (favoritism towards or prejudice against people of a particular race, gender, or group that influence's one's actions or perceptions) and working off your *white guilt* (remorse or shame felt by a white person with respect to racial inequality and injustice).

I enjoy playing with words, dear reader, and I doubt you will see me tire of it.

Neither do I expect any surcease in the assault on our reason, of which these new words are but the vanguard. Those uttering these inanities are not playing with us, either.

Rather than acknowledging objective truths and adapting themselves accordingly, they wish to redefine reality to suit their subjective wishes.

If wishes could create reality, would we live in paradise or hell? I fear we are on the path to finding out.

In the face of these assaults on my senses, I sought refuge by reminding myself what humankind has learned of existence.

The physics of classical mechanics that busied scientists for the last several thousand years was based on things that humans could observe and directly relate to, including space, time, matter, and energy, and our scales were above the size of the atomic and our speeds below the speed of light.

The high-energy physics of elementary particles departs from this familiar ground and, for many, starts to depart as well from common sense. In quantum mechanics, nature is no longer continuous but rather phenomena are discrete at the atomic and subatomic levels, with waves and particles existing simultaneously in probabilistic states.

Although there have been many attempts to popularize and explain the state of physics today, perhaps the last, best attempt that a layperson could hope to understand was that undertaken by Richard Feynman in the early 1960s in lectures given to undergraduate students at the California Institute of Technology.

Since then, physicists appear only to have added detail and complexity at the cost of clarity and understanding.

Sixty years on, and we are no closer to a grand model unifying relativity and quantum mechanics. Feynman was surely warning us when he said in his very first lecture:

> Everything we know is only some kind of approximation, *because we know that we do not know all the laws yet*. Therefore, things must be learned only to be unlearned again or, more likely, to be corrected.

Though the Standard Model is by far our current best theory, having stood the rigors of many tests, we know it is incomplete.

Indeed, some humility is in order when we admit we do not know what almost all of the universe is made of (dark matter and dark energy indeed), or how to explain the difference in the imbalance between matter and anti-matter.

What we do know is this: unlike its Greek name, the atom can be cut into sub-atomic particles, which are divided into even smaller constituents known as fundamental particles. The Standard Model describes the known fundamental particles and the forces they interact with.

Here is what we think they are.

The twelve known elementary particles of matter or fermions consist of six quarks, designated as up, down, top, bottom, charm, and strange; and six leptons, which can be electrons, muons, and taus, or their neutrino equivalents.

The Standard Model describes how these particles interact via elementary forces called bosons, generating so-called strong, weak, and electromagnetic interactions.

At present, a great unsolved problem is that we cannot account for the force of gravity, and the graviton boson is but hypothetical. The particles of matter exchange gauge bosons, which count among their number gluons, photons, and either Z or W bosons.

The famed Higgs boson, whose existence was predicted decades ago by Peter Higgs, stands alone as a scalar boson.

- After a fifty-year wait the European laboratory for particle physics, CERN, announced in 2012 its detection of the Higgs boson.
- At least the Nobel Prize committee was quicker in granting him recognition for his contribution to our understanding of the nature of existence.

"All well and good," you say, "but what does any of this have to do with living a good life or the meaning of life?"

Not a thing, I suppose, at least not directly. But indirectly, let me suggest the following.

Just as we happily subject ourselves to the stress of vacation travel, on the theory that a change is as good as a rest, so it is with thinking deeply on philosophy. When you need a rest from the strictures of our teaching, take a rest, but make it a change rather than total relaxation.

I have learned the power of continuous improvement can be applied in all areas of life. Small steps taken regularly will let you travel great distances over time, and so it is with your reading.

Steer clear not only of the self-help aisle of the bookshop, dear reader, but you may safely detour around the whole of the "summer reading" section. Though the sun is shining and you are sitting comfortably on the beach, still you may be studying up on some topic that has caught your interest.

If mathematics or physics are not on your Kindle reading list, then still you may enrich yourself with other meaty fare: the development of social and political systems in the Enlightenment, or art and architecture through the ages, to name but a few.

Truly the menu is well stocked despite all you have cut from the dessert section! Besides slowly but steadily adding to your wisdom, when you are thus challenged in your leisure, all the more willingly do you return to the embrace of philosophy when your pause has refreshed you.

We must be deliberate in our actions, whether we are in motion or at rest because this helps us to be consequent in our thoughts.

We humans are no elementary particles, and though our existence is probabilistically uncertain, it is certainly limited. To live long, you must first recognize that you are only living as long as you are living well.

Be well.

Chapter Two

On Fundamental Rules

Any person alive today may yield up answers to the questions that have propelled humankind's search for meaning and for reason

Did I leave you from my last letter with the impression that I am both master builder and in control of my emotions at all times?

You may assume I am prone to exaggeration, dear reader, not so different from the mass media you hear me lament, though my reasons are less vile. Unlike the news, I am not trying to drum up your anger so much as elicit your pity.

Pity me, though, not for failing to live up to my ideals at all times, but for feeling the need to hide that I am flawed. If I should not pretend to be perfect, I would not be so ashamed to miss the mark, thus failing doubly in my thinking.

To atone for my weakness, I will revisit another branch of thinking I have discussed with you before, fundamental physics.

The ancients were the masters of the human condition, and we have yet to match or exceed their analyses of virtue and values, emotion and reason, motivation and action.

But to modern eyes, their understanding of physics missed the mark. Or put differently, we have moved on from their thinking to develop fresh understandings of the workings of our universe.

To use my recent analogy, if the ancients found themselves building a guard's hut by the front gate, successive generations have expanded it to a fortified watchtower, only to abandon these defensive positions altogether for a handsome, full building on the grounds of the estate.

Whether today's knowledge is but a well-appointed guest house, or we have moved into a wing of the grand house itself, we do not know.

For all our progress, dear reader, I think humility is in order.

Despite all that we think we've figured out, we cannot answer fundamental questions about this structure we inhabit. Though to be fair to Seneca, when he asked Lucilius to be the judge of disputed questions, he asked him only to

> state who seems to you to say what is truest, and not who says what is absolutely true. For to do that is as far beyond our ken as truth itself.

Let's review how we've come to know what we presently think is truest, though it may not be the truth yet.

Just as our knowledge of the human condition has been built by accretion through the workings of generations of philosophers adding to the existing corpus, so has the advancement of science proceeded.

How wonderful that any can contribute! The physicist Richard Feynman described the supreme democracy of science in the first of his undergraduate lectures in physics at Caltech:

> We are not concerned with where a new idea comes from — the sole test of its validity is experiment.

What fundamental rules have we learned, first from intuition and hypothesis, and subsequently proven by experiment?

One of the most interesting things we've learned is that we cannot know at the same time both the definite location and the definite momentum of a particle.

This is called the Heisenberg uncertainty principle, and I find it fitting to start with a statement of fundamental uncertainty:

an inherent property of the quantum systems that make up our reality is that not everything can be determined with precision. For certain fundamental things, we must satisfy ourselves with probabilities.

We think it quite probable the following is a fundamental law: That mass-energy is conserved, which is to say although that mass can be transformed into energy and energy into mass, the quantity of both does not change; and energy [E] and mass [m] are related to one another via the speed of light [c] as captured in the famous formula $E = mc^2$.

Besides this mass-energy equivalence formula, Einstein also gave us

- special relativity (the laws of physics do not change if there is no acceleration between observers; and the speed of light is the same for all observers) and

- general relativity, improving upon Newton's laws of motion themselves to describe gravity as a geometric property of space and time, the curvature of which is related to the energy and momentum of matter and radiation.

Quantum mechanics has undertaken the description of properties of nature at the atomic and subatomic scale. It is from quantum mechanics that we are forced to accept uncertainty as a definite element of nature.

Objects have characteristics of both waves and particles and can be either or both depending on when and how we observe them. From probability amplitudes, we calculate probability density functions to predict where, for example, an electron will be found in an experiment.

Quantum mechanics describes the first three of what we believe are the four fundamental forces or interactions, namely the weak nuclear, strong nuclear, electromagnetic, and gravitation.

For gravitation, we still rely on Einstein's general relativity. Physicists would dearly love to extend quantum mechanics to explain gravitation and so create a "theory of everything," but quantum gravity has eluded our best efforts.

The physicist who finds a way to not just hypothesize but actually detect the as-yet hypothetical graviton particle will have performed weighty work indeed.

String theorists have proposed frameworks that are intellectually appealing because they give rise to the graviton, but they come at the cost of introducing additional dimensions to the four we currently know, for example, M-theory with its eleven-dimensional model.

The theories have so far yielded insights but no testable hypotheses. Can string theory be considered science at all, then, at least in the way that Feynman describes? Do we need better methods of experimentation, or have we reached the limits of science to explain nature?

I recall from my earlier letter on such topics what reaction I should hear from you now:

"Why are you spending your time on these questions? If they cannot be answered by today's methods, or perhaps ever, what point is there is pondering them? Surely your hours are put to better use in taming your passions and following the lessons that we know are valid."

If one purpose of the study of philosophy is a well-ordered mind, dear reader, then I accept no limits on the ability of my mind to take the lessons of other disciplines.

Indeed, to know that, though countless problems have been solved, countless still remain should give humankind purpose: we can make progress, we have made progress, and there is progress to be made.

Did nothing exist before a random fluctuation in quantum gravity created the universe from an infinitely hot and dense Big Bang singularity (the so-called no boundary proposal), or was there some First Cause in the form of God that set everything in motion as the Stoics believed?

We think everything we can observe and test today can be explained back to the first 10^{-11} seconds from the creation of the universe.

We speculate on what must have happened in the vanishingly small amount of time *before* this back to zero.

Though we change our scale from the incredibly vast and long to the microscopically tiny and short, the significance of the questions increases.

Any person alive today may yield up answers to the questions that have propelled humankind's search for meaning and for reason.

Although Heisenberg tells us in some realms we must be satisfied with uncertainty, I am sure that humans will never stop searching for meaning.

Is the scientific pursuit so different than our philosophical one? For centuries they were united.

Even though we cannot account yet for every fraction of every second for all time, I say training yourself in fundamental rules from whatever branches of human endeavor you find them is time well spent.

Be well.

Chapter Three

On Studying Beneath the Surface

Why is it so hard to understand what we want, what will make us happy, and how to take the actions that will bring us there?

I have been eagerly anticipating news of your trip to Iceland so that I can hear what you have learned about that island's unique geography.

I am particularly interested to know how your trip to Fagradalsfjall on the Reykjanes peninsula has progressed, and what you've been able to discover about the volcanic eruption ongoing there. This slow-moving and relatively quiet eruption is kind to the observer, allowing an unusually close approach.

How different from the eruptions a decade ago of Eyjafjallajökull, which shot an ash cloud directly into the jet stream resulting in the closure of the entire European airspace and the greatest disruption to air travel in generations.

Did you know that we know less about what the core of our own planet consists of than we do the composition of distant galaxies? We train our eyes on the heavens so that we may learn the mysteries of the universe, all the while standing on a mystery only incompletely grasped.

We hypothesize a mostly solid inner core made of an iron-nickel alloy, though we believe there must be other elements in unknown quantities. The inner core is no cold stone but burns with a temperature the same as the surface of the sun.

A liquid outer core surrounds this fiery inner ball, hiding it partly from our probing. Cooling iron at the edge of the core flows in convection currents in the outer core, creating the magnetic field. A great mantle then ensues, topped by a thin crust on which we carry out our lives.

Volcanic activity can be caused by two tectonic plates diverging from one another, allowing hot mantle rock to ooze up under the thinned crust stretched behind the plates; or by two plates colliding, with an oceanic plate typically being pushed under a continental plate, creating magma at the wedge.

Some geologists think that plumes sometimes rise from the core-mantle boundary, melting as they rise and creating volcanoes when plates drift across the plume. For all their fiery drama, most volcanoes happen out of human sight deep under the oceans. Because tiny Iceland perches over a rift in continental plates it has a wealth of volcanoes on display for curious eyes.

The study of philosophy for me is analogous to the study of the geology of the earth. The great volume of what makes us and drives us is hidden, and we spend our lives on the crust.

The surface matter of our lives that all can see is but the tail end of hot, deep processes playing out unbidden and mysterious. Even when we probe within, our senses do not penetrate far and we are left to hypothesize about causes, motivation, and meaning.

Psychologists posit fundamental archetypes found in our collective unconscious, unknown but powerfully shared by all, like the intense hot core at the center of the earth. And just like our knowledge of the earth is meager compared to what we know of the universe, what we understand of our motivations is a fraction of what we can observe of the consequences of our actions.

"What use is this meandering," you ask, "and why should we bother with it?" I will tell you, dear reader, and let me go with the flow of my analogy a bit longer for this purpose.

Just as we find it fascinating to study the flow of magma and explosive volcanic eruptions because they seem to reflect fundamental forces and are elementarily dangerous, so is the study of human motivation and actions of vital interest.

Why is it so hard to understand what we want, what will make us happy, and how to take the actions that will bring us there?

ON STUDYING BENEATH THE SURFACE

We continue a long tradition of explorers when we take up these questions. It is an honorable inquiry and pursuit. You need not fear that everything valuable about human behavior has been learned, or that the lessons are permanent.

Just like a cloud of volcanic ash can cover the landscape for thousands of miles hiding everything under a choking gray, the passage of time causes people to forget what their forebears have discovered and obfuscates basic truths.

We geologists/archaeologists of the mind are sifting the remains of great thinkers, each discovery giving us a chance to both relearn what was once known and to make our own contribution to the sum total of human wisdom.

We too are likely to suffer the fate of all people, which is not only to die but to be forgotten. The great majority are not widely known during their lifetimes, and what of it?

Is it not preferable to be anonymous during your lifetime though you do weighty things, than it is to have achieved temporary renown that fades almost as quickly as our tired and frail bodies? The former has lost nothing, while the latter supposedly progressed only to have the greater setback befall them.

I say our gaze is best directed to *future generations*, dear reader, and it is to them that we shall speak.

The ones who have gone before us are beyond aid. Those who currently share the roads with us are almost as hard to reach because they have a thousand distractions for every core of truth we unearth to shed light on.

Though our contemporaries are most welcome to sample what we have on offer, they have few reliable tools to separate the dishonest potions from the cure. The surest tool is time.

Just like the once choking volcanic ash later turns into a blessing upon nothing more than the passage of time, enriching the soil it blankets with vital nutrients, so too time's great sweep performs the function of separating the silly from the serious, the helpful from the hurtful.

Our good ideas will do the greatest good when they have stood the test of time and proven their worth after careful, considered reflection. We ourselves sift the wisdom of the ancients, which now stands out like volcanic basalt exposed after centuries of erosion have washed all else away.

For us to stand the test of time and have the greatest impact, we must thus spend our time within, applying the lessons of the ancients to our thinking, creating the conditions for well-ordered minds.

Thus honed, reason becomes the tool for humankind to faithfully identify and avoid folly and rather set its sights on building lives of substance.

Be well.

Chapter Four

On Studies of Substance

Rather than wishing you luck and fine things I will wish that you experience hardship, or at least a certain burden

I am not worried about your progress, dear reader, nor your fate. You may suffer bad fortune, illness, or injury because none of us is free from such risks while we are living, but I am confident you will not suffer harm from yourself.

Continue on as you have begun, with an eye towards living modestly and mindfully, and you will live well.

Rather than wishing you luck and fine things I will wish that you experience hardship, or at least a certain burden. This is through no ill will on my part. We become weak and soft in our pampered luxury, whereas privation teaches us to appreciate both what we already have and what is essential.

Your certain burden can come in many forms: It may take the shape of paid work, it may find expression in volunteering; your efforts may be spent on public works, or you may invest in private pursuits.

The end that many seek is an end to their toil, to put their burden down, and this can indeed be a worthy pursuit *provided* it opens the door to other pursuits.

Though you may fight your way free of all external entanglements and purchase your freedom, do not think that idleness is any kind of lasting reward in itself. Indeed, the longer you seek to enjoy idleness, the less you stand to gain from it.

The freer your hands are from manual labor, the more your mind is at risk from laboring under apprehensions and worries. You can be far removed from the dank salt mines where others toil but still feel as sharply the lash of your own expectations and fears.

Thus, I tell you do not put down all burdens when your time is more completely yours to direct. Turn once more to your studies to ensure that you do not lose your way and continue to progress.

Is it the study of philosophy that is required? Helpful, always helpful, but I would not say required, at least in the case of one like yourself whose lessons have been well learned and are never far from memory. By all means, refresh your recollection, and take pleasure in strolling even the best-known and well-loved by-ways of your favorite teachers.

But if you find your tastes turning to other things, let your mind roam freely and wander.

In your wandering, you will likely find that you do not know every path as well as you remembered. Though you stray in your contemplations, you will thus remain on the path to wisdom.

For this to happen you cannot be a passive tourist, watching new landscapes unfold from a safe distance and behind glass. Rather take your current learnings and see how they may be actively applied in new settings: Psychology, politics, physics, and more.

Will you make a connection between two fields that no one has managed to bridge before? Will you develop a wholly new line of thinking? Even if you provide merely a fresh perspective in an area previously believed to be fully understood, you will have acted nobly and invested the energy of your thoughts well.

And I ask you, at this moment is there any field as falsely believed to have been mapped as that of human motivation? We think we are entitled to talk about what drives others when we have the slightest idea of what drives ourselves.

Maslow's hierarchy of needs can be set out in a neat pyramid, with basic needs anchoring the bottom, psychological needs forming the middle, and self-fulfillment needs at the tip. Until the basic needs of food and water, safety, and shelter are satisfied, the theory goes, a person cannot work their way upwards to achieve a higher purpose.

In fairness, this is little different than what the Stoics and many other philosophical schools busied themselves with: What is the relative value of various human pursuits, and which should we pursue and why.

There have been as many interpretations of human motivation as there have been people who have pondered their own existence. Hundreds of serious schools of thought, some easily dismissed in hindsight, but others with enduring elements of the truth.

I do not doubt that generations to come will offer up additional valuable insights. No, we need not fear that the study of human motivation will be wasted time, for no matter whether you establish a new branch of wisdom, you will surely help yourself.

Or take the study of human intelligence and how inconsistently and even apprehensively modern theorists approach it.

Before they realized how their measurements would be misinterpreted and misused, psychologists developed quite reliable methods of measuring general human intelligence, or IQ (intelligence quotient). We are able to measure it more accurately than any other psychometric measure.

Not only can we measure it well, but psychologists have found that intelligence is the single most important determinant of life success. At least it is predictive in terms of educational and economic success, which we know is not everything, but it is also not nothing.

Psychologists also believe that intelligence is largely genetic and that although it can be influenced by environmental factors, the influence comes mainly in ways that either allow genes to express themselves or hinder the full development of potential intelligence.

Despite the weight of significant evidence, it is considered a cardinal sin in today's world to state that intelligence drives important life outcomes while also pointing out that people's individual intelligence differs.

Why is this so? We accept that people have physical differences that are apparent to the eye: the muscular athlete, the handsome actor, the model with symmetric features. Perhaps these differences are easier for us to swallow because we can tell ourselves that it is the steroids and supplements or the plastic surgeon's knife that have contributed to their enhanced natures.

Physical differences it seems are much easier to accept than the idea that our fates have been determined by a genetics lottery at birth, and that these gifts of fate are distributed unevenly.

Though we can no longer say it aloud, we can nonetheless silently observe that people also differ in their intelligence and temperament. To see something so important and yet restrict discussion because of the possibility of offending! Truly people can be willfully ignorant no matter what their intelligence.

I had despaired of advances in this field, dear reader, but I think there is a parallel path down which we might once again see progress. It concerns what is called artificial general intelligence, or AGI.

If the study of human differences is taboo let us heat up our brains in trying to make cold circuits and wires think. In trying to create intelligence in computer form, we may yet learn something about how humans think, though this is not the aim of the endeavor.

So become an indirect scientist, divining insights about human capabilities and motivation from our successes and, more likely, the failures of artificial intelligence research.

The most attractive aspect of working in this field is that we are perpetually on the cusp of breakthroughs. It is a magical feat that no matter how many decades we labor we are never further than a decade away from achieving AGI.

The last seventy years have at least humbled us to the point where we appreciate the magnitude of the problem. The human brain is no simple box of cells that we can replicate at will. By narrowing our ambition and our scope, we have unblocked a half-century's stall and seen rapid progress in artificial neural networks, pattern recognition, and machine learning.

And even if you want to leave the hard science to others, there is still a role to play for the philosopher with time on their hands. We have spent centuries experimenting to discover which models of societal governance best balance human weaknesses with human potential to let the most citizens thrive.

In AGI research the large majority of scientists are interested foremost in the question of *how*, as in how can we do it? A few have considered the question of *why*, and fewer still the question of *whether* we should do this.

We need but recall the mad dash to split the atom, with everything that was subsequently unleashed, to know that the smartest among us can also be the most reckless.

The long-term survival of humanity needs much more attention invested in the question of *control* of AGI.

Religions all assume an omnipotent creator, who is all-knowing and all-seeing, and has the power to direct all affairs. Consider though that if humankind had a creator, could it not be that our author was both unimaginably more powerful than us but similarly reckless? That in unleashing humankind on the world, they lost control and no longer have any say in determining our fate?

I do not mean to make humans think of themselves as gods if and when we bring AGI into being. My aim is more that we consider what sort of creators we would be if we had no means of directing the course of our new creation.

Chances are good that we will not have the luxury of centuries to experiment with how to control AGI. This genie being unloosed will not go willingly back into any bottle.

Thus, this would be a study worthy of serious pursuit by serious minds. Perhaps it will be you?

Be well.

Chapter Five

On Relative Values

I can't help but think how much the Stoics would have benefitted from exploring the beauty of set theory

No, dear reader, do not envy me for bidding farewell to my alarm clock. I can give you at least four reasons why not.

In the first place, envy is a known disturbance of the mind, an encroachment on your otherwise well-ordered reason. What another has is wholly irrelevant to what *you* have, just as your possessions, both material and immaterial, are irrelevant to the happiness of others.

It is the obsessive focus on the differences between people that arouses their passions. Once aroused, few of these passions are then put to the betterment of humankind.

We can level the field far more easily by tearing down those who excel than by raising up the many who cluster at the center of the bell curve, to say nothing of the long tail to the left.

If only we could bring ourselves instead to note all the ways in which we have already far exceeded others, and upon so noticing bend down a helping hand to pull them up. But instead, despite the hordes we have passed, we cast our envying gaze at the ones who remain ahead of us.

The additional reasons why you need not envy me can be enumerated as follows.

- My bladder and my prostate have conspired to create a more effective biological alarm than my digital clock ever mustered. And this all too human siren rouses me not just once a night like my prior electronic minder, but two, three, even four times.

- Then there is the fact that I seem to *need* less sleep than before. Though my labors are extensive, and I slip under my covers with an exhausted sigh, still my body sometimes pops awake before my mind thinks it suitable.

- And my mind itself presents the final reason for your pity and not envy: I *want* less sleep than I need. Though the measure of a life is whether it is well-lived and not whether it is long, I long to experience as much of my remaining life as possible. Thus, I have given up my alarm just when I find I need it least.

Sometimes when I am lying awake, I will nonetheless remain in my bed, for my body also knows when it is too early to rise even though my mind is already at work. A turn of phrase may spontaneously arise from which a train of thought starts chugging along.

These thoughts used to drive me unwillingly from my sheets to my desk to capture them in words, for fear that they would either keep me from sleep or that I would lose them altogether. My mantra of late has been to simply say, "Let it go. It's OK, let it go."

I seem to have no lack of thoughts or words these days. So, if the thought is worthy, I expect I will be reinspired soon enough. And if not, there has been nothing lost by letting these ephemeral night visitors float away.

Often my wandering thoughts turn to the Stoics, and how far we can follow their teachings before stumbling or, worse, running up against a brick wall. The simplicity and firmness of approach has its own appeal, but there is also danger in dogmatism.

Is there but a single virtue to be found in reason, and must all external things be considered of secondary value? Is it possible for the mind to be master of all circumstances, no matter what comes? And what does that make a person, and is it enough?

Given the importance the Stoics placed on the development of reason, and their use of deductive reasoning and logic, I can appreciate why they sometimes let their thoughts carry them to extremes.

Competing schools sought to tie each other in syllogistic knots, by taking an accepted proposition and extending it further and further until they produced a paradox. These paradoxes were then held out as proof that the whole proposition or value statement was untrue, or at least severely undermined.

On the one hand, the existence of a paradox presents us with a seeming problem. If the logic we have followed is sound, that must mean a defect in one or more of the propositions we began with. At the same time, paradoxes represent opportunities to reflect more deeply on what we think we understand and why, and possibly to advance the frontier of human understanding beyond where it currently lies.

For many serious students though, to say nothing of generations of casual readers, the insistence on following logic from set propositions to their inevitable conclusions sometimes led the Stoics to defend extreme positions that defied common sense:

- A single day lived according to the ultimate good of a reasoned mind was exactly equal to and as valuable as a hundred years in the same condition.

- Dying young upon the torturer's rack after betrayal and unjust accusations was no more to be feared than slipping away peacefully in old age.

It is the state of mind that matters: The wise man fears nothing that is inevitable and according to nature.

Short of seeking to conquer death, or at least the fear of death, the Stoics had much advice about avoiding vice, and all the things external to people that aroused their passions and cost them their self-possession.

The Stoic proposition is that living according to reason is the highest and only virtue. Further, that virtue is sufficient for a happy life. The instant you feel you are lacking something external you have disturbed your reason for something ultimately without value because the only thing of value is your well-ordered mind.

It does not matter what happens to you or what circumstances you find yourself in, it matters how you react to your circumstances. The virtuous person cannot be harmed by being poor, or ill, or any of the things that normally so trouble us.

I can't help but think how much the Stoics would have benefitted from exploring the beauty of set theory. I think they would have taken to it naturally, and found ways to extend even our modern understandings.

At a minimum, a Venn diagram illustrating the logical relationship between sets might have helped them work out from underneath at least a few of the seeming paradoxes that plagued them.

For example, though mathematical logic was put to use by philosophers hundreds of years before the earliest Stoics, it is only since the late 1800s that we have updated our understanding of infinity, using set theory to prove that although there is an infinity of infinities, some infinities are larger than others.

Set theory has had its own paradoxes to contend with, but our field of correct application is very broad though we limit ourselves to the von Neumann universe of pure sets.

Or take Bayesian probability, which introduces reasonable expectation to the concept of probability, instead of mere likelihood and frequency. The student of Bayesian statistics updates probabilities upon obtaining new data, computing conditional probability and distributions of probability.

Better answers are arrived at by taking prior knowledge but also personal beliefs into account. From a philosophical perspective, should we not welcome making room for human emotions and not requiring people to act like mere reasoning machines?

Armed with such theories and logical weapons, would modern Stoics find that no emotion or disturbance to reason could be tolerated? Would their belief in cardinal virtues and how they best expressed themselves have been shaken or extended by allowing relativity into their calculations?

I do not know the answer to these questions, dear reader, though these thoughts are much on my mind. Will you help me by sharing your perspective?

Wisdom is neither the possession of one people or one time nor a fixed thing. It is the individual pursuit by each of us who takes up the task of casting what light we can, building upon all who have gone before us.

Be well.

Chapter Six

On Philosophy's Dividends

Philosophy's domain is in guiding decisions about what we do with what we have, and how we respond to the circumstances we face

If there was a time when people lived in abundance and without any cares, perhaps it was when the first humans cavorted in the Garden of Eden.

From the time we ate of the Tree of Knowledge people have possessed reason. Since then, we were cast out of our period of easy plenty and have had to make our way in the world in lives of toil and struggle.

This has given many cause to ask the question "Is there any way for us to regain our carefree lives of abundance?"

The question I want to address today is whether and to what extent philosophy has contributed to the betterment of humankind in our wanderings through hard times.

If we have seen our lot improve over time, how much of it has come from philosophy and how much from other sources, including humankind itself through the application of science?

You could argue that intelligence is humankind's greatest gift, for all that it led to our losing paradise. Like all great things, intelligence is not one-dimensional. Its application can also be our greatest curse.

We have conquered the planet and have dominion over everything on it. But we have not conquered our desires. Further, by virtue of our nature to seek dominance over all things, we cannot avoid seeing hierarchy in everything.

Thus, having overcome the natural world our eyes turn to our fellow citizens. The result is that we are subject to a wealth of harmful emotions, such as greed, fear, jealousy, and anger.

Having "more," as in more wealth, beauty, possessions, or power, affords us greater stature in the hierarchy. This inclines us to always seek more. But no matter how much we have, we cannot make ourselves happy.

This is because in every hierarchy there are better off and worse off. Thus, everyone who sees someone above them is inclined to feel worse off than they otherwise might if they understood that peace of mind is the greatest possession of all.

In consequence, rather than being closer to regaining our carefree lives, the more abundance we acquire the farther we find ourselves from happiness and satisfaction. The pursuit of *more* thoroughly blinds most of us to seeing and understanding that to live a happy life one only needs that which is *enough*.

The aim of philosophy is to ensure we make proper use of our greatest gift, which is reasoning intelligently.

Humans alone are not forced to live as mere animals, subject to ungoverned emotions and physical urges. We can use reason not with the purpose of reigning in and extinguishing our ambitions, but to give them purposeful direction.

We should accept what we are given by nature and work to improve upon it. We should strive to theorize, invent, and explain but let it be in directions of our choosing after measured reason. If we seek to excel, to create, and to explore, let us do it knowingly, not blindly, and certainly not just because we can.

Do you honor someone who says they climbed a mountain just because it is there? That is as much of a reason as Cain saying he killed Abel because he was there. "I could, so I did" is not reasoned thinking.

Of course, there is a motive behind the climber and the killer, though they may not be able to articulate it aloud. Is it the place of philosophy to curb these impulses, to tame all humankind's passions? Just as intelligence is both a blessing and a curse, let us not consign reckless ambition to being entirely useless.

Who else but the ambitious would undertake dangerous missions that occasionally advance the human race by great leaps and bounds? Who else but the reckless would leap to the defense of their fellow persons at great cost to their own safety?

We should revel in our prowess as material creatures, not because physical prowess is virtuous in and of itself, but because it is part of our nature that allows us to overcome all obstacles.

So, intelligence and ambition are both fundamental parts of human nature. Philosophy can take no credit for our natures and everything that springs from them.

Philosophy's domain is in guiding decisions about what we do with what we have, and how we respond to the circumstances we face. It takes work to become wise because we need to learn to trust neither the surface appearance of things nor the opinions of the majority on most things.

All the greatest human accomplishments were achieved by intelligent people but not necessarily wise people.

The participants in the Manhattan Project understood in theory how to split the atom and they found a way to put their theories into practice. How often does humankind need to repeat the lesson that knowledge once gained is scarcely to be contained?

So, we suffered yet another fall from grace, again at our own hands. The fruit of that discovery has meant humankind living in fear not just of being yet further from a carefree life, but of life's very existence being extinguished from the earth.

I have written separately about the unchecked enthusiasm among artificial intelligence researchers. I see in them the similar bravado of the mountain climber facing a peak not yet summited. We will do it because it can be done!

Do you doubt for a moment that the joy researchers feel upon the first human-created intelligence emerging will be outdone many times over with bitter remorse at what we once again unleashed unwittingly on ourselves and the world?

Philosophy's dividends are this, dear reader: To first identify the right questions for humankind to be asking, and then to apply the very same reasoning the scientist uses in answering them.

- These questions include "What is of true value and how can we go about achieving it?"

- Not the question of what are all the things we *can* do, but "*Why* should we do what we do?"

- We do not question whether we can live in a world that is both easy and fair. It is clear we cannot remake the world fully to our liking. Rather we ask and answer the question "How can I conduct myself in every circumstance including, and even especially, hard and unfair circumstances?"

We do not lack clever scientists in the world. Intelligence has been fruitful and multiplied along with humanity and our ambition knows no bounds.

The world is overflowing with theories, inventions, and ideas. How many of them have made life better? I don't mean convenient, easier, or more productive. How many of our modern wonders have made us *happier*?

No, I tell you we do not need more intelligent scientists, we need more wise scientists. We need the philosopher-scientist to stop and think before acting.

"But" the scientific community will say, "if we do not pursue this line of inquiry, someone else will." They will continue, "You cannot hold back progress by refusing to study and to learn."

It is not all progress that we should be seeking to forestall, but progress in harmful directions.

We know there is pain and danger and risk in the world. Must we truly open every door that is closed and walk down every path that is shaded to relearn again and again that not every development is beneficial?

Philosophy would teach us that the ultimate power we can wield is not over nature but over ourselves.

Do you know what we will find when we set aside our lust for power, our greed for possessions, and our endless jealousy? The realization that we never left the

Garden of Eden and that we can return to it at any time if we simply open our eyes to see it.

Be well.

Chapter Seven

On Our Rotten Times

Just as advances and accomplishments belong to an age in history, so too do the embarrassments that the next generation takes but a few decades to clearly perceive

Have you noticed that each generation inevitably becomes convinced of two things, dear reader?

- First, they have reached the pinnacle of wisdom with current science and civilization; that their way of life and pursuits are correct and good and the one true path.

- And second, they simultaneously laugh at how their ancestors were so gullible and dangerously ignorant in so many things; while they lament that their children are both gullible and dangerously ignorant in so many things.

"Contemptible idiots behind us, and superficial fools ahead of us! Howsoever will the world survive when we are gone?"

It is not the times that give rise to such convictions. The folly is peculiar to humankind itself and so passes unbidden and unseen from generation to generation.

It is true that each generation finds a way to express its failings uniquely. Just as advances and accomplishments belong to an age in history, so too do the embarrassments that the next generation takes but a few decades to clearly perceive.

Humans are powerful in so many things but applying perspective to our *own* imperfections is not one of our inherent talents, nor do we seem to have any desire to develop it.

Is our own generation really the first to be free from error? Have we become enlightened as a whole, such that our every utterance deserves to be inscribed in the skies for all to wonder at?

Let us seek to be impartial judges and consider the evidence.

- We live in times where serious people seriously expound the idea that you can tell something important about the inside of a person by looking only at the outside of that person.

- That all of society can be explained by power, and that there is no objective reality behind power structures, only self-serving and self-perpetuating identity groups.

Consider the supposed attributes of "whiteness," which we are told have been invented and used to oppress non-white people.

- These include that whites value self-reliance, rational linear thinking, and the idea that hard work is the key to success.

- That it makes sense to plan for the future, delay gratification, and make progress.

- That we should have an action orientation and seek to master our circumstances.

Before you find yourself nodding along in agreement with the items on the list, recall that they are held out as symbols of oppression, not freedom.

Social justice movements hold out as heroes the victims of police brutality, as if somehow resisting arrest is the better example of virtuous conduct. Among the most exalted are the ones who have been martyred, and it does not seem to matter what their prior record may have been.

Mobs vandalize and burn city streets and we call it justice. Crowds loot stores and we call it redistribution of wealth. City councils tell you they expect to see *less* crime when they defund the police and stop prosecuting offenders.

For our own parts, we fill our bellies with junk food and we fill our heads with junk science. We buy junk products on credit and amuse ourselves with junk entertainment to tickle our ever-shortening attention spans.

We go into debt to pay for educations that fill our children's heads with dangerous nonsense. We borrow money to buy cars and houses that we don't need and can't afford.

All this brings us more sadness than satisfaction in both the pursuit and the possession.

On the national level, our politicians have elevated empty talk to a new art form. With one side of their mouths, they stoke our most base emotions and outrage.

So aroused, with our eyes burning red and our ears ringing, we do not notice when they utter out of the other side things like, "There are no limits on what we can spend and there is no consequence to running our deficit higher and higher."

As if! This is one time when future generations will look back not in amusement but in horror at the delusions we felt comfortable with, for we are burdening them with both our sins of omission as well as those we commit.

No, we would know on a moment's quiet reflection that ours is not the golden age, dear reader. At least, no more than any other age.

Despite our advancements in science, technology, health care, productivity, and more, we have spent little time in the laboratory of the human soul. For all our progress in external things, we have forgotten that the natural course of our minds inclines downward.

Stability in human societies is only ever temporary. We fail and we have never not failed.

The reason is that we have never removed our weaknesses and our vices from the equation. We have too few examples of virtuous behavior, and pay too little attention to the examples we have, for them to tip the scales in our favor.

In their hearts, people are not so easy to fool. We know when we are consuming garbage, though none admits it aloud.

We suffer in our hearts and our thoughts when we proclaim satisfaction with superficial things. These internal maladies do not remain suppressed but are expressed through ill health, depression, and turmoil in society.

Thus, we have sown the conditions for our downfall: Those who are told they are well-off are nonetheless unfulfilled and so restless and eager for change; while those who are told they are suffering are angry and mobilized to tear down the systems that have failed them.

Who will fight to preserve the good that humankind has achieved in its centuries of struggle? Who will ensure that the good humankind is capable of is not extinguished in the fire along with everything else?

In our rotten times, you cannot stand on the sidelines. You are either pouring water on the flames or you are fanning them. By your silence you let the rot spread.

By your words, do you seek to build and fortify or only tear down?

The early few may sacrifice themselves in standing up against madness, true. But if none stand, all will fall. And perhaps we will find that there are others who will stand with us to slow the fall.

Be well.

Chapter Eight

On What Survives Us

Serving as an example is more powerful than lingering in memory. What will people say about your conduct when you're gone?

In an earlier exchange, I gave you the argument for making plans for the future and doing your best to execute your plans.

You have reminded me of what I usually remind you, namely that we can take nothing with us past our own deaths. This leads naturally to the next question you have posed, "Does anything of our works survive after we are gone?"

If you grant me leave to first broaden your question somewhat, dear reader, I will give you my answer. The broader topic I wish to address is whether *anything* survives us, and if so what.

I have said that when we pass on our possessions remain. This was in the context of acknowledging that we cannot take material things with us into the immaterial zone beyond life.

So, it seems that while we do not survive our possessions, they survive us. We know not what will be made of them, though we may will them to others via our testamentary disposition.

Do we know if our wishes will be honored? We do not. You know I will continue on to say it does not matter, at least as far as the deceased is concerned.

Some of our friends and acquaintances can be expected to survive us, and children too if we have brought them into the world. They will each carry memories of us with them for a time.

We act according to reason for the sake of acting properly, and not to burnish our reputation. But if we have acted properly in our lives, it is appropriate for people who knew us well to hold positive memories of us after we have passed on.

Our conduct can also serve as an example to all those we encountered during our lifetimes. Pray let it be an example of good conduct rather than an example of what to avoid!

Serving as an example is more powerful than lingering in memory. The memory serves to remind someone of what *we* once did, whereas your example is an exhortation for what *they* are to do now.

If we are to be remembered, I would rather it was for conduct serving as a good example than mere memories of fine times and glad doings.

"What of our work" you ask, "and the things we have laid down in writing? Surely this is a more permanent record that will survive our demise."

I am not so sure, dear reader. I have seen many people come and go in the work setting. Some are tempted away by greener grass elsewhere, others are lured into early retirement.

Though the colleagues are soon gone their files remain stubbornly behind. Lawyers and accountants in particular trail great masses of paper behind them, like the wake of a supertanker.

The ranks of forests have been thinned if we take as evidence the organized rows of binders you are likely to find in the office of the tax specialist, to say nothing of the voluminous case files chronicling once important disputes shepherded along by lawyers.

These materials may be no more than a decade old. Have a stranger leaf through the volumes and they will be as indecipherable as hieroglyphics were to generations of Egyptologists.

"Well, what of our good deeds" you wonder, "and the things we have set in motion with our planning? Do our plans necessarily come to naught because we ourselves necessarily do?"

This is a more interesting question and again calls to mind some differences between our modern times and those of the ancients. If our ancestors made it seem that everything ended with their own existence it is because it must have seemed so to them.

When generals conquered territories, only to have them retaken a short while later, and Emperors could not rest easy on their thrones for a moment, what hope did the average person have that their works would endure?

We have been experimenting with different forms of society and political community for some time. At least since the Enlightenment we have created some that are more enduring than others.

The rule of law has been introduced and entrenched. It has brought with it the fantastic concept that we are nations ruled not by the whims of people but by written laws. No person is above the law and as a result, the creation of the law cannot be so easily undone by the undoing of a single person.

I refer to legal entities like corporations or foundations.

A legal entity is a real thing, dear reader, at least as real as our hopes, fears, and dreams. They have greater power than the thoughts that course through our minds because they can accomplish tangible things in the world through the human agents that work in their service.

A corporation may survive a succession of CEOs, each carried out the door by mandatory retirement age if not carried off before then by some other corporate intrigue. Though twenty CEOs have come and gone, the corporation is as vital as ever.

You can argue whether people dead for generations should have continued influence on the living, for example through their foundations. But you cannot argue that nothing of their will has survived their deaths.

The Swedish chemist Alfred Nobel died in the 1890s, but before leaving the mortal world he decreed the bulk of his fortune be used for the annual award of the Nobel Prize. It is given in multiple disciplines to persons who "have conferred the greatest benefit to humankind." What a legacy!

I could say the names Rockefeller, Wallenberg, and Duke; or Ford, Nemours, and Lilly, and chances are most people will have heard of at least some of them.

Foundations created by them all, with billions in endowment. They were created by people no person living today ever met, but they live on in their good works.

So yes, the good deeds that we have set in motion with our planning can indeed survive us, and for long after our deaths.

Your aim in setting long-term plans is not to enhance your reputation. Your reputation will be gone not long after you are.

No, you should make your plans to take advantage of the power of time to deliver the greatest good to the greatest number.

This can indeed bring you wide renown and many generations may know your name. Does it matter that *you* will not know it and your beneficiaries will never know you?

Be well.

Chapter Nine

On the Independence of Reason

A wise person's reasoned judgment must come to the same conclusion when presented with the same facts

You asked the question with such seeming innocence, "Does reason exist as an independent thing?"

I wonder if you know how important this question is. That we have arrived at the crux of what we have been discussing, and the implications of the answer are far-reaching.

Well, I need not build up your expectations for a grand answer too quickly. Let me rather start constructing the framework more modestly from the ground up.

To ask whether reason exists independently is to question whether it depends on the person or on the situation.

- In other words, will two people looking at the same situation come to the same well-reasoned conclusions?

- Will one person looking at two situations at different times come to the same conclusions both times?

- Does it matter who applies reason, what is the context, and what are the consequences of a decision?

Another way to ask the question is this. Assume we had before us a person of perfect wisdom, whose ability to apply the reason of their well-ordered mind was reliably demonstrated, Socrates say.

Could Socrates tell us the reasoned answer to every situation, for every person, every time? And assuming we have no trouble believing this to be the case, now ask yourself the question, "Would Aristotle agree in every case with Socrates?"

If two wise persons do not agree every time in every detail, is it the fault of the wise persons, or the fault of the situations they are discussing, or the fault of reason itself?

So, is the wise person not truly wise, in that their thinking has not attained true reason at least in part? Are some situations simply amenable to unvarying answers? Or is reason an entirely independent thing that gives us a consistent answer regardless of who applies it?

Having reflected on these questions, it seems to me at first glance that the teachings of philosophy and law suggest different answers to the question.

The philosophy of human thought has been a story of evolution, with ideas being proposed, debated, and refined by successive generations. If nothing else, our understanding of the physical world has advanced significantly, relegating early scientific theories to quaint historical footnotes.

And our understanding of the workings of the mind is also far advanced, though there remains much we cannot explain. This suggests a progression towards more perfect reason, rather than simply describing its operation.

But philosophers are not shy about suggesting their ideas are not just correct directionally, but also absolutely. You will no doubt recall how many times I have given you instruction by exhortation rather than entreaty.

Did you understand me all this time to be making mere suggestions for your improvement rather than commandments on how to live a good life? No, although they may disagree vehemently with one another, individual philosophers have not been shy about saying that they have found basic truths that apply in all circumstances.

Is this yet another paradox for which philosophy is famous? Not necessarily, dear reader. Although it is certainly possible that two sure-minded philosophers are both wrong, it is equally possible that they are both right.

"Now you are confusing me. How can you resolve a paradox with another paradox?"

I am not trying to be clever here. Consider that when two philosophers appear to disagree, they are often starting from different premises or describing alternative cases.

Much of what frustrates me about philosophical debates is that they devolve into petty disagreements about the meaning of words. Words have meaning, but if your case hinges on the definition of one word and mine depends on another, then it is more likely we are doing little more than talking past each other and missing the underlying truth.

I think this also explains the approach taken by the law. I said earlier that law and philosophy seem to supply different answers.

In philosophers, you will find many who say, "I have found the answer, and it is this." In law, you will hear rather "Reasonable minds can disagree."

People think lawyers are not humble, but in this case, I must concede that the lawyers' approach is the more modest one. But I give no profession a free pass, and for the moment I want you to consider that the statements of both philosophy and law are wrong.

Philosophy is wrong insofar as it suggests there is but one answer.

Take the hard science of math, which is built upon firm logical ground. Math is full of equivalents. These are terms or statements that represent a certain value and may be substituted for one another.

Why should something so complex as human affairs permit only a single, unvarying answer? Could there be many solutions to a problem, all equally correct? It is not so much that my answer is right and your answer is wrong, so much as perhaps both answers are right because they are equivalent.

If the purpose of philosophy is to help people lead good lives, then should not the answers offered up be as varied as the people they are supposed to aid?

As appealing as this line of thought is, dear reader, we should be careful in pursuing it too far. For you are but a single step away from saying that reason is relative. That it depends not only on the situation, but on the person, and thus must be entirely subjective.

If a solution works for a person, then it works. This person finds relief in reading, that person in shopping, another in drinking — they are each happy and who are we to say they are wrong? But this means there is no fundamental reason, just pragmatism applied to wishful thinking.

I say it is a step too far to conclude *all* answers are valid just because there may be more than *one* valid answer.

So, do the lawyers have the better take? When they say "reasonable minds can disagree," they do not mean that *any* interpretation is valid, but that there may be more than one reasonable interpretation. An objective judge or jury can still audit the chain of thought and see which conclusions reasonably follow.

If philosophers are criticized for assuming one answer applies to all situations, lawyers make another mistake: They assume one situation can permit many answers.

The fact that reasonable minds can differ is not because there are multiple interpretations of the same facts, but that the same situation has multiple facts in play.

So Lawyer A strings together a line of facts that support Conjecture A, and Lawyer B pulls a related but different set of facts from the same situational soup and finds the ingredients for Conjecture B. They are both reasonable in constructing their logical arguments. But they are not arguing different conclusions from the same facts, rather different conclusions from different facts.

"I am now thoroughly confused," you say. "You have told me philosophers are wrong for saying that a single solution applies in all cases, and lawyers are wrong in saying reason can be applied differently to the same facts. How does this help answer the question of whether reason exists independently, which I am now rather regretting asking you?"

Do not despair, dear reader. The conclusion of my argument is near at hand, as is the conclusion of today's letter.

What squabbling philosophers and squabbling lawyers have in common when they disagree is that they are arguing different cases (always assuming they are dealing honestly).

Socrates and Aristotle *would* come to the same conclusion if they were presented with the same facts in the same way. The reason is, in my view, that reason is *not subjective*. It only seems so because it is always interpreted by us as individuals.

- This person may have a harder time letting go of possessions because of their upbringing, the habits and vices they inculcate, and the friends they surround themselves with.

- That person may find it all too easy to scorn public opinion because they never found public favor and so placed little value on it.

Just as the situations we each face inevitably differ, we each have a unique history that creates the personal conditions we bring to each situation. Virtue is found in neither the person nor their situation but in their application of reason to their situation.

And this reason, I posit, never changes. A wise person's reasoned judgment must come to the same conclusion when presented with the same facts. When everything appears relative, it is only the observer that changes, and not the fundamental forces that apply to our actions.

Hence, I conclude that reason does exist independently and absolutely. It is our individuality that tricks us into wanting to give reason a sliding scale of application.

Apply your judgment to every situation by listening to reason and not emotion, and you will not be so easily led astray.

Be well.

Chapter Ten

On False Fronts

We take at face value the whole of our lives. In refusing to think for yourself, you resign yourself to accept the same fate as others

I remember going on an excursion with my family when I was a young boy. This would have been in the late '70s or early '80s, when we would spend six weeks of the hottest and brightest summer months away from the Kingdom of Saudi Arabia where my father worked and our family lived.

We traveled from an oasis in one arid country to a desert in another in the province of Almeria, Andalusia. This part of Spain is mountainous, rugged, filled with cacti and the crumbling remains of once vast industrial works.

The Mediterranean glinted invitingly, its clear blue water stretching out of sight into the horizon as if to mock the very idea that we sat baking in the middle of the driest part of the European continent.

Stay in any place for too long and you will take everything for granted. The iron-red mountains, with their herb-covered foothills running down to the azure sea, became so much painted backdrop to the boredom playing out within the four walls of our house.

So it was that my parents herded my brothers and me into the car one day for a drive to Tabernas, where the tantalizingly named Mini Hollywood nestled. This was where Sergio Leone filmed the spaghetti Western For a Few Dollars More, and where the drama of The Good, the Bad and the Ugly unfolded.

How could this not be a magical place to visit?

As an adult, dear reader, I can tell you the distance to the kilometer, but back then it was a journey into the unknown.

And like any journey when you do not know the destination, but whose arrival you eagerly anticipate, it seemed to take forever. I could not have spent half a day of my life staring out the window onto thousands of square kilometers of scrub and sand, but I felt older by the time we were freed from our four-wheeled prison.

Look! A genuine Western town, starting with the town square, watering trough for horses, and the storefronts facing it on all sides.

- The Yellow Rose Saloon, the Fire Company, Overland Stage Lines.

- A schoolhouse, the General Merchandise Store, and is that a church steeple I see?

A whole town laid out for us to walk through, not as spectators but as participants, transported directly into another world only ever seen on screen.

There was some sort of show, cowboy stunts, perhaps a recreated bank robbery. I don't recall exactly.

The appearance of actors and the carrying out of assigned roles had the effect, for me at least, of making it seem *less* real. No matter how lifelike, the play could not compare to the rich dramas concocted in my mind.

For the same reason, I suppose, that even the best film adaptation of a favorite book inevitably disappoints. "That's not how I imagined it when I was reading it," goes the resigned realization. The magic of books is that they allow each reader to create magic in their heads. Sometimes it's best left there.

Even at my impressionable age, I soon realized the actors were just people wearing costumes. That the magical town was just a quickly constructed set, and that half of the buildings were nothing more than false fronts, a single painted wall supported by struts creating giant empty right-angle triangles hidden from plain view.

Suddenly I could not see Mini Hollywood the same way, and I could not wait to get out of there. I wanted to keep the magic of my imagination intact. But it was too late, and not just for me in Tabernas.

Ever since then, I cannot visit a theme park or studio without immediately noticing the false fronts all around. Europa Park, Disney World, Universal Studios: No matter how artfully done, the entire experience is a set construction from beginning to end.

From the signage, the paint on the walls, the very flooring we walk upon, I see the craftsman's attempt to create worlds within worlds. It all seems so superficial because in my mind I know it has been built for effect. Sadly, the effect sought is less to create childlike wonder than to create the ideal conditions to separate weary parents from their money.

Why are these destinations still so popular, then, if we can easily recall at a moment's thought that they are nothing more than painted stages? Dear reader, it is because we want to be fooled.

We accept the false front as the reality because the reality behind the false front is just a hardscrabble desert or a reclaimed swamp. If life is hard and unforgiving, can we be blamed for wanting to believe in magic?

I suppose I can understand this, and could even forgive the impulse, if we did not take it so much further. We take at face value the whole of our lives.

We assume that what everyone else chases after must be valuable, so we chase after it too. We unquestioningly accept that buying things can bring us happiness, refusing to see the evidence before our eyes that though we are drowning in possessions we are no nearer to satisfaction.

We say "no good deed goes unpunished" as a cynical and self-serving way to justify focusing on our personal needs. I say, "No superficial thought goes unpunished," because in refusing to think for yourself, you resign yourself to accept the same fate as others.

How happy is your fellow person? How satisfied are they with their work, their pay, their politicians, their friends? How many suffer envy, greed, and misgivings, not to mention a hundred other maladies of the mind?

People say the Stoic philosophy is one of hardship and suffering because we try to see through the surface to the substance of things. When I compare the depth of mind of the average person with that of the philosopher, I must ask who is suffering the greater hardship.

What we gain from philosophy is deep peace of mind arising from confidence in our judgments and in our actions. The world is the same arid desert or reptile-filled swamp, but our steps are assured even though they are not always safe.

There is no greater achievement than to arrive at a point where you can look back on your life and say, "I would not change a thing."

Be well.

Chapter Eleven

On the AI Philosopher

Wisdom consists not just in making a correct decision, but in making it with an understanding of the reason why

You employ a most dangerous argument when you seek to use a lawyer's own words against them. In the present case, you have repeated back to me what I told you recently, namely that a wise person's reasoned judgment must come to the same conclusion when presented with the same facts.

You start with my conclusion, and you ask whether this means that a computer is wise. And taken a step further, will artificial intelligence become the ultimate embodiment of the wise philosopher, giving in to neither emotion nor temptation, providing consistently correct answers to all our problems?

Since it is my own words you employ, I cannot dismiss them lightly. Let me take you on a small journey before we arrive at our conclusion together.

Let us travel using one of the most impactful inventions of the Industrial Age, the combustion engine-powered car. The first modern automobile was invented in the 1880s by Karl Benz. If we could have an insight into horses' thoughts at that time, I wonder if they would have run something like this:

"Foolish humans. They have a perfectly reliable companion in us horses. We pull their loads, plow their fields, and take them to every corner of the earth. How much farther do they want to go, and how much faster do they want to get there? Can you ride two horses at once? Ten? And how will they feed them all? Mmmm, is that a carrot you're holding?"

Little did our faithful equine friends know how insatiable are our human appetites. Today mere passenger cars can sport more than a thousand HP, a veritable horde of horses to blanket the landscapes these supercars roar past.

Inside, their occupants are unseeing of anything they are speeding by beyond the tachometer and speedometer. My point is not to disparage the supercar or its owners, but rather to ask you this question: Is a horsepower equivalent to a horse?

"No one is suggesting that, and they never were" you say. "A horsepower is just a measure of power, the rate at which work is done."

All right. Is this a fairer comparison: Would you say a car is equivalent to a horse? Before you jump to answer, recall that it takes a combination of a car and a human to drive a car off a ferry landing and into a lake, something no horse would do.

You could say this is the fault of the human blindly following the GPS, but the car still ends up submerged. If a person sought to perform a similar stunt on their horse, the person is the one likely to end up spluttering wet.

"I know you said we were going on a journey" you say "but is it one that will take all day? Can we take a rest stop and stretch our legs?"

I am reminded of what young kids the world over say to their parents moments after getting in the car "Are we there yet?" And I will give the universal parents' response "Just a little bit further."

In place of our metaphorical rest stop and breath of fresh air let me just say that I am now preparing to compare the brain with the computer, our minds with the machine. I will even go so far as to give you the conclusion up front.

It is that today, and for the foreseeable future, I think, wisdom is a uniquely human attribute. Wisdom consists not just in making a correct decision, but in making it with an understanding of the reason why.

Humans make wise decisions out of more than short-sighted self-interest because they can anticipate consequences, both for themselves and others. A computer algorithm can make the same decision; indeed it cannot make any other, but there is no concern with consequences.

We talk of cold computer logic explicitly to distinguish it from humankind's reason, which is the result of overcoming our mess of constantly churning emotions. Though the resulting decision may be identical, the process by which we arrive at it couldn't be more different.

Some of the greatest advancements in artificial intelligence research came when we stopped trying to build algorithms to solve defined problems in their entirety and instead designed simpler systems patterned on human neural networks. This set the stage for deep learning and machine learning, where processing takes place in layers, each adding a piece of the puzzle and allowing higher levels of abstraction to emerge as a result.

In the case of both human infants and our fledgling machine systems, learning is the result of being confronted with data. Infants are amazing perception machines, taking in a flood of information from all their senses. This creates connections and associations among neurons in the brain, which are strengthened or weakened by further experiences.

The computer systems need to be force-fed their data like stubborn babies, and they need truly vast quantities of it to start drawing abstractions that a baby can do with ease.

It is when we observe how the two systems develop and learn from their steady diet of data that we come to the great distinction between humans and computers. Computers do not lack judgment. We humans build the rules in, or the rules for how rules will be learned, such that with a given input, the result will be the same.

What computers lack is perception. They do not sense the external world as we do, neither in quantity nor in quality. In fact, for any inputs to be made workable to the computer, they must be translated into the sterile binary code of zeros and ones. Humans do not lack perception. It is the judgment that we must learn through painful experience and repeated trial and error.

Because computers judge consistently but are limited in their perception, while humans have vast perceptions of situations that we judge inconsistently, we remain far apart.

And critically, when humans make judgments, it is the result of two things taken together: All of our past experiences and our anticipation of future results.

I have no doubt that we will steadily add to the situations in which computers outperform humans in tasks that appear to reflect perception, thinking, and judgment.

But until a computer takes the leap of making a decision not just because of past experience but because it desires a future outcome, I expect no wisdom to come from it.

Be well.

Chapter Twelve

On Nature as a Guide

The philosopher is playing the happiness game that Nature also allows us to pursue by virtue of our reason

You have pointed out another inconsistency in the Stoic advice. Or at least you have raised a question about their consistency when you reminded me of a basic teaching I like to repeat.

"You have stated that we should strive in all things to live in accordance with Nature. This means being satisfied with the basics and not being tempted to chase after luxury. You also said that a major cause of our unhappiness is looking to see our relative position in the hierarchy, because no matter how many people we stand over, so long as there is one above us, we will be miserable."

So far so good, and I see no fault in the argument.

You continue "You also say, do you not, that hierarchy itself is a fundamental feature of Nature, and that every society and every group of animals will organize themselves according to hierarchies. In hierarchies, more possessions and power mean more status, which means a longer, more secure life with better mating opportunities. When the Stoics counsel us to become wise by foregoing the quest for more, are you not advising us to act against Nature?"

Although most who make such an argument are looking to justify their own insatiable desires, I know you are looking only to understand the truth of the matter. So, I will give your question the attention it deserves.

The first point I would make is that to say we should live in accordance with Nature is not to say that everything Nature offers is equally valuable.

I would rather recommend you live on the verdant slopes of a dormant volcano whose caldera has long since exploded and become still than on the lava-strewn plains of its active cousin. Both mountains are creations of Nature, but you may confidently choose the one that will provide a safe home for you and your family.

So too would I tell you to steer clear of the trackless desert and to take your guidance from the plants that Nature has deposited all around us. If a land is barren, why should we humans thrive there? The desert is just as much a part of Nature as the Alpine valley, but I can easily tell you which one we are better off dwelling in.

When we say live in accordance with Nature, this means first understanding your *own* nature. You can then take advantage of the resources Nature offers that provide the best match for your nature.

If you love the warmth and the feel of the sun on your face, better that you incline toward the equator. If you thrive in the cold, the Northern regions are a more suitable home for you.

The point is that the natural environments we find ourselves in differ. We can and should choose those environments that will best suit us. And this speaks only to physical needs.

The question you have raised goes a step further. You are asking how the hierarchies we so readily perceive are to be considered in accordance with Nature when they have such an impact on our minds and our state of mind.

Here we have come to the crux of the matter, dear reader. When we move from the physical to the mental, we arrive at the point where Nature ceases to be the primary driving force and humankind takes the wheel.

It is by our thinking, whether reasoned or not, that we make all that Nature offers better or worse.

- Nature provides the instinct for us to acquire more possessions, assert our dominance, and ascend the hierarchies we find ourselves in.

- Our thinking serves as a mechanism to accelerate or slow our progress, or to steer in another direction.

Do not forget, our minds are also the product of Nature. Thus, the application of our minds to the situations we find ourselves in is also acting according to Nature.

Does it seem like a conflict to you that one part of Nature drives us unthinkingly down certain paths while another part gives us the ability to look ahead and plot a course? I say no more a conflict than for every carnivore who eats today another creature has been killed.

And for that matter, who said Nature itself needed to be consistent in all things?

It is because humankind developed such keen reasoning that we are at risk of acting against Nature.

The animals around us do not amass possessions far beyond their potential use. When they have satiated their hunger, they stop eating. When they have slaked their thirst, they stop drinking.

It is humans who override the signals from Nature and drive themselves to new heights of avarice, gluttony, and greed. A need arises naturally and is satisfied naturally. A luxury is fabricated and requires an elaborate system to create and maintain.

So far, we are still talking about satisfying physical needs. Consider that as thinking creatures, we also have mental and emotional needs. I would place the desire to be happy high among them.

The philosopher's aim is to help achieve the conditions to live a good life. Here we see humankind's greatest danger to itself arises from itself.

Descartes did not go far enough with his famous statement "*cogito, ergo sum*." He needed to add a further word at the end: "I think, therefore I am unhappy." We are unhappy because we realize we could have more, and we see that someone else does have more.

I assert this is not thinking, but merely instinct run amok in our minds. Pesky Nature seeking to ensure humans are fruitful and multiply, and that only the strongest and fittest survive.

We are fruitful, dear reader, but it is now mainly in multiplying our problems and our worries. When the Stoics say to live in accordance with Nature by developing well-ordered reason to understand the true value of things, they mean that we should place the greatest value on our peace of mind.

The physical things we torment ourselves with are necessary for physical survival, and that is all. If we can relegate them to their proper place, we will see that our physical needs are relatively easy to satisfy.

Having satisfied our physical needs, we can then turn our attention to the regulation of our mental processes.

Our thoughts can make us either happy or unhappy. We are fools to become distracted by anything that experience shows leads to unhappiness.

Playing the status game is a consequence of the hierarchies Nature has established. The philosopher is playing the happiness game that Nature also allows us to pursue by virtue of our reason.

Be well.

Chapter Thirteen

On Instincts and Archetypes

We have the capacity to respond to our circumstances, and some responses will bring better results than others

You are not happy with my recent description of how humankind is to live in accordance with Nature. You think I have too quickly brushed past the physical needs of people to arrive at the emotional chaos that can only be tamed by well-ordered reason.

Thus, you ask me to remain for some moments more in the realm of the physical and address a separate question. How is it that nature provides animals with instincts to drive their survival and these instincts work to great effect, but in people those same instincts lead us to terrible outcomes?

Even though it is dissatisfaction that drives your question, dear reader, I take it up with the greatest satisfaction.

Teaching and learning are two sides of the same conversation, and in our talks, I find I learn as much as I try to teach. So, let's discuss this together and see if we may both come to a better understanding. As our prior assault on the fortress of knowledge was unavailing, let us try another avenue of attack.

For over two thousand years it was understood that physical traits acquired by an animal during its lifetime could be passed on to its offspring. In this way, creatures developed over time from simple things to ever more sophisticated beings.

The idea of inheritance of acquired characteristics came to be associated with the French zoologist Jean-Baptiste Lamarck in the early 19th century. His reputation was then tainted by the increasing number of scientists who failed to find solid evidence confirming the idea and came to associate Lamarck's name with the singular failure.

Later that century, Charles Darwin proposed the mechanism of natural selection as sufficient to explain the variations between and among species. The variation in starting conditions (creatures differ in their constitutions from birth) and in the environments they find themselves in means that some animals will be better suited for survival than others.

Darwin's mechanism of natural selection driving evolution has served us well as a conceptual framework for the last 150 years. How interesting, then, that there are recent developments that demonstrate once again it can be fruitful to approach conventional wisdom with a dose of caution, if not skepticism.

One development in particular offered a bridge between Lamarckism and Darwinism. Named after the American psychologist James Mark Baldwin, the Baldwin Effect deals with the fact that animals change their behavior in response to their environments.

The ones that learn the most successful new behaviors are more likely to reproduce, and hence *the propensity for learned behavior* is itself a natural characteristic that is then passed on via natural selection to the next generations.

I find this component of the modern synthesis of our understanding of evolution wonderful, dear reader, because it not only takes into account our mental processes but embraces them as a key driver of our progress through life.

We have the capacity to respond to our circumstances, and some responses will bring better results than others. From a survival perspective, the creatures most able to craft successful responses will be most likely to reproduce. We have physical instincts that drive us, but we also have mental characteristics that allow us to respond to our environments.

One of the earliest explorers into the mental realms that dwell within people and drive our actions was the Swiss psychologist Carl Jung. From his interaction with and observation of patients, Jung hypothesized that people possess what he called a collective unconscious, shared across time and culture.

He described archetypes as universal and recurring mental images or themes. It is a simplification to call archetypes instincts for mental processes, but the analogy suffices for our purposes.

Just as animals inherit instincts that drive their behavior, for example in avoiding certain dangers automatically, so humans inherit archetypes, a kind of innate knowledge of human behavior across history, that drive mental processes without our being consciously aware of it.

I have not forgotten your question, dear reader, and I hope you see that we are getting nearer to an answer. Thus far we have suggested that humans possess both physical instincts and mental instincts of a sort. I don't suppose you will contest that the mental processes of most humans are more advanced than those of most animals.

I think this helps explain why human instincts do not always operate to the same good effect that animal instincts do. It is because we can use our minds to *override* our positive instincts. Or as Canadian psychologist Jordan Peterson put it,

> Only man will inflict suffering for the sake of suffering. That is the best definition of evil I have been able to formulate.

We do not need to posit evil deeds to see that people inflict suffering on others. It is, moreover, undeniable that we also inflict suffering on ourselves. Sometimes the harm comes from being unaware of the consequences of our actions.

Just as often, I would say, people are willfully blind to the long-term consequences because they are stubbornly pursuing short-term gain. Perhaps it is a question of listening to the wrong instincts, or impulses if you will.

One of the boons of philosophy is slowing down and taking time to think. By evaluating actions and considering consequences we increase the chance that we will listen for and hear the voice of the collective unconscious, the instinctual archetype, calling out guidance.

If these things exist, they can be of great benefit to humankind because they allow us to put our base, physical instincts in their proper place. I won't say we can learn to override our negative instincts because I think every instinct evolved for a reason.

But when we use reason to consider our highest and best purpose, and then take action in accordance with that purpose, we are surely taking steps along the path to wisdom.

Hence, the very thing that leads people astray (using our mind to override positive instincts) also holds the key to our salvation.

Be well.

A Little Philosophy Goes a Long Way

In our journey to living good lives, our highest purpose is to order our minds so that we can follow reason in all things

This marks the end of the Pragmatic Wisdom series, with its 124 compact lessons on Stoic philosophy. Congratulations on being a sincere student!

Stoicism asks us to challenge blind conformity to the current system, i.e. doing what everyone else does without questioning the underlying values of what everyone is doing.

The Stoic's task is initially the harder one: Taming one's passions and desires is a greater challenge than looking to change others. But the reward in determining the proper value of things is greater. The Stoic finds happiness by putting it firmly under the control of their reason.

Thankfully, we don't need to address all our needs at once. We make the most progress by taking little steps consistently:

> Consider every day as a session in the classroom of life. On most days you will be confronted with inconveniences, annoyances, or irritants. By applying your reason, you will put each stimulus in its proper place, and you will not be put out of sorts against your will. Either there is some validity to the thing that irks you or there is none.

Thus, in our journey to finding happiness, thinking for ourselves is the key.

We study philosophy with the aim of living good lives and being happy. What can bring about this state? It is the same thing that disturbs it, namely our minds.

Our highest purpose is to order our minds so that we can follow reason in all things.

I will end with one of my favorite gems of advice from Seneca himself. It is a lesson that bears repeating because so much of modern life pulls us in other directions and causes us to forget:

> Set yourself free for your own sake; gather and save your own time.
> While we are postponing, life speeds by.

Be well.

www.ingramcontent.com/pod-product-compliance
Lightning Source LLC
Chambersburg PA
CBHW052009290426
44112CB00014B/2172